O. HENRY

O. HENRY

RECENT BOOKS BY RICHARD O'CONNOR

The First Hurrah, A Biography of Alfred E. Smith
Pacific Destiny
The German-Americans
Ambrose Bierce, A Biography
Bret Harte, a Biography
Jack London, A Biography
Courtroom Warrior
Black Jack Pershing

O. HENRY

THE LEGENDARY LIFE OF

William S. Porter

BY RICHARD O'CONNOR

Doubleday & Company, Inc.
Garden City, New York
1970

Acknowledgment is made to the following for permission to reprint their material:

DOUBLEDAY & COMPANY, INC.
Excerpts from *The O. Henry Biography* by C. Alphonso Smith. Copyright 1916 by Doubleday & Company, Inc. Excerpts from *The Complete Works of O. Henry,* foreword by Harry Hansen. Copyright 1899, 1901, 1902, 1903, 1904, 1905, 1906, 1907, 1908, 1909, 1910, 1911, 1953 by Doubleday & Company, Inc. Copyright 1903, 1904, 1905, 1906 by The Ridgway-Thayer Co.; 1902 by The Era; 1902, 1903 by John Wanamaker; 1902 by Brandur's Magazine; 1903 by William Sydney Porter; 1904, 1907 by Associated Sunday Magazine; 1903 by The Pilgrim; 1909 by Hampton's Magazine, Inc.; 1910 by Semi-Monthly Magazine Section. Both reprinted by permission of Doubleday & Company, Inc.

E. P. DUTTON & COMPANY, INC.
Excerpts from *The Quiet Lodger of Irving Place* by William Wash Williams. Copyright 1936 by E. P. Dutton & Co., Inc. Renewal © 1964 by Mrs. Leone Scott Williams. Reprinted by permission of E. P. Dutton & Company, Inc.

GREENSBORO PUBLIC LIBRARY
Excerpts from *The Smith Papers*. Reprinted by permission of Greensboro Public Library, Greensboro, N.C.

THE MACMILLAN COMPANY
Excerpts from *Alias O. Henry* by Gerald Langford. Copyright © 1957 by Gerald Langford. Reprinted by permission of The Macmillan Company.

THE NEW YORK TIMES
Excerpt from the April 4, 1909, *New York Times* interview by George MacAdam. Copyright 1909 by The New York Times Company. Reprinted by permission.

Library of Congress Catalog Card Number 70–108035

Printed in the United States of America
First Edition

Acknowledgments

The author is particularly grateful to Miss Shirley Windham, assistant head of the reference department and in charge of the Caldwell-Jones Collection at the Greensboro, N.C., Public Library; and also to Robert Woodward, head of the Bangor, Me., Public Library, for obtaining books on loan. Also to Dale L. Walker of the University of Texas at El Paso for assistance in research on O. Henry's Texas years. Acknowledgment must also be made to previous O. Henry biographers: Prof. Gerald Langford for his splendid *Alias O. Henry;* Prof. Eugene Current-Garcia for his scholarly *O. Henry;* E. Hudson Long, *O. Henry, The Man and His Work;* Robert H. Davis and Arthur B. Maurice, *The Caliph of Bagdad;* C. Alphonso Smith, *The O. Henry Biography;* Ethel Stephans Arnett, *O. Henry from Polecat Creek.*

Contents

List of Illustrations

O. HENRY

"Along came my true lover about twelve o'clock
Saying Henry, O, Henry what sentence
have you got?"

—*Root, Hog, or Die,* Texas cowboy ballad.

I. THE WILL PORTER YEARS

Chapter 1. Salad Days

Like anyone else in the entertainment business a writer must find a suitable role to play. The Edwardian literary man in America was likely to adopt one of several personas tried and tested by the outstanding figures in his profession. Perhaps the most typical was that of the slightly pompous gentleman with Roman bangs over his forehead, who gestured with spectacles attached to a black ribbon and was given to expressing himself in carefully structured sentences; William Dean Howells or Richard Watson Gilder, for instance. The three-decker name was typical. Another type was that of the deliberately eccentric, publicity-conscious performer in a one-man circus, always quotable, embodied by that curly wolf of American letters, Mark Twain. There was also the professional adventurer, a role played with brio by Jack London in the Klondike, the South Seas, Manchuria and the waterfront bars of San Francisco, an expanding category which would one day include Ernest Hemingway and a procession of many others. In addition there was the dashing journalist, either a glamorous war correspondent or a big-city social crusader, like Richard Harding Davis, Stephen Crane, David Graham Phillips or Lincoln Steffens.

None of these stereotypes would suit the man who chose to call himself O. Henry, perhaps the drabbest pen name ever concocted, so obscurant that many literate people still believe his name was "O'Henry." It cloaked a man who could not indulge himself in the normal writer's passion for publicity and recognition. Unlike his more respectable colleagues, O. Henry was forced to conceal his past, even invent a partial biography for himself when the New York *Times* became inordinately inquisitive. The gaps he concealed with all the self-protectiveness of a proud and sensitive man included a stay in Central America as a fugitive from justice, a trial on charges of embezzlement and a term in a federal penitentiary.

It was a paradox of the sort that figured in many of his short stories that the more famous he became the more he feared the day that he would be exposed as an ex-convict. An even more excruciating irony was that none of the men with whom he served time in prison ever attempted to blackmail him; that despicable role was, from all indications, played by a prosperous broker's wife who had known him in the city from which he was sent to prison—all of which only testified to the validity of his theory that the higher the level of society you explored the more deplorable was the state of morality. From his own experience he could maintain that life itself provided as many trick endings as those which formed one of the more notable features of his storytelling. The coincidences of his own life more than matched those which the loftier critics condemned in his fiction. The good-bad men whom he fabricated, like the Cisco Kid and Jimmy Valentine, were drawn from life, though he was often accused of sentimentalizing outlaws and misfits. His villains were more likely to be silk-hatted hypocrites who robbed banks from the inside, and let someone else suffer the consequences, than honest working crooks. That, too, life had taught him.

But nothing he created as a writer was more amazing than the story of his own life, none of his characters more incredible than the man whom the newspapers and magazines promoted as The Caliph of Bagdad-on-the-Subway. One of those popular novelists with three-decker names who were his contemporaries could have worked wonders with that story, possibly titling it *The Regeneration of William Sydney Porter.* It had everything: the post-bellum South, Texas before the Colt .45's had cooled, tubercular sweetheart, precipitous fall from respectability, motherless daughter, prison, eventual success, and enough moral lessons to satisfy the editor of the *Ladies' Home Journal.* It would have had to eliminate, of course, his taste for low company, his association with streetwalkers in the Tenderloin, his heroic consumption of lager beer, and his sardonic views on the social system of his time.

In a sense he lived two lives: one as the amiable and obscure Will Porter, the family man of Austin, Texas; the other as O. Henry, the ex-convict who attained literary fame in the last eight years of a short life. Rehabilitation is hardly the word for the process by which Federal Prisoner No. 30664 stepped through the gates of the Ohio State Penitentiary with a few dollars and a railroad ticket in his pocket, and in less than a decade transformed himself into a world-famous author.

But this is not wholly a success story. It is the account of a man who clung to the shadows of the metropolis, the shabby streets of Chelsea and Hell's Kitchen, even while the spotlights of celebrity sought him out; the man who could not bear to have his past examined even by those he should have been able to trust. Between O. Henry and his New York friends there was a polite conspiracy of silence which allowed him to continue hiding behind his literary alias. This perhaps encouraged him to cling to his obsession with secrecy to such a degree that when he entered a hospital for the last time, almost through force of habit, he signed in under still another alias. "Why didn't someone speak out?" the journalist Will Irwin, who was his friend, asked. "Why did we all keep up the polite pretence of ignorance? Why didn't someone go to him and say, 'Bill, we know all about it and it doesn't make the slightest difference . . .'" The fact that no one could is also part of the paradoxical character of William Sydney Porter-O. Henry.

The principal focus of this biography is on those amazing last eight years, the years of O. Henry, but to show what formed O. Henry it is necessary to deal as cogently as possible with his alter ego William Sydney Porter. . . .

"May you live in interesting times" is an ancient Chinese curse. The fact that William Sydney Porter was born in the year

1862, in one of the Confederate States of America, promised excitement in his boyhood at least.

His birth took place on September 11, 1862, in Greensboro, North Carolina, a day on which General Robert E. Lee was massing his forces for the battle to be known as Sharpsburg to the Confederacy, Antietam to the Union.

Will, as he would be known in boyhood, youth and manhood, came of good middle-class stock, a cut below the cavaliers who were having their last fling just as he was born. His mother was the former Mary Virginia Jane Swaim, who had been graduated from Greensboro Female College and written the commencement essay on a subject that might have interested her son: "The Influence of Misfortune on the Gifted." Her mother was one of the prestigious Shirleys of Princess Anne County, Virginia. Her father was William Swaim, editor of the *Patriot and Greensboro Palladium,* which he had the good sense to change to the Greensboro *Patriot* soon after assuming the editorship. Swaim was a man of strong convictions and considerable moral courage. In 1830 he published a pamphlet titled *An Address to the People of North Carolina on the Evils of Slavery,* and campaigned editorially for the gradual emancipation of the Negro slaves.[1] In a ringing editorial he defied the slave-owning planters and declared that "we would sooner beg for bread and be free than to compromise our principles for a seat upon a tawdry throne of corruption."[2]

On his father's side of the house, there was a marked tendency toward tippling and a genial fecklessness. His father was Dr. Algernon Sidney Porter, who had not graduated from a medical college but had qualified for his profession, in those easy-going days, by clerking in a drugstore and learning enough about chemistry to lecture on the subject at the Edgeworth Seminary. Even without a legitimate M.D., he was regarded as the leading physician of Guilford County; more than that, he would answer any call in the county and take a good-natured attitude toward non-payment of bills. Dr. Porter's father, Sidney Porter, was a genial tippler who ran a repair shop and left his wife a widow at the age of forty-three.* His mother, the former Ruth Worth, was a practical, down-to-earth Quaker woman who turned her home into a boarding house after her husband's death.

Dr. Porter apparently inherited his father's weakness for the bottle. During the war, he labored long hours with the bone saw and scalpel at the Confederate base hospital established at the Edgeworth Seminary. At night, seeking relief from all the blood and agony of a military hospital, he would hole up in the barn behind his mother's boarding house—where he and his wife and children also lived—and work on an invention that preoccupied him until his death in 1888, a perpetual motion machine based on the principle of the water wheel. In the barn he also kept his private stock of whiskey, and though he was not a public drunkard, his son's schoolmates later testified that it was well known in the town (pop. 2,500 at the time) that Dr. Porter drank to excess; the doctor who turned to drugs or drink was a folk figure of nineteenth-century America.

Neither of his parents was a strong direct influence on Will Porter. His father was a gentle, self-effacing man, drunk or sober, but had little time for his children. His mother died when Will was three years old, in 1865, and it is doubtful whether he had more than the dimmest memory of her.

Will had two brothers, the younger of whom was born six months before their mother's death and died early in childhood. His older brother, Shirley, nicknamed Shell, was born two years before Will and there was never any love lost between them either as boys or men. From all accounts, Shirley Porter was a roughneck who bullied his younger brother. They had nothing in common. Shirley Porter spent much of his life as a construction worker in the Carolina lumber camps.

The strongest influence on the boy was exerted by his stern paternal grandmother, Mrs. Ruth Porter, whose character became

* Sidney Porter was also the agent for the C. and N. Jerome Clock Co., Bristol, Connecticut. Descendants of the Jeromes included Jennie Jerome, the mother of Winston Churchill, and William Travers Jerome, the fighting district attorney of New York, and a co-celebrity of O. Henry's.

all the firmer as that of her menfolk deteriorated, and his maternal aunt, Miss Evalina, who operated a small private school and also lived at the Porter boarding house.

Neither his grandmother nor his aunt resembled in the slightest the languishing southern lady of durable legend, thanks mostly, perhaps, to the fecklessness of their menfolk. Brusque and practical as any Yankee, Grandmother Porter once received the protest of two sisters against the bill she sent them for her son's medical services (Dr. Porter could rarely bring himself to send a bill). The sisters claimed that Dr. Porter had called on them socially.

"Social calls!" snorted Grandmother Porter. "I want you to understand that my son Algernon don't make social calls on maiden ladies at two o'clock in the morning and they a-suffering with colic!"

Greensboro was a quiet rural town in Will's boyhood, all but untouched by the war except that it had attracted every able-bodied young man. Towering elms arched over its streets. The only sizable building in town was the two-story wooden Southern Hotel. Just outside Greensboro were several ante-bellum mansions and the Edgeworth Seminary, where wounded Union prisoners and Confederates alike were brought for treatment from the field hospitals. The social center of the town, for men, was the drugstore, where Will's father had studied medicine and Will himself would become a boy pharmacist, and where the druggist kept a decanter for his friends.

The little mountain town experienced its one historic moment in the spring of 1865, when Will was less than three years old. Immediately after Lee's surrender at Appomattox on April 9, Jefferson Davis convened his cabinet, along with Generals Joseph E. Johnston and P. G. T. Beauregard, commanding his remnant of an army, in Greensboro. All through the war Greensboro had dozed under the shade of its elms. Suddenly, for a few days, it became the capital of the dying Confederacy. The town witnessed the farewell of President Davis to his troops before he continued on the flight that ended with his capture in the Georgia swamps.

The army which had marched under Sherman from Georgia to the sea was drawn up in battle formation only a few miles away. Greensboro was flooded with 37,000 weary and beaten Confederate troops, the last hope of the Lost Cause. If they resisted, Greensboro might be leveled by the federal artillery; O. Henry, or the boy he was, might have died in the wreckage of his grandmother's boarding house. But General Johnston knew a lost cause when he saw one, and quickly opened negotiations with General Sherman. The result was that the last sizable southern army lay down its arms in Greensboro, and 30,000 Union troops marched in to supervise the surrender.

The Reconstruction, and his people's resistance to it, figured largely in his boyhood. Shortly after the war a carpetbagger named Albion Winegar Tourgée appeared in Greensboro as Republican boss of the district. Soon thereafter the Ku Klux Klan was organized and enrolled eight hundred nightriding members in Guilford County to countermand Tourgée's rule of the law. The response, it seems, was out of proportion. Tourgée was neither a fanatic Abolitionist determined to overturn the social order nor an opportunist eager to line his pockets and clear out. A Confederate veteran wrote that Tourgée was an honest, fair-minded man, "not popular with the other carpetbaggers nor with prominent native scalawags—which speaks much for his honesty and independence." On his return North Tourgée published a novel, *The Fool's Errand*, based on his experiences as an administrator of the Reconstruction, which was widely praised (in the North) as a worthy sequel to *Uncle Tom's Cabin*. He wrote of living as "an outlaw in the land where he hoped to have made a home and which he desired faithfully to serve."

Compared to other northern administrators, Tourgée was a paragon; even the Ku Klux Klan was objective enough to spare him from one of its notorious midnight visitations. But to the boys of Greensboro he was the local ogre and tyrant. Naturally enough they had absorbed the attitudes of their parents and made heroes of the underground "invisible empire" sworn to restore the old white supremacy.

"Of course Will and I played Ku Klux Klan," his playmate Thomas H. Tate later recalled. "My mother was a past master at making masks out of newspapers which she folded and cut out with her scissors. I remember how the Negroes used to pretend to be terribly frightened and how pleased we were with our efforts. The old Presbyterian High School used to be the meeting place of the genuine articles and was always held in awe by us boys for a long time on that account . . . As to Judge Tourgée, we looked upon him as some sort of pirate, mysterious and blackened by a thousand crimes, and we glanced at him covertly when he happened to be around . . . but even we admired him for his courage and wondered at it, coming as he did from the North."[3]

It was hardly the KKK and its romantic ardors, however, which formed and influenced the first twenty years of Will Porter's life in Greensboro. The death of his mother, the amiable waywardness of his father, the preoccupations of his grandmother in holding her family together and running a boarding house left his upbringing largely in the capable hands of his spinster aunt, "Miss Lina," who was not inclined to spoil him. Miss Lina was a disciplinarian, in and out of her little school, and it was she who packed an education into young Will's resistant head.

His boyhood friend and official biographer, C. Alphonso Smith, recalled Miss Lina as a determined and intelligent woman "with none of her father's happy-go-lucky disposition but with much of her mother's directive ability and with a profound sense of responsibility for the welfare of every boy and girl that entered her school. . . . She did not, of course, spare the rod. It was not the fashion in those days to spare it. . . . But there was no cruelty in Miss Lina's disposition. She tempered justice if not with mercy at least with rigid impartiality and with hearty laughter. . . . To have been soundly whipped by Miss Lina is still regarded in Greensboro as a sort of spiritual bond of union, linking together the older citizens of the town in a community of cutaneous experience for which they would not exchange a college diploma."

Under her tutelage Will developed a considerable talent for drawing, which flowered in Miss Lina's schoolroom along with a growing sense of mischief. "She had a way of sending the arithmetic class to the blackboard while she paced the floor with a bundle of switches," as Smith remembered. "O. Henry would work his 'sum' with his right hand and sketch Miss Lina with his left at the same time. The likeness was perfect, not a feature or switch being omitted. The whole thing had to be done as she walked from one side of the little room to the other with her back to the blackboard."

During school hours Miss Lina was a stern taskmaster and did not flourish her bundle of switches purely for effect, but she was more than a teacher to the boys in her charge. Her attachment to and concern for her pupils was a continuing one, unbounded by the calendar or the clock. "On Friday night," Tom Tate would recall years later, "there was a gathering of the scholars at her home, and those were the good times. They ate roasted chestnuts, popped corn or barbecued quail and rabbits before the big open wood fire in her room. There was always a book to read or a story to be told. Then there was a game of story-telling; one of the gathering would start the story and each one of the others was called on in turn to add his quota until the end.

"In the summer time there were picnics and fishing expeditions; in the autumn chinquapin and hickory gatherings; and then in the spring wild-flower hunts, all personally conducted by Miss Lina.

"During these days Will showed a decided artistic talent, and it was predicted that he would follow in the footsteps of his kinsman, Tom Worth, the cartoonist, but the literary instinct was there, too, and the quaint dry humor and the keen insight into the peculiarities of human nature."[4]

Cartooning was his avocation throughout his life, and surviving samples of his work indicate that he might have taken it up professionally. But it was the written word that fascinated him from early in life; dime novels at first, then a wide range of more classical literature from Miss Lina's library. At the age of eight, Thomas Tate would recall, he and Will Porter had the largest collection of dime novels in town. A year or two later Will began to lose interest in the exploits of Deadwood Dick and to take up the novels of Charles Dickens and Sir Walter Scott.

Undoubtedly this literary bent was largely encouraged by his aunt. "She did not teach the history of literature," Alphonso Smith recalled, "but she laboured in season and out of season to have her pupils assimilate the spirit of literature. . . . She loved books as she loved flowers, because her nature demanded them. Fiction and poetry were her means of widening and enriching her own inner life, not of learning facts about the world without. . . . She did not measure literature by life but life by literature. So did O. Henry at that time, but he was later to transpose his standards, putting life first. . . ."

The adult Will Porter could later very well have been describing his aunt Lina in his story "A Municipal Report," while ostensibly delineating a character whom he called Azalea Adair: "She was a product of the old South, gently nurtured in the sheltered life. Her learning was not broad, but was deep and of splendid originality in its somewhat narrow scope. She had been educated at home, and her knowledge of the world was derived from inference and by inspiration. Of such is the precious, small group of essayists made. While she talked to me I kept brushing my fingers, trying, unconsciously, to rid them guiltily of the absent dust from the half-calf backs of Lamb, Chaucer, Hazlitt, Marcus Aurelius, Montaigne, and Hood. She was exquisite; she was a valuable discovery. Nearly everybody nowadays knows too much —oh, so much too much—of real life."

More directly he paid tribute to Miss Lina's influence when he confessed that "I did more reading between my thirteenth and nineteenth years than I have done in all the years since, and my taste at that time was much better than it is now, for I used to read nothing but the classics. Burton's 'Anatomy of Melancholy' and Lane's translation of 'The Arabian Nights' were my favorites . . . I never have time to read now. I did all my reading before I was twenty."[5]

At the age of fifteen his formal schooling ended; it was time for him to start contributing to the family's finances. Following in his father's erratic footsteps, he went to work as the apprentice pharmacist in the drugstore operated by his uncle, Clark Porter. Four years later, at the age of nineteen, he was registered as a licensed pharmacist.

In later years he told intimates that he detested working in his uncle's drugstore; it was confining, and it took little imagination or initiative to grind chemicals in a mortar and roll pills. But it was a fine place to study humanity in its unbuttoned state. The male citizens of the town gathered around the potbellied stove, smoked cigars, drank whiskey and generally let their hair down. Behind the store there were stakes for horseshoe pitching and a pistol range on which Will, in his spare time, developed into a marksman.

Between filling prescriptions, replenishing the decanter from the whiskey barrel in the basement and selling cigars and sundries, Will whiled away the time by drawing cartoons of the townsfolk. They were marked by a certain amount of wit and perception, a healthy dose of irreverence, and a dash or two of malice. A number of them were preserved and today are part of the Greensboro Public Library's exhaustive collection of O. Henry memorabilia.

One sketch in particular illuminates the state of morality in Reconstructed North Carolina generally and the sociology of Porter's Drug Store specifically. It shows his uncle Clark gloomily watching from behind his counter while one "customer" reaches for the jug of free whiskey and two others are looting the cigar case.

Porter's Drug Store may not have seemed likely to become anything more than the forum of the town's loafers, drunkards and philosophers in Will's youth, yet its subsequent history made it one of the glamour spots of the proprietary drug industry. In 1891 a man named Lunsford Richardson bought out Clark Porter.

He was too ambitious and serious-minded to tolerate the continued presence of layabouts, who were firmly expelled while the new proprietor busied himself developing a line of nostrums called Vicks Family Remedies. One of the products developed at the bench where young Will Porter once filled prescriptions was Vicks Vaporub. Today Richardson's Vicks Chemical Company, on the outskirts of the city, is one of Greensboro's leading industries.

During his pharmaceutical career Will was described in various accounts as a thin, pale youth with darkish hair and feverish complexion, about five feet six inches tall. Throughout his teens he suffered from a hacking cough, which caused the older people to nod to each other with melancholy significance. Young Will, in their opinion, wasn't long for this world. Both his mother and maternal grandmother, they reminded each other, had died of tuberculosis, and then there was that alcoholic strain in his paternal ancestry.

Aside from the doomed look which some fancied they could read in young Will's face, he was apparently a cheerful and popular youth. One contemporary recalled him as "holding court" in the drugstore among men two or three times older, because of his quick wit and unquenchable sense of mischief.

Several of his pranks were regarded highly enough to become part of the Greensboro legend. They were not particularly subtle jokes, but Porter's Drug Store was not the salon of Mme. Récamier. Once he poured a measure of syrup into a urine specimen left for testing by Dr. James K. Hall. It was the doctor's own urine. Dr. Hall returned later to conduct the test himself and from the sugared sample diagnosed himself as a diabetic on the verge of collapse. The physician was about to compose his will when someone—not Will—worked up the courage to tell him about the practical joke. Another prank that drew the guffaws of his seniors was doctoring the whiskey barrel with red pepper to teach the Negro porter, who had been tapping the barrel on his own hook, a lesson about the sanctity of the Porter liquor supply. Humorists have to start somewhere; Will Porter-O. Henry's proving ground was the circle of loafers around the drugstore's potbellied stove.

It was his racking cough, eventually, that rescued him from the fate of a small-town joker—that and the forgiving nature of Dr. James K. Hall. The physician had four stalwart sons, Lee, Frank, Dick and Will, all of whom were working the vast Dull brothers' cattle ranch in La Salle County, Texas. In March of 1882, Dr. and Mrs. Hall decided to visit their sons in Texas.

The physician had often shaken his head over Will Porter's constant cough, coupled with his medical history, and decided the youth needed a change. Many tuberculars had regained their health in the dry air of Texas, so he told Will a few days before he and his wife were scheduled to leave: "I want you to come with us, Will. You need the change, and ranch life will build you up."

It sounded like a good idea to Will, who had never been farther than a dozen miles from his birthplace. Then and always he lacked initiative, possibly because of his health, more probably due to the passivity of his character. He never made things happen. Things happened to him. His break with Greensboro and his long separation from his family were the work of exterior forces.

A family council consisting of his aged grandmother and aunt Lina—Dr. Algernon Porter was no longer consulted in anything important, having retreated long ago into alcoholic vacuity—decided in favor of the journey. With him on the long road that led to marriage, disgrace, imprisonment and eventual fame, he took little more than his clothing, easily packed into one suitcase, and a few dollars in pocket money—and a maturing sense of humor.

The last item was manifest in the letter Will wrote Mrs. Hall after she and Dr. Hall had returned to Greensboro, in which he recalled several incidents on the rail journey to Texas. ". . . I can see the conductor walking towards us with Dr. Hall's bottle of currant wine in his hands, which he let roll away from him down the centre of the car some 300 times on the journey, and which the conductor invariably brought to me, handing it in full sight of everybody, and saying, 'Here young man here's your bottle.' I think he always suspected the Dr. of dropping it but when he passed along by his seat, the Dr. would survey the bottle with such an indifferent, unrecognizing look that he always settled on me as the guilty party."[6]

Greensboro and the red-clay country of the Piedmont would see him seldom, and then only briefly, from then on. He was not particularly sentimental about the old hometown. Nevertheless, Greensboro remembers him today with pride. The mountain city may not be overrun by O. Henry statues, but the visitor is not likely to avoid being reminded that this is O. Henry's birthplace. There is an O. Henry Boulevard, and an O. Henry Hotel (though the misnamed Oh Henry! candy bar is manufactured elsewhere). The O. Henry-Richardson Room at the Greensboro Historical Museum is an exact reconstruction of the old family drugstore as it was fitted out under both the Porter and Richardson managements. A plaque marks the location of that drugstore. His cradle (about which there is confessed some doubt, though it was found in the old Porter homestead) and the Porter family Bible are on display at the Greensboro Public Library. Every scrap of journalistic and scholarly writing about O. Henry's career has been collected, pasted up and microfilmed in the Caldwell-Jones Collection at the library. And in the state capital of Raleigh there is a bronze tablet commemorating him at the Supreme Court building, its raised letters a quotation from one of his short stories, "Brickdust Row": "He saw no longer the rabble but his brothers seeking the ideal."

The Greensboro newspapers serve as the official guardians of his memory. On September 11, 1962, for instance, a memorial stamp was issued by the Soviet government to mark the hundredth anniversary of his birth. More in sorrow than anger, the Greensboro *Daily News* reflected editorially on the refusal of the United States Post Office to make a similar gesture, and called it an "embarrassing and puzzling omission." Downright outrage, however, was exhibited in the Greensboro papers when the stamp columnist of the Dallas *Morning News,* similarly brooding over the lack of an O. Henry commemorative issue, mistakenly referred to their native celebrity as a Texan.[7]

Loyally the citizens of Greensboro made a sizable celebration out of the "world premiere" of a 1952 Hollywood film produced from five of his stories. It was titled *Full House* and starred Marilyn Monroe among others, with John Steinbeck as narrator and glorifier of the author of the "original stories" on which it was based ("The Gift of the Magi," "The Clarion Call," "The Ransom of Red Chief," "The Last Leaf" and "The Cop and the Anthem"). O. Henry's eighty-four-year-old widow was unable to attend, and neither were any of the film's stars present, but it was a great night in Greensboro.

The fact that during his life he did not reciprocate the affection of his birthplace, which grew in proportion to his fame, was indicative of his feelings about childhood. Motherless and all but fatherless, he had no reason to look back on Greensboro with a choking nostalgia. He "lit out" for Texas with a sense of relief at having escaped from the confinement of Porter's Drug Store. If he hadn't, he might have wound up as an assistant chemist in the Vicks Vaporub factory.

Texas was then passing gradually from wild frontier to slightly tamer frontier. Except in a few of the larger towns, it was considered socially correct to wear a gun belt on all occasions. It was still cow country, with the first major oil discoveries a score of years away. The wide steppe from the bayous of eastern Texas to the Guadalupe Mountains in the western corner was slowly being brought under the rule of the law. Men like Ben Thompson, Jim Courtright, Bat Masterson, Luke Short and King Fisher who had displayed virtuoso talents with the six-shooter were regarded with the respect given in other places to supreme court justices and silk-hatted bankers.

Texas was still a fiefdom of the cattle barons, who exercised feudal powers over everything that moved on their vast spreads. In the early 1880's, when Will Porter migrated to Texas, the state was gripped in the old deadly controversy of the cattle country, open range vs. fence. The mountain men and other adventurers had opened up Texas, the ranchers had settled the endless range and with the help of the U. S. Cavalry had fought off the Comanches. Now came the little men with their plows and families and homesteaders' cabins to claim their bits of the range and fence off the cattle herds from the little water available. The range wars between the barons and the yeomanry were bitterly and mercilessly fought.

Little wonder that when the notation "Gone to Texas" was placed beside a man's name it was suspected that he was on the verge of bankruptcy, unwanted marriage, tuberculosis or some other disaster.

In Texas, Will succumbed to his first and possibly his last case of hero worship. The object of his youthful adoration was the red-haired, tall, tough but quiet-spoken Lee Hall. Hall was then thirty-two years old but had packed several lifetimes of adventure into those years. He had migrated to Texas as a boy, taught school briefly, then embarked on a career as a peace officer during the post-Civil War years, when order, if not law, had evaporated.

As marshal of Sherman and deputy sheriff of Denison, and later as captain of the Texas Rangers, Lee Hall became nationally famous as a scourge of gunmen, rustlers and dissident Comanches. Edmund King of *Scribner's Monthly* investigated Hall's career in 1874 and in a book published the following year recounted a number of Hall's exploits. As the peace officer of Denison, an unruly town in Grayson County, he made himself notable by arresting scores of desperadoes without first shooting them—the approved method—and "moving tranquilly every day in a community where there were doubtless a hundred men who would have delighted to shed his blood."

Lee Hall evidently possessed an extraordinary sense of authority. He exhibited this quality when he determined to put an end to horse thieves and rustlers pulling their jobs and then escaping across the Red River into Indian Territory. When one notorious outlaw attempted this maneuver, as King related, Hall stationed himself at one of the Red River crossings.

"In due time," King wrote, "the fugitive and two of his friends appeared at the river, all armed to the teeth, and while awaiting the ferryboat, were visited by Hall, who drew a bead upon them and ordered them to throw down their arms. They refused, and a deadly encounter was imminent; but he finally awed them into submission, threatening to have the thief's comrades arrested for carrying concealed weapons. They delivered up their revolvers and even their rifles, and fled, and the horse thief, rather than risk a passage-at-arms with the redoubtable Lee Hall, returned with him to Denison, after giving the valiant young constable some ugly wounds on his head with his fist. The passage of the river having thus been successfully disputed by the law, the rogues became somewhat more wary."[8]

Later he was appointed Captain Hall of the Texas Rangers and led an expeditionary force in the last sizable battle with the Comanches in northeast Texas. After these exploits, he had married and settled down to managing the Dull brothers' holdings, but he would always be remembered by Texans because, in the words of his obituary, "He did more to rid Texas of desperadoes, to establish law and order, than any officer Texas ever had. He has made more bad men lay down their guns and delivered more desperadoes and outlaws into the custody of the courts, and used his own gun less, than any other officer in Texas."[9]

It was a complex of sheep and cattle ranches which Hall, with the help of his three younger brothers, stocked and fenced. Their domain included 400,000 acres, mostly sand and brush, 12,000 head of cattle and 6,000 sheep. Despite the reputation of its manager, the ranch was constantly menaced by fence-cutting cattle thieves.

The young writer-to-be found it an excellent place for gathering material which later showed up in his short stories. For the most part, Will Porter led a rather sheltered life on the ranch, since it was understood that he was sickly, though according to Mrs. Lee Hall's recollection he "acted as cowboy for a period under Captain Hall about the year 1882." She also remembered "Willie Porter" as "a most charming but shy personality at this time."

A state of near-siege existed on the ranch during Will Porter's stay, according to Mrs. Hall. "We lived a most unsettled exciting existence. Captain Hall was in constant danger. His life was threatened in many ways, and the mail was heavy with warnings, generally in the shape of crude sketches, portraying effigies with ropes around the necks, and bearing the unfailing inscription 'Your necktie.' We usually travelled at night, nearly always with cocked guns. It was at this period of our life, during the struggle between the legitimate owners and the cattle thieves, that O. Henry saw something of the real desperado."[10]

The admiration Will felt for Captain Hall was reflected in a number of his stories in which a Texas Ranger appears, always in Hall's heroic mold. Lieutenant Sandridge in "The Caballero's Way," for instance, was described as "six feet two, blond as a Viking, quiet as a deacon, dangerous as a machine gun."

Mostly as a guest, seldom as a working hand, Will settled down on the sheep ranch managed by Lee Hall's brother Dick, about twenty-five miles from the headquarters ranch. It was a small log house with scant accommodations for the number of people it was supposed to shelter: one room divided by a curtain between living quarters (kitchen and dining room) and a bedroom for Betty Hall and her infant daughter. The menfolk, including Dick Hall, Will Porter and Mrs. Hall's brother, B. F. Hughes, slept out under the stars in their blanket rolls. When a blue norther roared down, they took shelter in an outbuilding.

A rugged existence, no doubt, but young Will remained something of a professional tenderfoot. He seldom participated in any of the heavier duties on the ranch, such as fence riding or sheep dipping, but sometimes earned his keep by taking over the kitchen duties, baby-sitting for the Halls and riding fourteen miles over to Fort Ewell for the mail once a week. Much of his time seems to have been spent in reading borrowed books from the libraries of Mrs. Lee Hall and a friendly lawyer in the nearest town, Cotulla, and in deep brooding. He spent the years between nineteen and twenty-one as a guest of the Halls and must have been concerned by what he was going to do with his life. The answer could hardly have been found in his intensive reading of Byron, Dickens, Shakespeare, Smollett, Scott, Milton, Pepys, Locke, Macaulay, Gibbon and Goldsmith, whose heavy volumes he borrowed from the Cotulla lawyer's library. But this, nonetheless, is how he passed his days.

A writer, in embryo or maturity, is necessarily a self-centered fellow, and Will inherited that tendency in full measure. His help must often have been needed in the grueling process of hacking a sheep ranch out of the brush, but Will lackadaisically remained a guest. Oddly enough Dick Hall and the other men accepted him as he was; it was Betty Hall, the pioneer woman, who expected something more from the male of the species, who resented his idling about, his long afternoons spent reading under the hackberry trees while the other men were out on the range.

Of young Will, Betty Hall later wrote that he seemed to possess "no sense of responsibility or obligation or gratitude." He was ungrateful in regard to his aunt and grandmother, she believed, nor had he ever "expressed any gratitude or repaid money advanced" to the Halls themselves. Even more harshly she judged him as "lacking physical and moral courage."[11]

It could hardly have been visible to Mrs. Hall that Will Porter, in his own way and at the expense of others, was simply gaining an education; subconsciously, perhaps, he was training himself for his eventual career. He kept up with his sketching. He sent back a number of stories and letters to a Greensboro literary society (some of them published in the *Patriot*). And he taught himself to speak Spanish, or its Mexican version, better than anyone in that section of Texas.

A more sympathetic assessment of the young Will Porter was made by Joe Dixon, a former Colorado prospector, who was compiling a book of reminiscences to be titled *Carbonate Days*, which, however, was never published. Dixon had heard of Will's talents with the drawing pen and made a trip out to the Dick Hall ranch to enlist his services as an illustrator for the project. "I found Porter to be a young silent fellow with deep brooding blue eyes, cynical for his years, and with a facile pen, later to be turned to word-painting instead of picture-drawing," Dixon recalled years later. "I would discuss the story with Will in the daytime, and at night he would draw the pictures. There were forty of them in all . . . good and true to the life they depicted."

Dixon spent three weeks with young Porter, roaming the chaparral plain, sleeping in a shack and discussing their work. "I became much interested in the boy's personality. He was a taciturn fellow, with a peculiar little hiss when amused, instead of the boyish laugh one might have expected, and he could give the queerest caustic turn to speech, getting off epigrams like little sharp bullets, every once in a while, and always unexpectedly."

At Betty Hall's suggestion, Dixon asked to read some of Will's stories, to which Will reluctantly agreed. Dixon found them first-rate. " 'Will,' I said to him one day, 'why don't you try your hand at writing for the magazines?' But he had no confidence in himself, and destroyed his stories as fast as he wrote them."[12] What Joe Dixon suspected was a lack of confidence, however, was simply an urge for perfection. Will had read the masters, and would measure himself against them. He would publish only when the artist's real and true critic—himself—judged that the time was right; the only opinion that mattered was his own.

The little of his work that reached anyone else's eyes went to Greensboro and its Vesper Reading Club, which had elected him to an honorary membership. Some of his developing style was apparent in a letter he wrote the club, rather breezily summing up his impressions of life on the Texas plain:

> "The people of the State of Texas consist principally of men, women, and children, with a sprinkling of cowboys. The weather is very good, thermometer rarely rising about 2,500 degrees in the shade and hardly ever below 212. There is a

very pleasant little phase in the weather which is called a 'norther' by the natives, which endears the country very much to the stranger who experiences it. You are riding along on a boiling day in September, dressed as airily as etiquette will allow, watching the fish trying to climb out of the pools of boiling water along the way and wondering how long it would take to walk home with a pocket compass and 75 cents in Mexican money, when a wind as cold as the icy hand of death swoops down on you from the north and the 'norther' is upon you. Where do you go? If you are far from home it depends entirely on what kind of life you have led previous to this time as to where you will go. Some people go straight to heaven while others experience a change of temperature by the transition. 'Northers' are very useful in killing off the surplus population in some degree, while the remainder die naturally and peacefully in their boots."[13]

The same gift for hyperbole, the essence of frontier humor, was evident in a letter he wrote Mrs. James K. Hall, back in Greensboro, about a year after he arrived in Texas. He described how he had taken over the commissary tent, filling in, at Lee Hall's request, for the man usually in charge of provisions. On taking over the tent, he wrote, he counted "nine niggers, sixteen Mexicans, seven hounds, twenty-one sixshooters, four desperadoes, three shotguns and a barrel of molasses. . . . Out of the rear of the tent they had started a graveyard of men who had either kicked one of the hounds or prophesied a norther. When night came, the gentleman whose good fortune it was to be dispensing stores gathered up his saddle-blankets, four old corn sacks, an oilcoat and a sheepskin, made all the room he could in the tent by shifting and arranging the bacon, meal, etc., gave a sad look at the dogs that immediately filled the vacuum, and went and slept outdoors. The few days I was there I was treated more as a guest than one doomed to labour."

In a subsequent letter to Mrs. Hall he sardonically confessed to being "consumed with a burning desire" to learn all the news of his hometown, whether "Julius A. Gray has returned from Fayetteville, if Caldcleugh has received a fresh assortment of canary bird cages, or if Fishblate's clothing is still two hundred percent below first cost of manufacturing . . ." In that letter, dated March 13, 1884—almost two years after his arrival in Texas —he advised Mrs. Hall that he was about to investigate a new science which "has but four letters and is pronounced Work." Somewhat cryptically he added, "Except my next letter from the busy marts of commerce and trade."

The reference was to the termination of his status as a guest of the Dick Halls, characteristically not willed by the youth himself. It was accomplished with southern tact. The cattle boom in La Salle County had ended, and the Dick Halls had decided to take up ranching in Williamson County. On their way to the new spread, the Halls simply dropped their idler-in-residence at the spacious home of Joe Harrell, Sr., on Lavaca Street in Austin. Harrell, a retired merchant, had migrated to Austin from Greensboro and had four sons about Will's age living with him. Once again Will found himself in cozy circumstances as a long-term non-paying guest. For him the term southern hospitality always had an especially truthful and heartwarming ring. This is not to say Will Porter was a parasite. He was as openhanded, ridiculously so, as he expected others to be.

At the time of his arrival Austin was beginning to live up to its pretensions as a center of culture as well as the capital of the state. It had crossed the 10,000 mark in the 1880 census, and a large part of its population was German-American, part of a flood of Germans migrating to Texas back in the days when it was a republic and bringing with them a considerable musical, literary and artistic tradition. There were theaters, opera, *Sängerfests* fueled by tides of lager, libraries and trolley lines.

But there was also considerable evidence of frontier woolliness, despite the claims of its businessmen that Austin definitely had been tamed and its wilder element either expelled or civilized. There were twice as many saloons as churches, for one thing. And there was a certain admiration for lawlessness still noticeable enough for Will to make the hyperbolic claim that the city had been founded not only by the sainted Stephen F. Austin but Daniel Boone, Davy Crockett, Ponce de León and Ben Thompson. This group, by Will's account, "got a gun and killed off the Indians between the lunatic asylum and the river and laid out Austin. It has been laid out ever since."

His inclusion of Ben Thompson was well merited, though respectable citizens liked to pretend Thompson was just passing through. Actually Ben Thompson was Austin's leading citizen, if you measured celebrity by the hush that fell on a barroom when he swaggered in, by the column inches of his publicity in the Austin *Daily Statesman*, by the number of citizens who ducked into doorways when they saw him coming down the street, by the sudden blanching of prominent cattlemen when his name was mentioned.

Will was able to study his career at close hand and make use of it in his stories. The Cisco Kid, among other desperate characters in O. Henry's portrait gallery, probably owed a lot to that study. Thompson was a mild-looking but quick-tempered gunman-gambler who had served in the Confederate Army and later in that of Emperor Maximilian during the latter's doomed reign in Mexico. He was said to have dispatched anywhere from twenty to fifty opponents in various showdowns and shoot-outs all over the Southwest, some of the forays undoubtedly traceable to his habit of drinking two quarts of brandy a day.

Shortly before Will arrived in Austin, Thompson had nominated himself for the office of city marshal, proclaiming that "I have always been the friend of the defenseless, and most of the difficulties attending the independent life I have led were incurred by sensitive love of fair play and an irresistible impulse to protect the timid and weak." As the Austin *Daily Statesman* delicately commented, he was a "formidable" opponent for Ed Creary, the longtime incumbent in that office. The forces of respectability, as opposed to the operators of saloons, gambling houses and dance halls around Congress Avenue and Sixth Street, prevailed against Thompson's candidacy. In his disappointment, Thompson raged up and down Congress Avenue, shot up the Iron Front Saloon, and fired a few rounds into the offices of the *Daily Statesman* to indicate his displeasure at its fainthearted support. At the next election the city sensibly placed him in the marshal's office and he served with some distinction.

Austin learned that it did not pay to trifle with Ben Thompson or his friends. An attorney named E. L. Edwards appeared at the annual banquet of the Texas Live Stock Association without an invitation. The cattlemen, presumably unaware that the lawyer was a bosom friend of Thompson's, booted him out.

Thompson arrived on the scene a short time later just when the merriment was reaching its crest. Whiskey had been flowing freely for the past several hours. Shanghai Pierce, the huge and testy-tempered cattle baron whose voice, it was said, "could be heard nearly half a mile even when he tried to whisper," was outraged because he had asked his fellow banqueters to pass the turkey and no one had complied. Pierce courteously removed his spurs, jumped up on the table and was walking toward the turkey platter when Ben Thompson appeared in the doorway, unlimbered his .45 and roared:

"Show me the rascal that don't like E. L. Edwards!"

A sudden hush fell over the roisterers in Simon's Cafe. Thompson began shooting the plates off the table. Most of the cattlemen stampeded for the nearest exits. Shanghai Pierce leaped through the nearest window and took the sash with him. All but Lee Hall and another man, who stayed at their places and merely stared at Thompson, had cleared out in less than sixty seconds.

Thompson then departed, and the banqueters crept back to their ruined feast.

Such consolation as was possible came from the toastmaster, who rose and offered thanks that Thompson hadn't been really mad and shot a few banqueters.

"Did he hold up the whole convention of a thousand cattlemen?" the toastmaster demanded. "No, gentlemen, he waited until he got forty or fifty of us poor fellows alone before he went into his shooting act."

Will never had the opportunity of meeting Ben Thompson in person, because shortly after he took up residence with the Harrell family Thompson and another notorious gunfighter named King Fisher went over to San Antonio one day to see a performance of *East Lynne*. After sobbing over the melodrama, the two men stepped across the street to a burlesque theater, where they walked into an ambush and were killed by several of their many ill-wishers.

The underside of Austin life, even minus Ben Thompson and King Fisher, fascinated Will from the beginning of his stay. Shortly after obtaining work as a registered pharmacist in a drugstore on East Pecan Street, he began roaming the town at night, particularly the saloon and dance hall district, a habit he later resumed in the New York Tenderloin. He called it "bumming," according to Dixie Daniels, a printer who worked in a shop near the drugstore and who often accompanied him.

"Night after night, after we would shut up shop," recalled Daniels, "he would call to me to come along and 'go bumming.' . . . We would wander through streets and alleys, meeting with some of the worst specimens of down-and-outers it has ever been my privilege to see at close range. I've seen the most ragged specimen of a bum hold up Porter, who would always do anything he could for the man. His one great failing was his inability to say 'No' to a man. He never cared for the so-called 'higher classes,' but watched the people on the streets and in the shops and cafes."[14] Subconsciously Will Porter was doing his research, soaking up the impressions and filing away the characters that were to people his three hundred short stories.

After two or three months he wearied of steady work in the drugstore and contented himself with enjoying the hospitality of the Harrell family. He indicated to his host that he was trying to think up some worthwhile vocation to pursue, but he seemed to spend most of his time reading, sketching, gazing at the ceiling or strumming a guitar. He did manage to employ his serviceable tenor as a member of the Hill City Quartet, but that could hardly qualify as a career. It was one of his hibernating periods when his metabolism seemed to burn low; only occasionally would he rouse himself and help out part-time behind the counter of Joe Harrell, Jr.'s, cigar store. Pointedly, perhaps, the senior Harrell offered to send Will to art school in New York City, but Will put him off with various excuses.

The role of the gay young bachelor suited him fine. He was one of a number of young blades who made up a serenading party and rendered their unique, and often unwanted, services to the community. "Our serenading party," he related in a letter May 10, 1885, "has developed new and alarming modes of torture for our helpless and sleeping victims. Last Thursday night we loaded up a small organ on a hack and with our other usual instruments made an assault upon the quiet air of midnight that made the atmosphere turn pale. After going the rounds we were halted on the Avenue by Fritz Hartkopf and ordered into his salon. We went in, carrying the organ, etc. A large crowd of bums immediately gathered, prominent among which were to be seen Percy Hicks, Theodore Hillyer, Randolph Burmond, Charlie Hicks, and after partaking freely of lemonade we wended our way down, and were duly halted and treated in the same manner by other hospitable gentlemen. We were called in at several places while wit and champagne, Rhine Wine, etc., flowed in a most joyous manner. It was one of the most recherché and per diem affairs ever known in the city. Nothing occurred to mar the pleasure of the hour. . . ."[15]

Without visible means of support—except the generosity of the Harrell family—he evidently cut a dashing figure in the capital's social circles. He was always well dressed and generally high-spirited. A photograph taken of him in his first years in Austin shows a fairly handsome young man with a sweeping gunfighter's mustache twisted at the ends, a slightly pudgy face and dark hair arranged in the fashion now associated with pre-Prohibition barkeeps. One associate credited him with being able to "drink more beer than any man his size"—about five feet six—that he had ever seen. The beer thirst was to stay with him almost to the end.

After about a year of lazing around, he bestirred himself and accepted a position as bookkeeper with the real estate firm of Maddox Bros. & Anderson. One of the partners, Charles E. Anderson, adopted Will as a sort of protege. His salary was $100 a month, a lot of money in those days for an apprentice bookkeeper.

He stayed with the firm for two years, until January 1887, when Dick Hall—benefactors always kept popping up in Will Porter-O. Henry's life—became state land commissioner. Hall made a place for Will on the state's payroll as an assistant draftsman at the same salary he had been receiving as a bookkeeper for Maddox & Anderson. And the four years he spent in the Land Office were probably the happiest of his life. Some of his experiences were included in such stories as "Witches' Loaves," "Georgia's Ruling" and "Buried Treasure."

His work in the Land Office, which was housed in a castellated building on a hill across from the capitol, was filled with importance and human drama, he believed. "People living in other States can form no conception of the vastness and importance of the work performed here and the significance of the millions of records and papers composing the archives of this office. The title deeds, patents, transfers, and legal documents connected with every foot of land owned in the State of Texas are filed here . . .

"The honest but ignorant settler, bent on saving the little plot of land he called home, elbowed the wary land shark who was searching the records for evidence to oust him; the lordly cattle baron, relying on his influence and money, stood at the Commissioner's desk side by side with the pre-emptor, whose little potato patch lay like a minute speck of island in the vast, billowy sea of his princely pastures, and played the old game of 'freeze-out,' which is as old as Cain and Abel."

In his story "Bexar Scrip No. 2692," he detailed just how the "quick hand of the land grabber" reached out to defraud the unwary, in this case a widow and her only son. "Twenty years ago there was a shrewd land agent living in Austin who devoted his undoubted talents and vast knowledge of land titles, and the laws governing them, to the locating of surveys made by illegal certificates or improperly made, and otherwise of no value through non-compliance with the statutes, or whatever flaws his ingenious and unscrupulous mind could unearth. . . . He found a fatal defect in the title of the land as on file in Bexar Scrip No. 2692 and placed a new certificate upon the survey in his own name.

"The law was on his side. Every sentiment of justice, of right, and humanity was against him. The certificate by virtue of which the original survey had been made was missing. . . . Under the law the land was vacant, unappropriated public domain and open to location. . . . The railroad had surveyed a new line through the property, and it had doubled in value. . . ."

The larcenous land agent eventually had to commit a murder to make good his fraudulent claim to the widow's property, but "The last two years of his life were clouded with a settled melancholy for which his friends could assign no reason."[16]

Much that he witnessed in the Land Office undoubtedly reinforced a resentment of the privileged class which figured, in varying degrees of subtlety, in his work and which made his stories so acceptable to Soviet Communism that he is regarded, along with Jack London, as a proletarian crusader. This is a misapprehension, but there is no doubt that he acquired a sense of social justice from all the attempted trickery and land-sharking he saw in the Land Office. In his small way, he could help the small landowner defend himself against the range barons and this made him feel, for the first time in his life, that he was doing something worthwhile.

Even the place where he worked delighted his artistic eye with its medieval conformation rising out of the raw young city. "You think of the Rhine; the 'castled crag of Drachenfels'; the

Lorelei; and the vine-clad slopes of Germany. And German it is in every line of its architecture and design. The plan was drawn by an old draftsman from the 'Vaterland,' whose heart still loved the scenes of his native land, and it is said he reproduced the design of a certain castle near his birthplace with remarkable fidelity.

"Under the present administration"—he was writing three years after leaving the Land Office—"a new coat of paint has vulgarized its ancient and venerable walls. Modern tiles have replaced the limestone slabs of its floors, worn in hollows by the tread of thousands of feet, and smart and gaudy fixtures have usurped the place of the time-worn furniture that has been consecrated by the touch of hands that Texas will never cease to honor. But even now, when you enter the building, you lower your voice, and time turns backward for you, for the atmosphere which you breathe is cold with the exudations of buried generations. The building is stone with a coating of concrete; the walls are immensely thick; it is cool in the summer and warm in the winter; it is isolated and sombre; standing apart from the other state buildings, sullen and decaying, brooding on the past."

The old building was converted into a museum eventually but continued to testify to the "consecration" which young Will Porter believed to dwell there. The sacredness of boundary lines may seem a little difficult to understand today, but they were a matter of life and death to the settlers of Texas, and he regarded his work on their behalf as anything but that of a bureaucratic drone.

Chapter 2. The Girl in Dimity

About six months after entering the Land Office, Will Porter, then in his twenty-fifth year, married a nineteen-year-old girl named Athol Estes after a courtship strewn with obstacles. The romantic aspects of that courtship, in which he won out over a more prosperous rival favored by the girl's parents, delighted the younger element of Austin. But the older people shook their heads over the affair because Will Porter seemed something of a lightweight to them, not particularly promising.

Will met Athol when she was a seventeen-year-old high-school girl. She was born in Tennessee, where her father died of tuberculosis, the scourge of the nineteenth century as cancer is of the twentieth. Her mother had remarried, and her stepfather, P. G. Roach, had moved to Austin with his new family.

Judging by her photographs, Athol was not a beauty but was an attractive girl with light brown hair, blue eyes and a "peachbloom" complexion. There was a vivid aura about her often noted in those with a tubercular strain: an almost unnatural vivacity, a determination to live at high pitch. Her romance with Will Porter was described in rather sugary terms by one of her girlhood friends, Frances Maltby, in *The Dimity Sweetheart*—a portrait of Athol. "Athol," wrote Frances Maltby, "was a belle from babyhood to maturity by sheer right of charm." She usually wore dresses of dimity, a thin cotton fabric, and many of O. Henry's heroines also wore dimity. His explanation was simple enough: "Athol always wore dimity."

Will met the belle at a dance sponsored by the Austin Grays, a state militia company, and apparently fell in love with her at first sight.

The first ostacle to their relationship was the girl's parents, particularly her mother. Mrs. Roach wanted "the best" for Athol, and young Mr. Porter's prospects did not seem to fit into that category.

The second obstacle was a suitor with prior claims. He was a darkly handsome, dashing young man with the un-dashing name of Zimpelmann, the type who drove a fancy carriage with fast-stepping horses. Lee Zimpelmann was the son and heir of a wealthy German-American family, utterly respectable, and with the manners likely to endear him to a prospective mother-in-law.

Mrs. Roach considered that her daughter was too young to be engaged, which may have been a tactical mistake on her part. Zimpelmann, with Teutonic foresight, had established his claim to be the first to ask for her hand by giving Athol a locket and an opal ring. His handicap was a certain stolidity, an inability to imagine that a mucker like Will Porter could steal the girl from him.

From various accounts, especially Mrs. Maltby's, it is apparent that Will moved in fast and with a dogged determination. If the Roaches objected to him as a suitor, their attitude was balanced by that of the girl's friends, female, who sighed over the stylishly waxed points of his mustache, his melodious voice and his drollery. "Isn't he adorable?" the girls would sigh when he passed, according to Mrs. Maltby's recollection. Athol thought so, because they shared one indelible quality—a high-spirited romanticism of the sort long vanished from the relations of young American men and women.

Soon Athol was seeing more of Will than of his rival, despite her mother's warnings that Will was "too sporty" and that there was tuberculosis on his mother's side of the family as there was on Athol's father's side. Any children they might have would be doubly endangered. But Athol could not resist Will's charm and wit, his habit of showing up with the Hill City Quartet and singing under her bedroom window to the further annoyance of Mr. and Mrs. Roach. By the time she graduated from high school in June 1887 they were unofficially engaged.

The Roaches, however, were still withholding their consent and approval. Athol and Will decided they would have to proceed on their own. They met downtown and Will persuaded the girl to elope with him that night. It was late afternoon before they made the decision, and Will had to enlist the help of his former employer, Charles Anderson, in obtaining a marriage license after hours at the county clerk's office. They then rented a carriage from a livery stable and drove to the home of the Rev. L. K. Smoot, pastor of the Southern Presbyterian Church. Rev. Smoot was presiding at a church meeting and did not return to his home until about ten o'clock.

The minister was appalled at the idea of Athol's marrying without her parents' permission but finally yielded to the argument that they were both old enough, had a license and would be married by someone else if necessary. After the brief ceremony, they went to the home of the Charles Andersons, where they lived for the next six months. Anderson, at midnight, was delegated the unhappy role of bringing the news to the Roaches. Mrs. Roach was enraged, no less so the next day, when the *Daily Statesman* carried a story under the headline "HEARTS UNITED" which made it plain enough that they had married without her approval.

The Roaches finally came to accept what they couldn't change, and more than once befriended Will when he had no one else to turn to.

There was that charm of his in full operation, able to turn away the wrath even of an outraged mother-in-law, perhaps the severest test to which it could be put. His appeal to men and women alike, his ability to win their confidence, trust and support under the most adverse circumstances, was one of his most notable characteristics. People couldn't help being attracted by his high-heartedness, his gaiety and his wit, which could be penetrating but was never malicious. There was nothing small-minded or mean-spirited about him.

And there was more than mere surface charm, the easy flattering manner of a southern gentleman, because he kept the friends he made so quickly and frequently. If he sometimes asked much of friendship, he was also willing to give much. Someone who needed money could rely on him to turn his pockets inside out.

Most of all he had the ability to make people laugh, whether they felt like it or not. He was a born entertainer with a vaudeville actor's repertoire of songs and jokes. In his company, ordinarily sobersided people like his father-in-law suddenly found themselves sparkling, apparently, with a wit to equal his own. This sort of talent naturally flourished in a saloon, but Will could turn it on with equal facility in the parlor or at a church social.

In its early stage the marriage was happy enough. Athol encouraged her husband to make something of himself as a writer, and was probably as tolerant as most young wives would have been when he stayed out late singing beerily with his friends. The sentimental author of *The Dimity Sweetheart* would testify that it was the love match of the ages. But Athol was a "belle," a southern belle at that, with a habit of command that would grow firmer with every passing year, and more than a little possessive.

Will Porter, by then O. Henry, told his closest confidante many years later in New York that Athol was the only woman he ever loved.

But love was one thing, marriage another. The institution, he once declaimed to his editor and friend, Robert H. Davis, ought to be abolished. "In all matters of the heart the word o-w-n-e-r-s-h-i-p should be expunged," he explained. "Friends of mine, who have forced confidence upon me, are a unit in the conclusion that romance is a form of proprietorship, that is to say a gent supposedly living a free and unencumbered existence casts a languishing eye upon a fair woman, lets a few kind words slip into his conversation, allows her hand to repose in his for a split second and then finds himself on a par with the leading character in *Uncle Tom's Cabin*. . . .

"In chains . . . Manacled, clanking in a lock step with his fate. Thus old Uncle Tom comes to, with the discovery that his Simon

Legree is a perfect lady who owns him body and soul. . . . Ambrose Bierce sized it up when he drafted that masterful toast: 'To woman. O that we could fall into her arms instead of her hands.'"[1]

One great merit of Athol Porter was that she believed in him and his embryonic talent when few others took him seriously. He began selling a few sketches to the Detroit *Free Press,* a New York periodical called *Truth,* the McClure Syndicate, the Houston *Daily Post,* for which he received checks of less than ten dollars each. At least it was a beginning. Doubtless Athol was determined to show her mother that she was wrong about Will's "sporty" inclinations. He trotted along with her to sing in a church choir, though undoubtedly he would have preferred the less sacred music and sprightlier company of the Hill City Quartet. By their friends' account they were a happy and well-mated young couple.

They lived in a small frame house on East Fourth Street, a block away from the commercial bustle of Market Square and from the horse trolley cars on East Fifth. Just down the block was the larger house occupied by the Roaches. Carefully restored, the Porters' home is now the O. Henry Museum and has been moved to 409 East Fifth. Hermann Becker, his landlord, donated it to the city in 1934.

The little house with its elaborate scrollwork is a tourist attraction drawing about three hundred visitors a month, according to Mrs. Maree Larson, the curator, who is particularly amazed by the number of foreign visitors making a long out-of-the-way trip to Austin. They testify, perhaps, to his greater popularity abroad in modern times than in his own country. "I think every foreigner who comes to town visits here," Mrs. Larson said recently. "I'm continually amazed at the languages O. Henry has been translated into. One man said he'd read O. Henry's complete works in Rumanian!"

It is evident that Mr. and Mrs. Will Porter lived in modest comfort. In the parlor there is a concert grand piano made of rosewood with mother-of-pearl inlay above the keyboard.

The small mahogany desk where Will wrote his first "bits and pieces" once belonged to Sam Houston's secretary, whose daughter gave it to the Porters. In the kitchen is the heavy iron "fluting" machine on which Athol put ruffles in her dimity dresses and bonnets. Over the bedroom door is the true O. Henry touch —a horseshoe Will nailed there as his talisman.

The horseshoe, however, proved incapable of warding off the bad luck that began to afflict the little house on East Fourth. The Porters' first child, a boy, was born in their big Victorian bed but lived only a few hours. Athol's health began to decline after that, and she barely survived the birth of their second child, Margaret, in 1889. By then her tuberculosis had flared up for the first time.

The possessiveness which Will deplored in women also made an early appearance, possibly heightened by the fact that Athol was Mrs. Roach's only child and had been spoiled. When Will came home late, Betty Hall would recall, Athol would "lie on the floor and scream." Later, Mrs. Hall observed, Athol became downright shrewish and delighted in starting quarrels with Will in public, a humiliation that made him visibly cringe.[2]

It seemed a bad omen, too, when Will lost his job at the Land Office due to a change in administration. Once again, however, Charles Anderson came to his rescue, this time by getting him a job as teller at the First National Bank, again with a salary of $100 a month. He held that job for the next three years, from 1891 to 1894, though he must often have wondered whether he was permanently chained to minor office jobs, each of them paying exactly the same salary. He was still a bank teller when he passed the age of thirty, usually a time for personal stock taking and serious pondering of the future.

His prospects must have seemed dim, with an ailing and often ill-tempered and unreasonable wife at his side, a young daughter to care for, and his highest probable attainment the desk of the chief cashier at the First National. To bring in a little extra money he occasionally wrote a short humorous piece for a magazine or newspaper, and also provided the twenty-six illustrations for a book by J. K. Wilbarger titled *Indian Depredations in Texas: Reliable Accounts of Battles, Wars, Adventures, Forays, Massacres, Murders, Etc., Etc.*

One summer while he was working at the bank he scraped up enough money to take Athol and their daughter to meet his family in Greensboro. His grandmother had died but Aunt Lina was still alive and vigorous. The old hometown only depressed him, as he described the visit a few years later in a magazine sketch: "I got off at the old depot, and then commenced the strange feeling of loss, depression and change that so much alteration wrought. I walked down the old familiar streets and gazed in deepest wonder at the scenes around me. The streets seemed narrower, the houses smaller and meaner; every prospect had shrunken and grown into ruin and decadence. I met men in the street by whose side I had grown up from my earliest boyhood. They all passed me with either a curious stare or a careless glance. . . ."[3]

Back in Austin his life wasn't any less depressing for a young man of imagination. Banking was not suited to his temperament; he could not regard United States currency as something sacred and a column of figures as something of surpassing beauty. Often in the teller's cage he whiled away the time by making sketches and drawing caricatures. Word also got around town that he liked to sit in on a poker game fairly often and occasionally to roister in the saloons. On one occasion, he later admitted, he experimented with absinthe, a concoction of wormwood and alcohol now prohibited in the United States, and was fascinated by its effect—"an exalted sense of non-participation in worldly affairs."

Actually a dreamer had no business behind the bars of a teller's cage in a Texas bank. A man needed his wits about him if he hoped to stay out of trouble. Banking practices were irregular, to say the least, in keeping with the freewheeling atmosphere. Large overdrafts were allowed to the bank's better customers, and its officials had a habit of helping themselves from the tellers' cash drawers, often without leaving a slip to indicate the informal transaction had taken place.

His short story "Friends in San Rosario" has often been cited as providing an insight into the kind of slipshod banking methods which may have been partly responsible for his own subsequent difficulties. In the story Bob Buckley, president of the Stockmen's National Bank, is surprised by a visit from the federal bank examiner to San Rosario. The examiner goes first to the bank across the street. Buckley sends a note over to the president of the other bank asking him to stall the man while he gathers up enough cash to replenish his bank's reserves. The note reads: ". . . We've got just $2,200 in the bank, and the law requires that we have $20,000. I let Ross and Fisher have $18,000 late yesterday afternoon to buy up that Gibson bunch of cattle. They'll realize $40,000 in less than thirty days on the transaction, but that won't make my cash on hand any prettier to that bank examiner. Now I can't show him those notes, for they're just plain notes of hand without any security in sight, but you know very well that Pink Ross and Jim Fisher are two of the finest white men God ever made, and they'll do the square thing. You remember Jim Fisher—he was the one who shot that faro dealer in El Paso. I wired Sam Bradshaw's bank to send me $20,000, and it will get in on the narrow-gauge at 10:35. You can't let a bank examiner in to count $2,200 and close your doors. Tom, you hold that examiner. Hold him. Hold him if you have to rope him and sit on his head. Watch our front window after the narrow-gauge gets in, and when we've got the cash inside we'll pull down the shade for a signal. . . ."

While still working at the bank, he got the ambition to edit and publish a humorous weekly of his own. He tried to raise the money for such a project but failed. Then in the spring of 1894 came the chance to buy the printing press on which William C. Brann ("Brann the Iconoclast") published his vituperative monthly. Brann's sheet, called *The Iconoclast*, had failed to find much favor in conservative Austin. Later he re-established it in Waco and attained a nationwide circulation of 90,000 through a constant and calefactory eruption of Brann's adverse opinions of humanity and its institutions. The Iconoclast's career was ended with a bullet in 1898. Now, however, in 1894 he was willing to sell his press for $250 cash, which Will raised from friends. Will, with a partner named James P. Crane, went into production immediately with a weekly called *The Rolling Stone,* which in the course of a year's publication gathered considerable moss from Will's father-in-law and friends in the form of loans its publisher was unable to repay.

Surviving copies of that periodical are now collector's items, but during its brief life, from April 28, 1894, to April 27, 1895, it tottered continually on the verge of bankruptcy. Until the end of 1894 Will worked at the First National Bank daytimes and wrote and edited *The Rolling Stone* after hours, an exhausting schedule that must have astonished friends who considered him a rather lackadaisical young man. The business and production side of the operation were handled by various persons, including Dixie Daniels, the printer, with whom he "bummed" around in Austin's night life, his father-in-law, who was also on tap for loans, and Athol herself, who helped around the office.

The Rolling Stone was a loosely compiled weekly, usually eight pages, sometimes twelve, five columns wide, which included comments on local and national events, satirical jabs at local personalities, humorous sketches and squibs. It was modestly introduced to its paying and non-paying subscribers—never numbering more than 1,500—by its conférencier as a paper which "will endeavor to fill a long-felt want, that does not appear, by the way, to be altogether insatiable at present. The idea is to fill its pages with matter that will make a heartrending appeal to every lover of good literature, and every person who has a taste for reading print and a dollar and a half for a year's subscription. . . . Each number will contain stories, humorous sketches, poems, jokes, properly labeled, side-splitting references to the mother-in-law, the goat Governor Hogg, and the States of the Weather and Texas."

Will wrote most of the paper, except for material bought from the syndicates, including Bill Nye's column, and drew its illustrations. Some of his comments, satirical and otherwise, reflected the editor's attitudes on social problems, which veered from comparatively liberal to crusty southern conservative. The invasion of Washington by General Jacob Coxey's army of the unemployed drew enough of his sympathy to satisfy the claims of his present-day Russian admirers that he detested the capitalistic system:

"General Coxey has made a great blunder. He and his fellows should have gone to Washington clad in broadcloth and fine garments, and backed by a big bank roll, as the iron, steel, sugar and other lobbyist delegations do. He should have taken apartments at the Arlington, and given receptions and dinners. That's the way to get legislation at the hands of the American congress. This thing of leading a few half clothed and worse fed working men to the capitol grounds to indulge in the vulgar and old-fashioned peaceable assemblage to petition for redress of grievances, with not a dollar of boodle in sight for the oppressed and overworked members of congress was of course an outrage and so the perpetrators were promptly squelched by the strong hand of the 'law.'"[4] Coxey and some of his followers, in fact, were arrested on charges of walking on the grass of the Capitol lawns.

On the other hand, Porter's views on lynching were certainly such as to satisfy the most orthodox Southerner of his time. Commenting on a lynching in the town of Corsicana, he wrote: "Of course, northern papers will teem with misrepresentations of the affair and will indulge in abusing the South generally and the State of Texas in particular. But what do we care for their strictures? Southern manhood has a method of dealing with this class of crime that is at least satisfactory to those who mete out justice. . . . Our people will pursue the even tenor of their ways until it again becomes necessary to make an example of some brute of northern proclivities, and they will then prove themselves equal to the emergency."[5]

The main target of his satire, it appears, was the German-American element, its appetite for music and thirst for beer.

Since it was well known that Will Porter shared those proclivities in full, if not Teutonic, measure, he could see no reason for any of the burghers to be offended; especially since some of his best friends were German.

Will began irritating some of his German readers almost from the first issues. In his account of the *Sängerfest* in Houston during the joyous bock beer season of 1894, he reported that "Yesterday was the first day of the Saengerfest, and today is universally acknowledged to be the second. Tomorrow, if the beer holds out, will be the third." A number of German readers wrote in protest, declaring he had insulted their nationality by inferring that they swilled beer day and night. Will more or less apologized in print and explained that his reportage from Houston had been "conceived in a spirit of pure fun and printed without a wish or thought that it would possibly give serious offense to anyone."

He was not content to lay aside his barbs, however, and several weeks later published the imaginary reply of his imaginary Houston correspondent, "Gottlieb Kremhauser," answering the editor's charges that he had distorted the facts about the *Sängerfest* and protesting amazement that some of the Austin Germans had complained. ". . . I not de half of it you told . . . It vas der krandest wunderschon, most peautiful, high-doned und boetical dime efer seen in dis country. We trink tree hundert kegs peer. De music vas schveet und knocked most all der blastering from der walls in de opera house. . . ."

Will followed that up with the humorous account of a detective named Hans von Pretzel, who was assigned to check out the report that a notorious diamond thief was hiding on a schooner. Von Pretzel's search led him to a beer garden and a schooner of beer instead of the waterfront.

He also zeroed in on what ladies' magazines and other social commentators called The New Woman—the girl of independent spirit, with brashly modern ideas, who left home and took a job. *The Rolling Stone* came down heavily on the side of the old-fashioned girl who stayed home and waited for Mr. Right. Will provided an acidulous profile of the young woman who would soon be parading with the suffragists and demanding the right to vote:

"Her conversation is embellished with such expressions as 'You bet your life,' 'You ain't in it,' 'I should smile,' 'Rats,' and 'Come off.' She chews gum. She wears shirts and ties, and either cuts her hair short or blondines it. She will not refuse a glass of beer, if insisted upon and not more than fifteen persons are looking. She chews gum. She says 'hello' and catches young men by the sleeve on the street when she talks to them, which is every time she meets them.

"She rides a bicycle if her figure justifies it, and sometimes whether or not. She chews gum. She goes on excursions to other towns and up the river with young men whose reputations and intentions are well known. She is losing that delicacy and spotlessness which a man may not look for in a companion for a boat ride, but demands in a wife. She is cheapening her charms by advertising them, and the day will come when she will be 'marked down' in price."[6]

Will was leading a double life as a journalist and a bank clerk, and his habits became more bohemian and therefore more distressing to Athol, who had never been inclined to view them with indulgence. After banking hours and between editorial chores at *The Rolling Stone* offices in the Driskill Hotel block, he would adjourn to the Bismarck Cafe, where the heavily Germanic atmosphere, including portraits of Kaiser Wilhelm and Prince Bismarck glowering at each other across the room, seemed to please him. He had his own table at the Bismarck, where he consumed immense seidels of Pilsener and placed himself on a sybaritic diet of Hungarian goulash, sweetbreads, cream puffs and preserved ginger. Dixie Daniels, his printer and drinking companion, recalled that "One of his favorite amusements was lounging about a cafe, eating caviar sandwiches and throwing dice for beers."

The admiring Daniels also remembered that Will could "drink half a gallon" of beer "without taking the vessel from his mouth."[7]

People began talking about him and wondering whether his heavy drinking—and the reported poker games over which he presided in *The Rolling Stone* office—were compatible with his position as a teller at the First National Bank. Presumably the buzz of gossip only increased when, on several occasions, Athol appeared at *The Rolling Stone* office around midnight and tried to break in the locked door which confronted her. It was alleged in whispers that Athol's anger was aroused because he had another woman in the locked office, with whom he may not have been reading the galley proofs.[8] Later the local moralists would be able to conjecture that Will's growing waywardness during the period of his editorship of *The Rolling Stone* was only one symptom of the pressures he was experiencing, which would become even more evident when the word got around that there was a shortage in his accounts at the First National.

Will Porter was thirty-two years old when the cruncher came. From all the testimony of his friends, he was ill equipped to deal with any kind of adversity, particularly that of his own making. Consistently, since early youth, he had exerted his considerable charm and used his friends and in-laws as a crutch whenever necessary. Charm had got him by thus far, but it wouldn't work with the law. He was winsomely irresponsible when it came to handling money, either his own or someone else's, but a federal bank examiner would not be impressed by his blithe and boyish personality. With an alcoholic father and a mother who died when he was three years old, he had survived a harder life than most; yet it had only made him more resistant to maturity. The strongest element in his character, and the most enduring, was the way he clung to the privilege of youthful irresponsibility.

The first sign that there was something wrong with his accounts at the bank—that he had been using bank funds, as most of his closest friends believed, to make up the deficits in *The Rolling Stone*'s chronically depleted treasury—came in mid-December 1894. He suddenly resigned as teller. Inevitably word spread around the city that there was a shortage, since his resignation more or less coincided with the visit of a federal bank examiner.

Will, perhaps wisely, behaved as though nothing disastrous had happened. He announced that he was going to start up a San Antonio edition of *The Rolling Stone.* After making that bravura announcement, he left Austin for San Antonio. On December 20, he wrote a somewhat enigmatic letter to James P. Crane, who had served as Will's partner on *The Rolling Stone*'s staff during its early issues but had since gone to Chicago. He rather breezily informed Crane that he had arrived in "the City of Tamales" the previous night to "work up the *Rolling Stone* a little over here. Went over the city by gas-light. It is fearfully and wonderfully made. I quit the bank a day or two ago. . . ."

Despite his plans to expand his paper's circulation to the San Antonio area, Will surprisingly, in the next paragraph, suggested that Crane find him a job on a Chicago newspaper. This would indicate, possibly, that he didn't intend to hang around Texas and face charges over the shortage at the First National.

". . . I tell you what I want to do," he wrote Crane. "I want to get up in that country somewhere on some kind of newspaper. Can't you work up something for us to go at there? If you can I will come up there any time at one day's notice. I can worry along here and about live but it is not the place for one to get ahead. . . ."[9]

No encouragement about the prospects in Chicago came from Crane, however, and Will returned to Austin after making arrangements for publication of a San Antonio edition of *The Rolling Stone* (which was short-lived). Meanwhile there was that business of the shortage in his accounts to be straightened out.

Despite all the intricate defenses of Will Porter he erected in his later manifestation as O. Henry, it would appear that technically, at least, he was responsible for the shortage.

Some of his sympathizers went to extraordinary lengths, including an essay in amateur psychology, to "prove" that Will Porter simply couldn't have tapped the till. These included an elaborate theory that he was so hurt, so crushed by the accusation that he was unable to speak up in his own defense; that he characteristically wilted under attack and was psychologically unable to defend himself. Another theory is that he was covering up for someone else. But he would have had to be remarkably masochistic or extraordinarily chivalrous to submit himself to the probability of a prison sentence, the disgrace to his ailing wife, their daughter, his in-laws and friends, merely out of supinity or misguided friendship.

The more reasonable of these theories constructed on his behalf, of course, is the one suggesting he took the fall for someone else. The bank itself admitted that during the noon hour another person, George W. Brackenridge, the cashier, took over Will's cage while he went to lunch.

Self-incrimination, however, may be noted in the cold officialese of F. B. Gray, the federal bank examiner, in his report to the Comptroller of the Currency and the Department of Justice.

Gray, who was to insist on Will's prosecution over the initial protests of the United States attorney in Austin and of the bank itself, reported that a conference was held between Frank Hamilton, vice-president of the First National, and Carr Lucy, a representative of the company which had bonded Will Porter. Hamilton formally requested that the surety company pay off, but Lucy pointed out that there was no definite proof that Will took the money. Gray's report continued:

". . . It looked a little formidable to Hamilton and he saw at once that he had a law suit on his hands with the possibility of losing the case. He then applied to Porter and a Mr. Roach who is a relative of Porter's wife and gave them to understand that he must have his money. Circumstances go to show that, to avoid the law suit, the three, Hamilton, Lucy and Roach, held a conference and agreed upon the following settlement:

"Roach agreed to pay $1500 provided Lucy would pay $1500 and the Bank lose the remainder and provided further that both Hamilton and Lucy should use the utmost endeavors to get Porter released from the complaints I had filed against him. Hamilton told the U.S. Attorney that it was his opinion that Porter intended no wrong, what he did was only *a series of mistakes* and he should not be prosecuted."[10]

It was generally understood that the case of *U.S.* v. *William S. Porter* would be submitted to the July session of the federal grand jury. Until then, Will was free to do as he pleased. The community, on the whole, was sympathetic; Athol and her family were loyal to him, and joined in the chorus protesting his innocence. And his cause was aided when the officers of the First National let it be known they couldn't believe that Will had embezzled the missing funds.

As a man of gambling instinct he evidently operated under the theory: when in trouble double your bet. Instead of closing down the money-losing *Rolling Stone*, he went through with his plan to establish a San Antonio edition. He was not always the best judge of people, and appointed as his editor-in-charge in San Antonio an Englishman who happened to be passing through Austin and proclaimed himself to have been the "amanuensis" of Charles Dickens. (The Dickens family said they never heard of him.) His name, he said, was Henry Ryder-Taylor and he had formerly been dramatic editor of the London *Telegraph* as well as Dickens' associate. Ryder-Taylor soon demonstrated his incompetence, and Dixie Daniels later recorded, "How Taylor had any influence over him I never was able to make out, for he [Porter] used constantly to make fun of him. 'Here comes that man Taylor,' he'd say. 'Got a diamond on him as big as a two-bit piece and shining like granulated sugar.' "[11]

With no banking duties to occupy him, Will made an effort to improve the quality of *The Rolling Stone*. One added feature was "The Plunkville Patriot," a section made up in imitation of a backwoods weekly full of typos and transposed lines. The humor was bucolic, one item being a broadside from his fictitious editor against a grocer who had withdrawn his advertising: "No less than three children have been poisoned by eating their canned vegetables, and J. O. Adams, the senior member of the firm, was run out of Kansas City for adulterating codfish balls." He also produced parodies in verse, such as that of Thomas

Hood's *The Bridge of Sighs,* which may have been a rueful recap of his own experiences as a husband with many late homecomings on his record:

> One more unfortunate,
> Weary of breath,
> Chewing cloves hastily,
> Scared half to death.
> O, it was pitiful,
> He left the city full
> Quarter past one.
>
> Prop him up tenderly
> By the hall stair,
> On a big bender, he
> Needs some fresh air.
> Now run! His wife's got her
> Hands in his hair.

In the last weeks of *The Rolling Stone*'s existence Will got so desperate over its prospective collapse that he and two friends, one of them the faithful Dixie Daniels, went out looking for buried treasure. The three men investigated an old legend that a Mexican army paymaster's funds—$400,000 in gold pieces—had been buried on Shoal Creek several miles outside Austin after he was ambushed and murdered. They began digging near a tree with mysterious markings cut into its bark, working by lantern light and pausing frequently to swig from a bottle of whiskey. Their labors were interrupted by weird cries on the perimeter of their diggings, and they began to wonder if the paymaster's ghost was on the prowl. The howls so unnerved them that they gave up the treasure hunt and fled back to town. Next day they learned of the source: an inmate who had escaped from a nearby mental hospital.

The Rolling Stone was a lost cause. In March 1895, two issues failed to appear, and the March 30 number contained an explanation from the editor: "The person who sweeps the office, translates letters from foreign countries, deciphers communications from graduates of business colleges, and does most of the writing for this paper, has been confined for the past two weeks to the underside of a large red quilt with a joint case of la grippe and measles. . . . People who have tried to run a funny paper and entertain a congregation of large piebald measles at the same time will understand something of the art, finesse, and hot sassafras tea required to do so. We expect to get out the paper regularly from this time on, but are forced to be very careful, as improper treatment and deleterious after-effects of measles, combined with the high price of paper and press work, have been known to cause a relapse."

A month later *The Rolling Stone* finally collapsed. Will had run out of financial support, and according to Dixie Daniels a final jab at local German-American sensibilities cost the paper readership and revenue it could not afford to lose. The main difficulty had been apparent from the beginning: Austin was simply too small, too conservative in its tastes and too provincial to support a satirical weekly.

The last straw, according to Daniels, was a woodcut of a fat German conductor leading his orchestra with wild gestures of the baton and underneath it the verse:

> With his baton the professor beats the bars,
> 'Tis also said he beats them when he treats.
> But it made that German gentleman see stars
> When the bouncer got the cue to bar the beats.

Daniels later recorded that "that issue alienated every German in Austin from *The Rolling Stone*, and cost us more than we were able to figure out in subscriptions and advertisements."[12] *The Rolling Stone* folded at the end of April, and Will was not only unemployed, but living under the shadow of a possible indictment by the federal grand jury that summer. For almost six months he was out of work, and he and Athol and their daughter lived on a dole from his stepfather-in-law.

In July, the grand jury was convened and considered the evidence against Will on the insistence of Bank Examiner Gray, who was determined that Will would be tried and, if possible, convicted of embezzlement. Gray became all the more determined when the U.S. attorney, R. U. Culberson, balked at prosecuting the case and the First National's officers demonstrated an equal reluctance to have Will punished. Vice-President Hamilton of the bank was allowed to appear before the grand jury and explain matters in Will's favor; that is, he testified that procedures at the bank were so casual it was difficult to say who was responsible for the missing funds.

Gray himself appeared before the jurors and painstakingly presented his evidence against Porter, charging that Will had embezzled a total of $5,654.00 from the bank's funds, and concluding that "to my mind conclusive evidence that he embezzled the money" was available.

He was shocked, as Will and his supporters were delighted, when the grand jury returned a no——bill. It seemed as though the threat of imprisonment was now lifted. Shortly after that exoneration Will received an offer to edit a comic weekly in Washington, D.C., and he was eager to accept the post. Just as he and Athol were in the midst of preparations to move, bad luck struck again. Athol's health had been declining for several years, and doubtless the anxiety and excitement of that summer only hastened the progress of her disease. She became seriously ill, and the Washington offer had to be turned down.

She was a little better in mid-October, when Will received another offer of employment—this time from Col. R. M. Johnston, the editor of the Houston *Post,* who had been impressed by the quality of Will's writing in *The Rolling Stone.* Johnston offered Will a job as "general utility writer" at $15 a week. It was less than he had been making as a bank clerk, but he eagerly accepted. Athol, however, was still too ill to accompany him to

Houston and stayed with her stepfather and mother, along with their daughter Margaret.

For once, on the Houston *Post*, Will made good on his own, without any friendly shoulders to lean on. He stayed with the *Post* for nine months, starting out as an ordinary reporter jumping to orders from the city editor. Almost immediately, the management of the *Post* recognized that he had more talent than that required for chasing fire engines or covering Chamber of Commerce luncheons. He was given a column, first titled "Tales of the Town," then, "Some Postscripts," and his salary was raised from $15 to $20 and eventually to $25 a week, the top wage for a newspaper writer in Houston.

His column was mostly made up of the usual local paragrapher's trivia and occasional scraps of verse, such as the stanzas he wrote in tribute to Eugene Field when the hard-drinking "poet of childhood" died November 4, 1895, which concluded:

> So, when they laid him down to sleep
> And earthly honors seemed so poor;
> Methinks he clung to little hands
> The latest, for the love they bore.
>
> A tribute paid by chanting choirs
> And pealing organs rises high;
> But soft and clear, somewhere he hears
> Through all, a child's low lullaby.[13]

The *Post* got its money's worth out of Will. In addition to the "Postscripts" column, he had to help with the society page and often was called upon to draw cartoons and other illustrations. The *Post's* editors apparently considered his cartooning ability equal to the humor he produced in his column, and noted in their obituary of him, "As a cartoonist Porter would have made his mark equal to that he attained as a writer had he developed his genius; but he disliked the drudgery connected with the drawing and found that his sketches were generally spoiled by anyone else who took them to finish. . . . The generality of the result was at times disheartening to the artist and Porter never followed his natural knack for embodying his brilliant ideas in drawings."[14]

Athol and their daughter joined him in Houston late that fall and they lived in a boarding house on Caroline Street. According to the reminiscences of Elbert Turner, who served on the *Post* staff with Will, he fitted in neatly with Houston in the nineties: "It was the day of the open saloon, sawdust floors, and the gastronomical gamble, the free lunch. . . . It was a wild time in the old town. Bloomers and bicycles were agitating the press. Somebody was fighting somebody else in Europe, but nobody seemed to care much, for everybody seemed to think it was just another Balkan operetta, with a bad score. . . ."

Will, as Turner remembered him, was usually self-effacing and withdrawn; undoubtedly he had every reason to be repressed, with his seriously ailing wife, a six-year-old daughter to be concerned about, and, from reports he had received from Austin, the Javert-like bank examiner, F. B. Gray, still clamoring for his prosecution. At times he seemed to forget his troubles momentarily, Turner recalled, and then "his conversation bubbled with witticisms. He made no effort at being funny. Jokes just oozed out of him, and he never laughed at his own sayings. Sometimes there was just a small smile."[15]

Will's case was resubmitted to the federal grand jury in February 1896, on orders from Washington and at the instigation of F. B. Gray. This time U. S. Attorney Culberson apparently made a more vigorous presentation of the evidence, and the result was an indictment on four counts of embezzlement. Will was immediately arrested in Houston and taken to Austin. His father-in-law and an old friend, Herman Pressler, posted $2,000 bond for him and he was allowed to return to Houston. Athol suffered a severe relapse as a result of the indictment. Her mother came over from Austin to care for Athol while Will returned to his duties on the *Post*.

The next months were grimly shadowed, with Athol rallying

only slightly and with his trial placed on the calendar for the July term of the federal court. His friends were puzzled by his failure to consider how he would defend himself at the trial. Was he already planning what the federal statutes frowningly term a "flight to avoid prosecution"? He did not consult with any attorneys, and he refused to discuss with anyone else how he planned to meet the government's charges of embezzlement. The only insight into his attitude—which was that he was innocent, that he was taking the blame for someone else—was provided by Mrs. Lollie Cave Wilson in her memoir *Hard to Forget*. She had known him since his earliest days in Austin, and he had often confided in her. Mrs. Wilson quoted him as telling her:

"The guilty man, if charged, would take the stand and call me a liar. He is not, as I thought, a man of honor, or he would have kept his word to me and straightened the matter out when I left Austin and the bank.

"Therefore when he is caught in a trap he will take the crook's viewpoint and clear his own skirts. His word will be taken against mine, because my word is the only thing that accuses him—the books, those silent accusers, are pointing fingers of guilt at me. You know those men at the bank are too close together to give an outsider a chance. . . .

"I was not cut out for that kind of work. But I took the job and held a position of trust. I failed that trust when I permitted such an outrageous thing to happen. Since I did not report the shortages as they occurred, I can legally be held as an accessory to the fact."[16]

That, incidentally, is as definitive a defense as Will ever made for himself.

It may have been a Freudian slip—he may already have been meditating on a non-legal solution to his difficulties in Austin—but in one of his Houston *Post* columns he referred to Honduras, which was then widely advertised as the most progressive of the Central American countries and the center of a banana boom. Honduras possessed another virtue well known to the American underworld: it had no extradition treaty with the United States.

In his column, at any rate, Will presented what he claimed was a typical Honduran menu: "Pale ale, chicken with herbs, rum, fricassee of young monkey, rye whiskey, green turtle with broth, brandy and soda, oysters, pale ale." He may also have been secretly congratulating himself on the fact that he had a thorough knowledge of Spanish.

As the date of his trial approached, it appeared that everyone who mattered in his life was convinced that he could prove his innocence. Athol was firmly loyal; so was her mother; and her stepfather had believed in Will enough to help put up bond. The federal prosecutor had proceeded against his will, and his former employers were equally unenthusiastic about prosecution. And in Houston Colonel Johnston, the editor of the *Post*, and other members of the staff raised a fund of $260 and handed it to Will to help out with the expense of standing trial. Everyone was confident that he would be able to clear himself—except the accused man himself.

On July 6, 1895, Will Porter boarded a westbound train headed for Austin. Athol and their daughter, about two weeks earlier, had gone to visit friends in Brazoria while he stood trial. No one can say what Will was thinking of when he boarded that train with $260 in his pockets which had been raised by men who believed in him. There was a deeply pessimistic streak in him which had been confirmed by most of the events of his life; perhaps he convinced himself, if innocent (as he had maintained to Lollie Cave Wilson), that fate had him by the throat and would see to it that the trial resulted in his conviction.

Anyway, he got off the train in Hempstead, about fifty miles from Houston, waited for hours until an eastbound for New Orleans came along and then boarded it. New Orleans was the jump-off point for Central America. He could hide down there, free of any fear of extradition, until the statute of limitations expired. He took the plunge and became a fugitive.

Years later he told a friend in New York that he identified himself most strongly with the hero of Conrad's *Lord Jim*, who abandoned his ship and its passengers when it was about to sink, because of what Conrad analyzed as "this extreme weariness of emotions, the vanity of effort, the yearning for rest."

"I am like Lord Jim," Will explained to his friend, "because we both made one fateful mistake at the supreme crisis of our lives, a mistake from which we could not recover."[17]

New Orleans in the nineties, undoubtedly, was a fine place for opting out if you had your choice of options. It still had a lazy Creole charm, especially in the French Quarter across Canal Street. Will spent several weeks—so far as can be reconstructed—in the city before putting more space between himself and the agents of the federal government. Long afterwards it was a legend among New Orleans newspapermen that Will worked for a week or two on the old *Picayune.* The only certainty about that brief period before he shipped out for Honduras is that he stayed long enough to absorb the atmosphere of the old quarter, which he later conveyed in half a dozen short stories with a New Orleans locale. Like Lafcadio Hearn, who had preceded him there by a number of years, also in flight from an unhappy past, he found the city a treasure of local color with its still visible traces of a more glorious ante-bellum history.

In "Blind Man's Holiday," for instance, he would tap his memory for a description of the Rue Chartres as a street of ghosts. "It lies in the quarter where the Frenchman, in his prime, set up his translated pomp and glory; where, also, the arrogant don had swaggered, and dreamed of gold and grants and ladies' gloves. Every flagstone has its grooves worn by footsteps going royally to the wooing and the fighting. Every house has a princely heartbreak; each doorway its untold tale of gallant promise and slow decay. . . . The old houses of monsieur stand yet, indomitable against the century, but their essence is gone. . . . Once men gathered there to plot against kings, and to warn presidents. They do so yet, but they are not the same kind of men. A brass button will scatter these; those would have set their faces against an army."

The atmosphere of the *Vieux Carré,* the genteel dilapidation of its wrought-iron balconies and magnolia-shaded courtyards, the melancholy residue of lost fortunes and ruined hopes that drenched post-bellum New Orleans struck a responsive note in a man with little but rueful memories to show for his past. He could sympathize with those ghostlike aristocrats of the French Quarter like Grandemont Charles in "The Renaissance at Charleroi," a Creole gentleman of thirty-four. "By day he was a clerk in a cotton broker's office in one of those cold, rancid mountains of oozy brick, down near the levee in New Orleans. By night, in his three-story-high *chambre garnie* in the old French Quarter he was again the last male descendant of the Charles family, that noble house that had lorded it in France, and had pushed its way smiling, rapiered, and courtly into Louisiana's early and brilliant days. . . . Perhaps Grandemont was even Marquis de Brasse. There was that title in the family. But a marquis on seventy-five dollars per month! *Vraiment!*"

But it was the story "Blind Man's Holiday" which closely paralleled Will's own circumstances while in New Orleans and gives some insight into his feelings. The central character, Lorison, an embezzler in flight from the law, sometimes "appeared to himself to be the feeblest of fools; at another he conceived that he followed ideals so fine that the world was not yet ready to accept them. During one mood he cursed his folly; possessed by the other, he bore himself with a serene grandeur akin to greatness. . . ."

Lorison, as his presumed alter ego would write, "saw himself as an outcast from society, forever to be a shady skulker along the ragged edge of respectability; a denizen *des trois-quarts de monde,* that pathetic spheroid lying between the *haut* and the *demi,* whose inhabitants envy each of their neighbors, and are scorned by both. He was self-condemned to this opinion, as he was self-exiled, through it, to this quaint Southern town a thousand miles from his former home . . . knowing but few, keeping in a subjective world of shadows which was invaded at times by the perplexing bulks of jarring realities."

He falls in love with a girl of the old quarter and feels he must tell her why he has "abdicated" from the respectable world. "The story, pruned of his moral philosophy, deserves no more than the slightest touch. It is no new tale, that of the gambler's declension. During one night's sitting he lost, and then had imperilled a certain amount of his employer's money, which, by accident, he carried with him. He continued to lose, to the last wager. . . ." And he adds, in his confession to the girl, "from the moment I staked the first dollar of the firm's money I was a criminal—no matter whether I lost or won."

He marries the girl, even though she confesses that her own past has been "wicked." Through a fortuitous turn of the plot, Lorison discovers that he wants the "rewards of the virtuous" again. "To what end, he vehemently asked himself, was this fanciful self-accusation, this empty renunciation, this moral squeamishness through which he had been led to abandon what was his heritage in life . . . ? Technically, he was uncondemned; his sole guilty spot was in thought rather than deed, and cognizance of it unshared by others."

Will Porter, unlike the fictional Lorison, decided to resume his flight from the law, probably on a fruit steamer bound for Central American ports. He wound up in Trujillo, Honduras, which became the setting for the stories in the volume *Cabbages and Kings* (in which Honduras is Anchuria and Trujillo is Coralio, "a little pearl in an emerald band").

Honduras was a wise choice for any fugitive. It was prosperous, with a booming market for the bananas, indigo, rubber and mahogany it exported. It was indulgent toward the American bank presidents, swindlers, confidence men, gold mine promoters and others who found it necessary to seek a respite from North American life, and hospitably refused to extradite any of them. Politically it was more stable than most of its neighbors. And best of all, from the viewpoint of a man who would glean a volume of short stories from his brief Honduran stay, it was redolent with atmosphere, with lingering traces of the grand larceny practiced in the days of the Spanish Main. "The game still goes on," as he observed in "The Proem." "The guns of the rovers are silenced;

but the tintype man, the enlarged photograph brigand, the kodaking tourist and the scouts of the gentle brigade of fakirs have found it out, and carry on the work. . . . Gentlemen adventurers throng the waiting-rooms of its rulers with proposals for railways and concessions. The little *opéra-bouffe* nations play at government and intrigue until some day a big, silent gunboat glides into the offing and warns them not to break their toys. . . . Add to these a little love and counterplotting, and scatter everywhere throughout the maze a trail of tropical dollars. . . ."

Trujillo, as he remembered his refuge in "Fox-in-the-Morning," was "like some vacuous beauty lounging in a guarded harem. . . . In front the sea was spread, a smiling jailer. . . . The waves swished along the smooth beach; the parrots screamed in the orange and ceiba trees; the palms waved their limber fronds. . . ."

Aside from the glimmerings of remembrance in those stories, his life as a fugitive in Honduras may be glimpsed in the colorful but imprecise recollections of Al Jennings (*Through the Shadows with O. Henry*). Jennings and his brother Frank, who arrived on a tramp steamer shortly after Will Porter, were also fugitives and much more highly prized by the U.S. government, though they were not inclined to be snobbish about it. The last gasp of the Old West, they were successors to the James and Dalton family enterprises of train and bank robbing. Recently they had relieved a bank in Texas of $30,000.

As Al Jennings described his meeting with Will, he and his brother walked up from the quays of Trujillo suffering horribly from a 3-Star Hennessy hangover. They came to a bungalow in front of which the American flag was displayed. On the wide front porch "sat an ample, dignified figure in immaculate white ducks. He had a large, nobly set head, with hair the color of new rope and a full, straight-glancing eye that noted without a sparkle of laughter every detail of my ludicrous makeup. [Mr. Jennings had fled the U.S. in a full-dress suit, which he still wore. One of the tails was missing and only the rim of his top hat was intact.] He was already serene and comfortably situated with liquor, but he had about him an attitude of calm distinction. A rather pompous dignitary, he seemed to me, sitting there as if he owned the place. This, I thought, is indeed a man worthy to be the American consul."

Will Porter's luck with new-found friends was amazing. Someone always popped up to join the Society for the Preservation of William Sydney Porter, it seemed. He had come to Honduras almost broke, obviously, and had no source of income. Just at the propitious moment there appeared Al Jennings and his brother with $30,000 in fresh loot.

Jennings announced that he had used up his appreciation for brandy and asked whether Porter knew where an honest drink of whiskey could be obtained. Will immediately led the way to the nearest cantina. On the way Jennings asked if he were the U.S. consul in Trujillo. "No," replied Will. Jennings asked what line of business occupied him. "I entertain the newcomers," Will said.

Over drinks, sizing up each other, Will asked Jennings what had caused him to depart from the States in such a hurry.

"Perhaps," Jennings retorted, "the same reason that routed yourself."

He noted "the merest flicker of a smile" on Will's face in response.

"You probably wonder who I am and why I'm here," Will remarked.

"Oh, no," Jennings assured him. "In my country nobody asks a man's name or his past. You're all right."

Warmed by whiskey, they discussed plans for the future which could only be carried out with the Jennings brothers' loot. "Several hours we sat there, an ex-highwayman in a tattered dress suit and a fugitive in spotless white ducks, together planning a suitable investment for my stolen funds. Porter suggested a cocoanut plantation, a campaign for the presidency, an indigo concession."[18]

In Will's story "The Fourth in Salvador" (included in the *Roads of Destiny* volume) he describes a whimsical Fourth of July celebration. According to Jennings, he and his brother and Will decided on a belated Fourth of July celebration in Trujillo, with revolvers substituted for firecrackers. "Porter, Frank, two Irishmen who owned an indigo concession, the American consul, myself and a negro brought along for the sake of democracy, made up the party. . . . We started to shoot up the town in true Texas fashion, prepared to wind up the fireworks with a barbecued goat in the lemon grove near the beach. We never got to the barbecue. A revolution intervened." By Jennings' account—he was a great teller of tall tales—the Fourth of July celebrants inadvertently quelled the revolution by making so much noise that the rebels thought they were being counterattacked. There was almost as much fiction in Jennings' story, undoubtedly, as in Will's literary fabrication.

For all the escapades they shared and all the whiskey bottles they mutually emptied, and even the plans they made for a joint future, Jennings came to realize that there was an invisible class barrier between him and his new friend.

"Will," he wrote, "had all the proud sensitiveness of the typical Southern gentleman. He liked to mingle with the masses; he was not one of them. Gladly he threw in his lot with a pair of bandits and fugitives. It would have cut him to his soul to have been branded as one of them."[19]

There was no echo of his escapades with the Jennings brothers in Will's letters to Athol. These, of course, had to be sent circuitously. They were enclosed in envelopes addressed to Mrs. Louis Kreisle, their neighbor in Austin. "Mrs. Porter used to read me selections from her husband's letters" from Honduras, Mrs. Kreisle related. "They told of his plans to bring Athol and Margaret to him as soon as he was settled. He had chosen a school for Margaret in Honduras and was doing everything he could to have a little home ready for them. At one time he said he was digging ditches. He also mentioned a chum whom he had met. Sometimes they had very little to eat, only a banana each."

(This would have greatly surprised the "chum," presumably Jennings, who was spending his Texas loot with a reckless generosity and who never observed Will Porter doing anything more strenuous than lifting a drink.)

While Will was sojourning in Honduras, Athol was bravely providing for herself and her daughter, despite her increasingly desperate struggle with tuberculosis. Her stepfather was more than willing to support them, Mrs. Kreisle said, but "Athol did not want to be dependent. She said she did not know how long they [she and Will] would be separated, so she planned to do something to earn some money. She commenced taking a course in a business college but ill health interfered. When Christmas came she made a point-lace handkerchief, sold it for twenty-five dollars, and sent her husband a box containing his overcoat, fine perfumery, and many other delicacies. I never saw such will power. . . ."[20]

Meanwhile, the Jennings brothers, presumably with Will's assistance, had run through the $30,000 in bank loot and there was only $417 left. Al, a reckless, garrulous little man with a shock of red hair, proposed that Will join them in another bank robbery, the proceeds from which would allow them to buy a ranch outside San Antonio.

Will begged off, however, telling Al Jennings, by the latter's account: "Colonel, I think I would be a hindrance in this financial undertaking."

"Well, you needn't take the gun," Jennings replied. "You just stay outside and hold the horses. We really need you for that."

"I don't believe," Will said after thinking it over, "I could even hold the horses."[21]

A continued lotus-eating existence in Honduras would evidently have pleased Will more than an outlaws' ranch in Texas or anything else he could think of at the moment. Regarding an American exile in Honduras, he wrote in "The Lotus and the Bottle":

"He was happy and content in this land of perpetual afternoon. Those old days in the States seemed like an irritating dream. . . . The climate as balmy as that of distant Avalon; the fetterless, idyllic round of enchanted days; the life among this indolent, romantic people—a life full of music, flowers and low laughter;

the influence of the imminent sea and mountains, and the many shapes of love and magic and beauty that bloomed in the white tropic nights—with all he was more than content."[22]

The "fetterless" days for the escapist, however, were coming to a close. The obligations of a husband and father followed him to Trujillo, and his conscience would not allow him to shake them off. Letters came from their friends and from his mother-in-law reporting that Athol's health had started declining rapidly and that her temperature often rose to 105 degrees.

Early in January 1897, he took a ship back to New Orleans, and from there wired his father-in-law for $25 to pay his rail fare to Austin. The fugitive had come home to find his $2,000 bond forfeited, his wife near death, and very few people still believing in Will Porter's innocence.

Chapter 3. Federal Prisoner No. 30664

Will returned to Austin about a week before the legal machinery began moving toward his trial. A motion to quash the indictment was filed to postpone the proceedings. Meanwhile, he was free on a $4,000 bond again signed by his stepfather-in-law and Herman Pressler, two men of abiding faith. The earlier bond had been declared forfeit, but had not been collected. In view of Will's demonstrated slipperiness, the federal court insisted that it be doubled.

Athol was so overjoyed at his return that her condition improved temporarily, but she was only a thin, feverish ghost of the belle he had married. Soon her condition relapsed and she was so weak that Will had to carry her to the buggy in which he took her for afternoon rides. Athol was simply wasting away; the girl in dimity could look forward only to her shroud. She was then twenty-nine years old.

In May 1897, Will's Aunt Lina died, and late on a Sunday evening, July 25, Athol drew her last tortured breath . . . the two women who had most deeply influenced his life were gone. "She made many friends while yet a young girl in this city," the *Daily Statesman*'s obituary noted of Athol, "and her married life was but a continuation of that girlhood so far as the molding of friendship's chain is concerned." Will and his daughter rode to the burial service in a carriage by themselves, and for weeks and months afterward he seemed to isolate himself from other people.

He and the Roaches remained on the closest terms, and an office in which he could write was improvised for Will in the attic above P. G. Roach's grocery store. Here, for the first time, he began taking a serious approach to making himself a writer. He turned out a number of stories between the time just after Athol's death and his trial in federal court, which was scheduled for February 1898. One result of those solitary labors was his first sale of a short story to a national outlet, the S. S. McClure Company of New York, which on December 2, 1897, wrote him:

"Your story, 'The Miracle of Lava Canon,' is excellent. It has the combination of human interest with dramatic incident. If you have more like this, we should like to read them. . . . The other stories we return herewith. They are not quite available [sic]."

"The Miracle of Lava Canon" was a fairly routine western story telling of a cowardly sheriff who is steeled to gun down the local badman through the love of a courageous woman.

Its acceptance was the one bright spot in the weeks preceding his trial. Toward that ordeal he had adopted an abjectly hopeless attitude; he was certain that he would be convicted, knowing that his flight to Central America would count heavily against any protestations of innocence. Again the lethargy that marked him in times of trouble took a firm grip on him, and he did little or nothing to prepare a defense against the government's charges. One of his lawyers later remarked that he had never known so "non-communicative" a client.

The complete stenographic transcript of the trial was lost, but enough court records and newspaper accounts survive to show that—despite the claims of those eager to exonerate the man who became O. Henry—it was fairly conducted by Federal Judge Thomas S. Maxey before a jury. It was only a coincidence, though again O. Henry partisans would not have it so, that the day his trial began in Austin, February 7, 1898, the great French novelist Emile Zola was facing a Parisian tribunal on charges growing out of his defense of Captain Dreyfus.

There were three days of highly technical testimony concerning the shortage of funds at the First National, which was attributed to Will Porter. The testimony on how the funds disappeared, and how Will's books were falsified, has been analyzed by experts. Whether he was covering up for someone else, as some of his admirers believe, can never be determined. Before the trial jury rendered its verdict, he had already been convicted in the minds of many who knew him longest and best. In 1914 Hyder Rollins, a retired professor of English at Harvard, talked to a number of surviving persons connected with him and the case. Their opinion was almost unanimous: technically, at least, Porter was guilty. U. S. Attorney Culberson, the reluctant prosecutor, considered that the "evidence against him was overwhelming." Herman Pressler, who was co-signer of Will's bond, said that at first he believed Will was innocent, but that he changed his mind when Will refused to "go over the bank books with his attorneys." Such former benefactors as Mrs. Betty Hall and John Maddox agreed that Will must have been guilty of taking the money, but they did believe that he meant to put it back. Even his old drinking companion Dixie Daniels was convinced of Will's guilt. Others less intimate believed that Will took the money and unsuccessfully gambled on cotton futures in hopes of keeping *The Rolling Stone* afloat.[1]

The jury officially charged with determining the matter concurred, and found him guilty on all three counts. On March 25, Judge Maxey sentenced him to five years in the Ohio Penitentiary at Columbus, which was handling an overflow of federal prisoners from Leavenworth and Atlanta.

William Sydney Porter, as Federal Prisoner No. 30664, was inducted into the Ohio Penitentiary on April 25, 1898, while thousands of his contemporaries were joining the army or navy to fight in the Spanish-American War. His specifications were entered on the prison records. His age was recorded as thirty-three (actually he was thirty-five); he was five feet seven inches, hat size seven and one eighth, shoe size six, hair chestnut sprinkled with gray. It was also noted that his education was "good" but his personal habits were "intemperate." His primary occupation was listed as that of a newspaper reporter; second, a pharmacist.

It was lucky for him that he listed himself as a registered pharmacist. There was no prison newspaper, but the infirmary could always use a pharmacist and thus Will was relieved of drearier prison chores and less pleasant associations.

Almost from the beginning of his sentence he began to make use of the experience in a literary way; the Ohio Penitentiary, along with every other way station of his life, was made to serve that purpose. First, however, he had to throw off what was described as an acute depression. Aside from imprisonment itself, he had every reason to be depressed, his wife having died less than a year before, his daughter being cared for by her grandparents, whatever career he had now shattered.

Even behind prison walls Will found people eager to befriend him; his melancholy charm worked even under the most adverse circumstances. One was the chief physician, Dr. John M. Thomas, whose initial impression of Will was that of a shy, sensitive man extraordinarily humiliated by being sent to prison.

"Most convicts," Dr. Thomas would recall, "would tell me frankly how they got into jail. They did not seem to suffer much from mortification. O. Henry, on the other hand, was very much weighted down by his imprisonment. In my experience of handling over ten thousand prisoners in the eight years I was physician at the prison, I have never known a man who was so deeply humiliated by his prison experience as O. Henry. He was a model prisoner, willing, obedient, faithful. His record is clear in every respect."

As a trusty, Will made the most of his opportunities to gather material for his stories, which he began writing soon after entering the penitentiary. "O. Henry liked the western prisoners, those from Arizona, Texas and the Indian Territory," Dr. Thomas remembered, "and he got stories from them all and retold them in the office. Since reading his books I recognize many of the stories I heard there. . . . He was an unusually good pharmacist and for this reason was permitted to look after the minor ills of the prisoners at night. He would spend two or three hours on the range or tiers of cells every night and knew most of the prisoners and their life stories."[2]

In his letters to the Roaches during his first months in prison,

Will indicated that the only thing keeping him alive was the hope that the appellate court would reverse his conviction. "I can stand any kind of hardship or privation on the outside, but am utterly unable to continue the life I lead here. I know all the arguments that could be advanced as to why I should endure it, but I have reached the limit of endurance. It will be better for everyone else and a thousand times better for me to end the trouble instead of dragging it out longer."

The reason for the implied suicide threat was provided in a subsequent letter to Mrs. Roach, in which he admitted that "as far as physical comfort goes I am as well situated as anyone here." He had books available, decent food, work to keep him occupied. As night druggist, however, he was deeply troubled by "misery and death and all kinds of suffering around one all the time." He then gave his mother-in-law a graphic picture of prison conditions as seen from the hospital.

"We sometimes have a death every night for a week or two. Very little time is wasted on such an occasion. One of the nurses will come from a ward and say—'Well So and So has croaked.' Ten minutes later they tramp out with So and So on a stretcher and take him to the dead house. If he has no friends to claim him—which is generally the case—the next day the doctors have a dissecting bee and that ends it. Suicides are as common as picnics here. . . ."

He related that the night before last a professional boxer had gone mad in his cell, and it took Will and six other trusties to hold the man down while the doctor jabbed him with a hypodermic needle. "These little things are our only amusements. I often get as blue as anyone can get and I feel as thoroughly miserable as it is possible to feel, but I consider that my future efforts belong to others and I have no right to give way to my own troubles and feelings."[3]

Meanwhile, in his letters to his daughter Margaret he kept up the pretense, agreed upon with her grandparents, that his work had taken him away from Austin. "I think it is a shame some men folks have to go away from home to work and stay away so long

—don't you? But I tell you what's a fact. When I come home next time I'm going to stay there. You bet your boots I'm tired of staying away so long. . . ."

Shortly after Will was imprisoned, Al Jennings, the little bank and train robber with whom he had shared the exile in Honduras, "took the fall," as prison argot had it, and was also sent to the Ohio Penitentiary, convicted of robbing the U.S. mails. They had a quietly joyous reunion. Jennings, who could adopt the manner of a divinity student, was made a transfer clerk and a trusty like Will.

In his two memoirs, *Beating Back* and *Through the Shadows with O. Henry,* he confirmed Will's description of prison conditions. Aside from the brutality of their treatment, according to Jennings, the prisoners had cause to resent a class system by which those with money and influence were allowed to serve their time in comparative luxury on what was called Bankers' Row. "These were the largest, airiest cells in the place; and here were confined men of means, like cashiers, directors, and the like, who had gone up for embezzlement or juggling funds. Of course, they had money; and, of course, they used it. Hence their special privileges. This prison, as I learned soon afterward, was run on a strict political system, and hadn't escaped graft. The bankers were allowed to decorate their cells and to buy special food." For the less privileged, the food was so bad it occasionally caused riots. Any prisoner who got out of line was taken to the basement and subjected to a high-pressure stream of water from a hose, which often knocked him senseless.[4]

Will himself was spared mistreatment because his services as a pharmacist were so valuable, and besides, he was considered a model prisoner. He worked directly under the night physician, Dr. George W. Williard, who remembered him as an unusually reticent and reserved man. "He seemed to like me personally because I did not ask him personal questions and because I showed that I felt as one intelligent man must feel toward another under such circumstances.

"He was as careful and conscientious as if the drug store at the prison had been his own property. His hours were from six in the evening to six in the morning. Often I left at midnight with Porter in charge and I knew things would run as regularly and effectively until morning as if I had remained. . . . Although nearly every drug clerk at the prison was at some time or other guilty of petty trafficking in drugs or whisky, Porter as always above approach. He always had the keys to the whisky cabinet, yet I never heard of his taking a drink."

On one occasion Dr. Williard credited Will with having saved him from an assault. "One night a huge negro to whom I had refused a drug became abusive. The guard who had brought him in had stepped away for a moment and the prisoner directed at me a fearful torrent of profanity. I was looking around for the guard when Porter . . . went over the counter like a panther. All of his hundred and seventy or eighty pounds were behind the blow he sent to the negro's jaw. The negro came down on the floor like a ton of brick. Instantly Porter was behind his counter again. He did not utter a word."[5]

In prison, it appears, Will Porter developed a sense of responsibility, a determination to make the best of things that the closest observers had never noted in him outside the walls. He was determined, above all, to repay the Roaches and to provide for his daughter (who later was sent to finishing school); and to behave so circumspectly that he would get all possible time off for good behavior. Drs. Thomas and Williard both noted that he refused to have anything to do with the other convicts—except Al Jennings—and that he particularly was careful not to become involved in the prison's incessant intrigues and quarrels. He held himself rigorously aloof.

The only time Dr. Thomas could remember his losing his calm, reserved attitude was when the chief physician found it necessary to investigate an abnormal increase in the use of medical alcohol. "I requested that he wait for me one morning so that I could find out how much alcohol he was using on his night rounds, and after asking him a few questions he became excited when he thought I might be suspicioning him. 'I am not a thief,' he said, 'and I never stole a thing in my life. I was sent here for embezzling bank funds, not one cent of which I ever got. Someone else got it all, and I am doing time for it.' You can tell when a prisoner is lying as well as you can in the case of anybody else. I believed O. Henry implicitly. I soon discovered that he was not the offender in the matter of the alcohol. But the question disturbed him and he asked me once or twice afterward if I really thought that he ever stole anything."[6]

During his first year in prison, in December of 1898, Will wrote his mother-in-law that he had started writing again and would send her any proceeds from the sale of his stories. It was while he was in the Ohio Penitentiary that he adopted the pen name O. Henry. There have been many guesses at the inspiration for that drab pseudonym. Will himself never elaborated on the matter, and one guess is probably as good as another, inconsequential as the question is. One seemingly sensible guess is that he adapted the pseudonym from an old cowboy song he probably heard while a guest of the Dick Halls in Denison County; at least there is a certain ironic aptness about one verse of *Root, Hog, or Die:*

"Along came my true lover about twelve o'clock
Saying Henry, O, Henry, what sentence have you got?"

While a federal prisoner he produced fourteen short stories which critics have rated as being among his best. Three of those—"Whistling Dick's Christmas Stocking," "Money Maze" and "Georgia's Ruling"—were published while he was in prison. The others, published later, included "A Medley of Moods," "A Chaparral Christmas Gift," "An Afternoon Miracle," "The Marionettes," "No Story," "A Fog in San Antone," "A Blackjack Bargainer," "The Enchanted Kiss," "Hygeia at the Solito," "Rouge et Noir" and "The Duplicity of the Hargreaves."

With the establishment of O. Henry as a writer, as a trade name, he began the second phase of his life. Only his family, some of his former friends in Texas and elsewhere and a very few intimates would know that O. Henry had been born in the Ohio Penitentiary and that the first thirty-six years of his life were to be filed away in the secret archives of his memory. William Sydney Porter, unsuccessful publisher, disgraced bank clerk, failed husband and convicted embezzler, was purposely disappearing with every story O. Henry wrote in his cell and published under his new guise.

Will Porter, as such, still lived only for his young daughter Margaret, to whom he would write fanciful letters, so heavily whimsical the child must have wondered what he was trying to hide. "Don't you remember me?" her father wrote. "I'm a Brownie, and my name is Aldibirontiphostiphornikophokos. If you see a star shoot and say my name seventeen times before it goes out, you will find a diamond ring in the track of the first cow's foot you see go down the road in a snow storm while the red roses are blooming on the tomato vines. . . ." It must have caused him considerable anguish to wonder how long he could keep up the pretense that he was away "working"—at least three years if he was given time off for good behavior. The Roaches meanwhile were doing their best to keep Margaret from learning that her father was actually in prison. Mrs. Roach took her granddaughter back to Tennessee and waited on her brother's farm while Roach disposed of his grocery store and other holdings in Austin. Then the elderly couple and the child moved to Pittsburgh, where Roach established himself in the hotel business.

The Ohio Penitentiary was located downtown, with some of its administration offices in a separate building outside the walls. Only a few of the most trusted inmates were allowed to work as clerks in that building; they attained a special status that was the next thing to freedom. Will wanted to join that extra-privileged group and applied to Dr. Thomas for help.

"I have never asked a favor of you before," Dr. Thomas quoted him as saying, "but there is one thing I should like to ask you now. I can be private secretary to the steward outside. It depends on your recommendation."[7]

Dr. Thomas recommended him for the post, and twenty minutes later it was his. Two weeks later he jubilantly wrote Mrs. Roach that "I am now in the steward's office keeping books, and am very comfortably situated. The office is entirely outside and separate from the rest of the institution. It is on the same street, but quite a distance away. I am about as near free as possible. I don't have to go near the other buildings except sometimes when I have business with some of the departments inside. I sleep outside at the office and am absolutely without supervision of any kind. I go in and out as I please. At night I take walks on the street or go down to the river and walk along the paths there. The steward's office is a two-story building containing stores and provisions. There are two handsomely furnished office rooms with up-to-date fixtures—natural gas, electric lights, 'phones, etc.

"I have a big fine desk with worlds of stationery and everything I need. We have a fine cook out here and set a table as good as a good hotel. The steward and the storekeeper—very agreeable gentlemen both of them—leave about four p.m. and I am my own boss till next morning. In fact, I have my duties and attend to them, and am much more independent than an employer would be. I take my hat and go out on the street whenever I please. I have a good wire cot which I rig up in the office at night, and altogether no one could ask for anything better under the circumstances."[8]

He became friendly enough to several other inmates, including Al Jennings, all of them members of the privileged trusty class, to form what they called the Recluse Club. According to Jennings, it was Will's idea. Probably the exclusiveness of the group was too. It was limited to Will, Jennings, another train robber, two embezzlers and a forger, all of whom had some claim to gentlemanliness and an instinct for the finer things. They were, as the English say, clubbable, and shared the founder's fastidious taste in food, dress and conduct. They also had to prove themselves adept at scrounging the necessary items for their weekly feasts.

The Recluses were a dining club. They had Sunday afternoons off, so that was the day designated for banqueting. "Every

Sunday," Jennings (the club's historian) related in one of his books, "the president appointed a dinner committee. It was their duty to find what supplies were needed for next Sunday and to collect them. The committee prowled through the prison all the week, using every trick and device. Frankly, they often stole the stuff. Morals are the rules of the game, and the prison game is decidedly peculiar. I for one didn't regard this quite as larceny. More often, we wheedled the guards. . . . No one liked to antagonize us—we knew too much, and we handled too many little privileges for the guards and convicts alike. Yet often, as the week went on, we'd still find ourselves short of some little thing, like salad oil or cloves or garlic. The whole committee would start out as though this was their one object in life. No one can know how much this little interest did to lighten our lives. When news went about that we'd secured a roast, a turkey, or some other special delicacy for next Sunday our mouths watered for two days ahead."

Will, whom Jennings called "Bart" in his narrative, was the finest scrounger of all. In a culinary emergency the president-founder of the Recluses would be called into action. "Bart, from his position and talents, could get more provisions in a day than all the rest in a week. He had made slits in the lining of his coat, and there he carried his plunder. I can see him yet, walking through the gate, looking neither to right or left, his coat bulging with a Mother Hubbard effect. As he passed the patrol guard, he would cast one quiet glance, and the guard would look in the opposite direction. Had the gate closed on him suddenly, his coat would have resembled the wreck of a grocery wagon. Once he even brought in six bottles of wine."

The members of the Recluse Club obviously were running the risk of losing their trusty status if the higher prison officials ever learned of the club's existence. The center of their activities was a small compact kitchen designed by one of the members, an embezzler and ex-bank official from New Orleans, and built into the loft above the construction office. It was concealed by a false wall and fitted out with a gas stove connected to the prison's mains. "The club and its layout was distinctly against prison rules," Jennings admitted. "At a moment's signal, gas stove and its range could be hidden out of sight. A false wall had been built and the kitchenette was hidden like a long telephone booth behind it. It was stocked with silverware, napkins, flavouring extracts, flour and every necessity, enough, in fact, for a small hotel. All had been stolen or bargained from the head clerks in other shops and from the chief cook in the kitchen."

All members wore white shirts at their weekly dinners, but there was no way they could avoid the sartorial disaster of a prison stripe down the trousers. Much as they tried to ignore it, they were still prisoners of the federal government. The table was set formally, with flowers, and a typical menu included tomato soup, a roast meat, corn, green peas, potatoes, mince pie and bread pudding. The dinner was conducted with some punctilio. At each place setting there was a copy of the club's rules and a card, both Will's work. For the place cards of each of the four members who proclaimed that they were innocent —including himself, presumably—he drew a cherub or a lily.

One of the members was a southern bank president, in for embezzlement, whom Jennings identified in his informal history of the club as "Carnot." Perhaps he had been elected to membership for the sake of variety. He was an elderly man with the crusty ante-bellum manner of a plantation aristocrat.

"He was a curious convict—I believe he never realized he was in prison," Jennings wrote. "The president used to assign, turn about, the duty of setting the table and washing the dishes —but never to the old bank president. He'd have smashed club property if anyone had suggested this common labor. He treated us as his employes, and the guards as his servants. He criticized the cooking of principle. . . ."[9]

His inclusion was probably Will's doing. The old gentleman was ripe for study as a character and undoubtedly served that purpose in various guises in Will's stories. Certainly he possessed no other visible charms as a fellow clubman.

A whole gallery of characters, and dozens of story ideas, were whispering to Will every day he spent in the Ohio Penitentiary. Prison was the making of the writer—not for the first time in literary history. It gave him time to reflect and to solidify his style and to provide himself with a viewpoint: looking up at American society from the underside. The stories he heard from other convicts, particularly the western outlaws, and the characters he observed behind bars were to appear in quite recognizable form in such collections as *The Gentle Grafter, Roads of Destiny* and *Heart of the West.*

One of the most poignant and certainly the most celebrated characters he created was Jimmy Valentine in "A Retrieved Reformation." As *Alias Jimmy Valentine* it was adapted for the theater and became one of the greatest hits on Broadway in the pre-World War I years. The character was drawn precisely from a safe-cracker Will met and worked with in the Ohio Penitentiary. Just how accurate was Will's observation of 'Jimmy Valentine' may be gathered from the account of their supervisor before Will went to work outside the walls in the steward's office.

"The moment I read O. Henry's description and character delineation of Jimmy Valentine in 'A Retrieved Reformation,' I said, "That's Jimmy Connors through and through,'" Dr. George W. Williard wrote for O. Henry's authorized biographer. "Connors was in for blowing a postoffice safe. He was day drug clerk in the prison hospital at the same time Porter was night clerk. The men were friendly and often, early in the evening, before Connors went to bed, he would come and talk to Porter and tell him of his experiences.

"Although Connors admitted himself guilty of many other jobs he claimed not to be guilty of the one for which he was serving time. Another man who resembled Connors had blown a safe and Connors was arrested and sent to prison for it. Because of fear of implicating himself in other jobs of which he was guilty, he never told on the other man but went to prison innocent. This statement was borne out early in his term in the penitentiary by the arrival of the sheriff who had sent him up and who, in the meantime, had arrested the right culprit and secured from him a confession. To right his wrong the sheriff went to Washington, but the inspectors knew Jimmy Connors and said he doubtless was guilty of some other jobs and had best stay in prison for safekeeping. . . ."[10]

Dr. Williard recalled that there seemed to be a special bond between Will and Connors because both believed themselves innocent of the crimes for which they had been imprisoned.

During his stay at the Ohio Penitentiary, the services of Jimmy Connors as a highly skilled cracksman were enlisted by the law. The treasurer of the Columbus *Press-Post* Publishing Company had locked up the company's books in the safe, to which only he had the combination, and then fled before he could be arrested on charges of grand larceny. The company needed those books to find out how much it had lost, and the state needed the evidence. By Al Jennings' account, Connors filed his nails to the quick, and below, so they would be sensitive enough to catch the slightest click of the tumblers. In a few minutes he opened the safe. In Will's fictionalization of the incident, however, he had Jimmy Valentine using a set of tools for the job. It "chilled my teeth," he later explained to Jennings, to think of Connors filing away most of his fingernails, and "I don't like to make my victims suffer."

The real-life ending to Jimmy Connors' story was supplied by Dr. Williard: "Poor Jimmy! He never lived to try any sort of reformation on the outside. He died of liver trouble in the penitentiary hospital, May 19, 1902, which was after Porter left and before Jimmy Valentine became famous in story, play and song. . . ."

From those hours Will Porter spent with Jimmy Connors in the prison hospital, a lucrative sector of the entertainment industry would develop. *Alias Jimmy Valentine* established a vogue for what were then called "crook plays" on Broadway; the underworld became fascinating to mass audiences, and that was the genesis of the gangster films of the thirties and all the hundreds that followed, down to *Bonnie and Clyde,* a saga of the Texas highways that would certainly have astounded Will Porter-O. Henry in all his Edwardian innocence. Bank robbers were never anything like that in his day.

In other stories stemming from his prison experience and included in the volume titled *The Gentle Grafter,* he developed the theme, perhaps partly in self-justification, that there wasn't really much difference between the outright crooks then residing in Ohio State and the great financiers, whom a later generation would regard as "robber barons."

In "The Man Higher Up," with himself cast as the narrator, he tells of his annual reunion with a swindler named Jeff who comes to New York every winter for a vacation from crime. He reveals his own attitude toward the analogous positions of crime and wealth in the following dialogue abstracted from the story:

JEFF: "There are two kinds of grafts that ought to be wiped by law. I mean Wall Street speculation, and burglary."

NARRATOR: "Nearly everyone will agree with you as to one of them."

JEFF: "Well, burglary ought to be wiped out, too. . . . About three months ago it was my privilege to become familiar with a sample of each of the aforesaid branches of illegitimate art. I was *sine qua grata* with a member of the housebreakers' union and one of the John D. Napoleons of finance at the same time. . . . Let me tell you about these barnacles that clog the wheel of society by poisoning the springs of rectitude. . . . Three months ago I got into bad company. There are two times in a man's life when he does this—when he's dead broke, and when he's rich. . . ."

A description of Will's working methods as a writer-prisoner was provided by J. B. Rumer, the night guard in the hospital while Will acted as drug clerk. Rumer recalled that Will began writing shortly after midnight, when his pharmaceutical chores were finished and he and the guard had shared a supper. "He always wrote with pen and ink and would often work for two hours continuously without rising. He seemed oblivious to the world of sleeping convicts about him, hearing not even the occasional sigh or groan from the beds which were stretched before him in the hospital ward or the tramp of the passing guards. After he had written for perhaps two hours he would rise, make a round of the hospital, and then come back to his work again."[11]

There is evidence that Will hardened himself, as prison time slowly passed, to the misery and cruelty which surrounded him in a day when prison reform, or the theory of prisoner rehabilitation, were mentioned only by the most dedicated humanitarians. His mind acted as a filter to those experiences and he made use of them in his own literary manner. A bluntly realistic treatment of those experiences was not his way; instead, they were sentimentalized as in the Jimmy Valentine story, when he had Jimmy using tools instead of his filed-down nails because the thought was too painful for him even to write about. He began writing in the muckraking era of Lincoln Steffens, but refused to take advantage of his inside knowledge of prison life to write about it realistically—perhaps because that would have exposed the fact he had "done time," and also because the escapist tendency in his character would not allow him to face things squarely.

Upton Sinclair, who made fictional use of the muckrake, wrote a mawkish, unproducible, self-published play based on those experiences as related by Al Jennings and also making use of a number of Will's stories. In the melodrama Sinclair titled *Bill Porter: A Drama of O. Henry in Prison,* he has Athol's ghost appearing in his cell and excusing Will's refusal to expose the brutality of prison life on the grounds that his sentimental and humorous stories about life on the outside would be for the greater good. "Write about them, Will!" Athol's ghost implores him, referring to the masses who needed to be uplifted by the sunnier type of literature. "Write *for* them! I see them, eager, hungry, craving just the sort of pity mixed with laughter that is your gift. . . . Faces! Faces! Millions of faces—and all of them your lovers. . . . Go forth, Will Porter! Do your work and take your place as their story teller—the voice of the Four Million!"

His attitude toward the suffering he witnessed changed from

the raw sensitivity demonstrated in the letters he sent the Roaches early in his term to a more calloused attitude as expressed in an exchange with fellow members of the Recluse Club one Sunday evening.

Jennings told his friends about an incident which had occurred a few hours earlier in the prison morgue. An Indian prisoner had been taken to the morgue in the belief that he was dead, and had been placed in an ice-filled trough in which the bodies were preserved for the dissecting table. "He had tried to climb out," as Jennings told the story. "His clawing, terrible, long arms were flung forward. His body hung over the board, his head resting on the cement, as though he had lost his balance and half toppled out. The face, one cheek pressed against the ground, was twisted toward us—the mouth agape, the eyes staring."

Except for Will, the club members were horrified by the story, and one said, "We should write to the President of the United States about it. It's an outrage."

Even Carnot, the crusty old banker, was outraged and told Will: "Mr. Porter, you should exercise your best ability as a writer on this subject. You should enkindle the world about it. You should put it in an article and send it broadcast."

Will, however, crisply made it clear that he did not intend to make himself an agent for bleeding-heart humanism. "I do not understand you, sir," he told Carnot. "I am not here as a reporter. I shall not take upon myself the burden or responsibility. The prison and its shame are nothing to me."[12]

His sentence, with time off for good behavior, ended on July 24, 1901. Just before his discharge he and Jennings one night discussed what they had to look forward to "outside," since the little Oklahoma train robber was also due for discharge soon.

Jennings said he was going to "take the bull by the horns. I'm going back to Oklahoma, where my criminal record is known, and grow up with the country. I'm going to tell every new acquaintance exactly who and what I have been. I'll manage somehow for a year. Then I can get my citizenship restored and hang out my shingle."

He suggested that Will "face the music" in similar fashion and return to Austin.

"I can't, Al," he quoted Will as replying. "Perhaps it's the only method, but I'm too reserved where you're forward, and besides I'm too sensitive."[13]

As the time for his release drew nearer Will's most excruciating concern seemed to be whether he would be able to step through the prison gates properly attired. He had always been a dapper, well-tailored fellow who liked to sprinkle a little perfume on the handkerchief in his breast pocket. It distressed him that the well-cut tweeds in which he entered prison could not be found and it appeared that he would have to sally forth in the cheap suit furnished all released prisoners. He had made so many friends among officials, guards and inmates at the penitentiary that somehow, according to Jennings, he was provided with a good brown worsted, a black derby and pigskin gloves in which to face the world.

The testifying witness to his discharge—a scene more touching than most such leave-takings of the convict from the walls which have both imprisoned and sheltered him—again was Al Jennings, who described it with feeling:

"Even the warden was nervous when Porter came into the office for his discharge . . . Porter's face was slightly lined. He looked older for his thirty-nine months in prison, but even so, his was a head and a bearing to attract attention anywhere. There was about him an attitude of confidence, of self-sufficiency, of dignity. He looked more like a well-educated, cultured businessman than like an ex-convict."

Jennings was then secretary to the warden, and wrote, "There were visitors in the outer office. The warden stepped outside, telling me to give Bill his discharge papers. As soon as we were alone the intense strain became unbearable. I wanted to cram everything into those last moments. I wanted to say: 'Good luck—God bless you—Go to hell.'

"The coaxing smile on his lips, he put out his strong, short hand to me. 'Al, here's a book. I sent to town for it for you.' It was a copy of 'Omar Khayyam.' I handed him the discharge and his $5. Porter had at least $60 or $70—the proceeds from his last story. He took the $5.

"'Here, Colonel, give this to Billy—he can buy alcohol for his locomotor ataxia.'

"That was all. He went toward the door and then he came back, the old drollery in his eye.

"'I'll meet you in New York, Colonel. You might beat the brakes there before me. I'll be on the watch. Goodbye, Al.'

"Porter's voice lapsed into a low whisper at the end. He went to the door, and, without looking back, went out. I felt as though something young and bonny—something lovable and magnetic—was gone forever."[14]

Thus Will Porter stepped into a world which, even in the three years of his imprisonment, had changed more than its citizens would ever know. America had entered the twentieth century and almost simultaneously had become an empire, though few would be brazenly honest enough to admit the fact. In that short time, the United States had landed its armies on Cuba and Puerto Rico and had acquired the Philippine Islands and other Pacific possessions through the victory over Spain. Historians have declared that period the last years of American innocence, but perhaps that innocence actually was lost when the troop transports sailed for the Philippines and American forces began a bitter twelve-year campaign to subdue the Filipino insurgents.

In other ways, too, America was changing fast. One symbol of that change was the first snorting, bucking automobiles venturing on the streets; they would transform the face of America more than any of its wars. Electricity and telephones were becoming more commonplace. Even in literature there were fresh winds blowing, with the publication of the novels of Stephen Crane, Theodore Dreiser and Frank Norris and the first short stories of young Jack London—all of them heralding the development of realism and naturalism in American writing, the importance of being serious and having a social viewpoint. Into this fast-changing literary world Will Porter, as O. Henry, would bring innovations of his own, but essentially, as he made quite clear to his prison mates, he was an old-fashioned storyteller, an entertainer committed only to the demands of the marketplace.

Immediately on leaving the shelter of the Ohio Penitentiary, he took a train to Pittsburgh for a reunion with his daughter Margaret, now twelve years old and dismayingly strange and different, and with the Roaches. His father-in-law was now managing the slightly run-down Iron Front Hotel, and Will moved in to be close to his daughter and her grandparents.

Largely for his daughter's sake, he stayed in Pittsburgh for eight or nine months, but he detested the place. He kept himself in walkaround money by free-lancing for the Pittsburgh *Dispatch* and selling on the average of a story a month to the magazines, whose editors were beginning to regard him as a possibly important discovery. For those stories he received seventy-five dollars each. The stories he had written in prison were submitted through an intermediary in New Orleans, so the editors had no idea that O. Henry, author, was also Will Porter, convict. Now that he had moved to Pittsburgh he was able to submit his stories directly.

If Pittsburgh was his first taste of freedom after three years in the penitentiary, he indicated, he would almost prefer going back to the walls. Al Jennings was the only prison mate with whom he corresponded, and to Jennings he confided that Pittsburghers were the "most ignorant, ill-bred, contemptible, boorish, degraded, insulting, sordid, vile, foul-mouthed, indecent, profane, drunken, dirty, mean, depraved curs" he had ever known. In short, he would "linger here no longer than necessary." He was even disillusioned in the delights of freedom, and wrote Jennings that in his opinion "the only difference between P. [prison] and O.P. [outside of prison] is that they are allowed to talk at dinner here."

He and Jennings had agreed to try peddling an article to be titled "The Art and Humor of Holding Up a Train," for which

Jennings supplied the technical information and Will, the actual writing.

In September 1901 he wrote Jennings his instructions on the rough draft, which Will would then rewrite and polish. ". . . We have got to respect the conventions and delusions of the public to a certain extent. An article written as you would naturally write it would be regarded as a fake and an imposition. Write in as simple, plain, and unembellished a style as you know how. Make your sentences short. Put in as much realism and as many facts as possible." Then, Will added, he would "put it into the shape my judgment decides upon . . . we'll whack up shares on the proceeds. . . ." A little more than a month later Will was able to report that *Everybody's* had accepted the piece. "When you see your baby in print don't blame me if you find strange earmarks and brands on it . . . but I followed your facts and ideas, and that is what made it valuable. . . ."[15]

The story, published as "Holding Up a Train," constituted a short course in that difficult and tricky criminal art, but in his preface it was noted: "The man who told me these things was for several years an outlaw in the Southwest and a follower of the pursuit he so frankly describes. His description of the modus operandi should prove interesting, his counsel of value to the potential passenger in some future 'hold-up,' while his estimate of the pleasures of train robbing will hardly induce any one to adopt it as a profession."

Indeed, the Jennings-as-told-to-Porter story is full of tribulations, not least the evanescent quality of the loot. "I never could account for a tenth part of it after it was spent. It goes fast and freely. An outlaw has to have a good many friends. . . . With angry posses and reward-hungry officers cutting a hot trail after him, he must have a few places scattered about the country where he can stop and feed himself. . . . Sometimes I have, at the end of a hasty visit at one of these havens of refuge, flung a handful of gold and bills into the laps of the kids playing on the floor, without knowing whether my contribution was a hundred dollars or a thousand."

Several months after his discharge from prison and arrival in Pittsburgh, he moved out of the Iron Front Hotel for undisclosed reasons. Perhaps he didn't want to live under the watchful, possibly apprehensive eye of the Roaches, or to meet the questioning, puzzled glances from an intelligent and sensitive daughter who was still asked to believe that Papa had been away on "business" for three years. Also he had begun doing more work for the *Dispatch,* a morning paper, and his hours (due in great part to the conviviality of the newspaper business in those years) were irregular.

The circumstances of his employment by the *Dispatch* were distorted, as he maintained in the only newspaper interview he ever granted, in a story written about them after he became famous. The story claimed that "I blew into the office looking like a tramp, offered manuscripts for sale, and before blowing out again borrowed a dollar. That story is an embroidered fib. Why, I was the best dressed man in the office unless it was the editor, whose shoes were a little more pointed than mine.

"It was a year after the story was printed before I saw it. Then I made a special trip over to Pittsburgh. I sent in my card to the editor. 'Sir,' said I when I at last found myself face-to-face with this libeler of my solvency, 'Sir, I have come over to lick you.' 'But wasn't it a bully good story?' asked the editor. I admitted that it was, and instead of licking him we went out and lunched together."[16]

Even if that tale of his first appearance in the city room of the Pittsburgh *Dispatch* wasn't quite accurate, he was by all accounts chronically broke during that period. Despite selling a magazine story a month on the average and working on space rates for the *Dispatch,* he lived from check to check. His taste for alcohol seems to have been unimpaired by his prison stay and must have taken a large share of his funds.

He moved into shared quarters on the second floor of a rooming house at Wylie and Fullerton streets in what was then described as Little Harlem. His roommate was a young man named

2. The house where O. Henry was born, Greensboro, North Carolina.

3. William S. Porter at age two.

4. Dr. Algernon Sidney Porter, Will's father.

5. Mary Virginia Swaim Porter, Will's mother, who died when he was three years old.

6. Will's Aunt Evelina, his teacher, guiding influence and foster mother in the years of his youth.

7. The Porter family drugstore where Will worked as an apprentice pharmacist.

8. Left to right: Shell Porter, Will's brother; Tom Tate, Will's best friend; and Will as a young boy.

9. Will at age twenty-two in Austin, Texas. He was working for the State Land Office at the time the photograph was taken.

10. Athol Estes Porter, Will's first wife —the girl in dimity.

11. The Hill City Quartet, with which Will took great pleasure in singing. He is seated on the left in the first row.

12. Will Porter as a sporting young man in Austin.

Samuel C. Jamison, then the clerk in a drugstore across the street and later the coroner of Allegheny County.

Almost thirty years later Jamison (in a newspaper interview) remembered his roommate as "a mighty fine fellow . . . I was then in my last year at the Pittsburgh College of Pharmacy. I had lots of room and didn't mind sharing it with Bill. We occupied the same bed—one of those high old walnut fellows—and together, when necessary, fought the insect life. Bill never rolled in before three o'clock in the morning. His work at the paper kept him that long. He didn't do much but work and play cards occasionally. He played a good game of poker, but as we played five-cent limit, he never won much.

"At that time there was a saloon at 79 Fulton street, known as Angloch's, and there one could get a fine sandwich for five cents. Beer was also a nickel, and they threw in a bowl of soup. That's where O. Henry ate most of the time he was here. He was fastidious about his dress and tried to look as English as possible. He liked yellow kid gloves, carried a cane and wore spats, which in those days were something of a rarity. We used to kid him about his clothes, but he didn't mind."[17]

He stayed on in cold, grimy Pittsburgh, with its eternal fog of soft-coal smoke through the winter of 1901–2, and then early in the spring decided to leave for New York. Oddly enough, for a man who was to be renowned as the most poignant chronicler of New York's "Four Million" of his time, he knew nothing about the city where he would spend the last eight years of his life except that it was the literary marketplace and that the closer he worked with its editors the more stories he might sell.

Some encouragement came from that quarter, particularly from Gilman Hall, a senior editor of *Ainslee's Magazine,* which had bought "Money Maze" from him (via the New Orleans mail drop) while he was in prison. That first story, at the editors' insistence, appeared under the by-line Olivier Henry, since they considered O. Henry too plain in a time when most authors (Richard Harding Davis, David Graham Phillips, Richard Watson Gilder, etc.) flourished under the triple-barreled by-lines.

Ainslee's also bought "Rouge et Noir" and "The Flag Paramount," and its senior editors, Richard Duffy and Gilman Hall, considered O. Henry very promising.

Hall suggested a "visit" to New York so they could talk over his writing plans. This encouraged Will to write in reply that he'd rather make a "move" than "visit" to New York. He also asked *Ainslee's* to advance him $100, against future story purchases, to enable him to make the move. Hall persuaded his publisher to agree to the advance. Somehow the money evaporated—a characteristic quality it acquired in proximity to Will Porter—and Will somewhat brashly asked that *Ainslee's* send him another $100. *Ainslee's* did, and this time Will actually boarded a train for New York. It was a bargain no one would have cause to regret.

Thus began the New York years, the productive and triumphant years of O. Henry.

II. THE O. HENRY YEARS

Chapter 4. One of the Four Million

On the day in early April 1902 that O. Henry arrived in the great city it would have been a reckless gamble to take hundred-to-one odds on him to become the most popular chronicler of contemporary New York and its growing masses. He had never set foot in the city before and his previous experience with urban life had been in such relatively sleepy southern towns as Austin, Houston and New Orleans. Aside from one or two editors with whom he had corresponded, he knew no one in the publishing world. His formal education was scant, his literary apprenticeship haphazard, his working habits irregular, his personal life a shambles. Even with those qualifications, he might have seemed a better bet if he had been charged with ambition or a sense of dedication; if he had been driven by the determination of a Balzac to create a body of work that would capture the spirit of his time and place.

But his artistic aim was deliberately sighted on the commercial level and he would not be affronted by anyone who called him a hack. "Writing is my business," was the way he defined his attitude; "it is my way of getting money to pay room rent, to buy food and clothes and Pilsener. I write for no other reason or purpose." In addition, he was no eager youth full of a bright vision and fresh insights, but a man in his fortieth year with few illusions and little delight in humanity as a whole. His only real aim in coming to New York was not to find a new creative field but a more comfortable corner in the marketplace.

The melting-pot New York in the early years of this century was a sociological nightmare. For the past several decades the "golden door," which for many opened on the sweatshop and the dead-end ward at Bellevue, had been entered by successive hordes of immigrants from Ireland, Germany, Italy, eastern Europe and Russia. It cried out for a man with the conscience and creative power of a Zola or a Tolstoy to convey the reality of the human baling machine which the city had become. But William Sydney Porter did not aspire to fill such a gigantic role and he pleased a large readership by looking on the city as the capital of a fantasy, a modern revival of the Thousand and One Nights, which he would variously call "Bagdad on the Subway," "Noisyville on the Hudson" and "City of Too Many Caliphs." In his own oblique way, aiming at nothing more than pleasing the reader for half an hour, he did make something of a social historian of himself. One of his earlier biographers was probably not exaggerating the overall achievement of O. Henry when he claimed that if all the records were lost, a future historian, using the stories with a New York background, "might rebuild a grotesque and alluring city that would somehow be the city of that decade from 1900 to 1910, echoing its voice, expressing the moods of its four million. . . ."[1] In his own offhand manner, he was a more effective muckraker than Lincoln Steffens or Ida Tarbell. What the social reformers raged at with a shower of invective and a fusillade of statistics O. Henry depicted in his own storyteller's voice.

In "The Unknown Quantity," for instance, Dan Kinsolving, the heir to a bakery fortune, is taken on a tour of the slums by his old college friend, Kenwitz, a Socialist watchmaker. They enter a "poverty-haunted" tenement on Varick Street. "In that almost bare room a young woman sat sewing at a machine. She nodded to Kenwitz as to a familiar acquaintance. One little stream of sunlight through the dingy window burnished her heavy hair to the color of an ancient Tuscan's shield. . . . 'How many shirts this week, Miss Mary?' asked the watchmaker. A mountain of coarse gray shirts lay upon the floor. 'Nearly thirty dozen,' said the young woman, cheerfully. 'I've made almost $4. I'm improving, Mr. Kenwitz. I hardly know what to do with so much money. . . .'"

But when Kinsolving declares he will give away his father's tainted fortune, Kenwitz tells him, "You can't do it! One of the chief punishments of you men of ill-gotten wealth is that when you repent you find that you have lost the power to make reparation or restitution. I admire your good intentions, Dan, but you can't do anything. Those people were robbed of their precious pennies. It's too late to remedy the evil. You can't pay them back . . . If you had a hundred millions, you couldn't repair a thousandth part of the accumulated evils produced by misapplied wealth. Every penny that was wrung from the lean purses of the poor reacted a thousandfold to their harm. . . ."

Only rarely did O. Henry raise the pitch of his storyteller's voice to the level of indignation, because he considered himself an entertainer, not a pamphleteer or social reformer. Yet on occasion he could be searingly effective in showing his readers what lay below the surface of metropolitan life. There was his brief sketch of a working girl about to quit the sweatshops for a prostitute's career:

"Nancy you would call a shop-girl—because you have the habit. There is no type; but a perverse generation is always seeking a type; so this is what the type should be.

"She has the high-ratted pompadour and the exaggerated straight-front. Her skirt is shoddy, but has the correct flare. No furs protect her against the bitter spring air, but she wears her short broadcloth jacket as jauntily as though it were Persian lamb! On her face and in her eyes, remorseless type-seeker, is the typical shop-girl expression. It is the look of silent but contemptuous revolt against cheated womanhood; of sad prophecy of the vengeance to come. When she laughs her loudest the look is still there. The same look can be seen in the eyes of Russian peasants; and those of us left will see it on Gabriel's face when he comes to blow us up. It is a look that should wither and abash man; but he has been known to smirk at it and offer flowers—with a string tied to them. Now lift your hat and come away, while you receive the sardonic, sweet smile of Nancy that seems, somehow, to miss you and go fluttering like a white moth up over the housetops to the stars."[2]

In similar vignettes and side-glances, imbedded in stories that otherwise were designed for entertainment, he produced for his readers a chilling, poignant and penetrating view of the world they might walk through every day without noticing its underlying tragedy. The America of those early-century years was bursting with hope for social progress, with faith in what scientific and industrial advances would bring. It is looked back upon as the "good years," the last of the age of innocence, but no one can read O. Henry and believe those years were more than the mere illusion of the comfortable and the established.

O. Henry's forebodings about the "vengeance to come" were nurtured in the rich compost of the section of New York City which might have been called O. Henry Country. Roughly it was the area on the West Side of Manhattan from Hell's Kitchen down through Chelsea to lower Manhattan and the Bowery (but well north of Wall Street); the other boroughs of New York City were all but ignored by him. His turf could be covered by a brisk walker in a few hours. A number of landmarks survive, of course, but Hell's Kitchen, the Tenderloin, Battle Row and other colorful areas have long since changed their character; the elevated railways which roared overhead on the north-south avenues have disappeared into the scrapyards to be replaced by the vexations of an endless traffic jam, and Sixth Avenue, the Boul. Mich of O. Henry Country, has been romantically restyled the Avenue of the Americas.

Even during O. Henry's time, however, New York could have been called "fun city," depending on your definition of fun. Then as now it was in a state of perpetual crisis. Crime and street violence were so prevalent that the city had been rocked by police scandals for the past twenty years. There were an estimated 25,000 prostitutes on the streets of New York with every whore, pimp and madam operating virtually under license from the New York Police Department. The rectangle known as Satan's Circus or the Tenderloin, extending from Fourteenth almost to Forty-second Street between Fifth and Seventh avenues, was a nightlong saturnalia, seven nights a week, a vast Sodom of barrooms, dance halls, parlor houses and concert saloons. The character of those establishments was conveyed by their names: Paddy the Pig's, the Burnt Rag, the Bohemia, the French Madame's, Sailors Hall, the Pig's Head, Dan the Dude's, the Buckingham Palace, the Tivoli, the Haymarket and the Seven Sisters (seven parlor houses in a row on West Twenty-fifth operated by seven sisters from New England). Down in the Bowery was McGurk's Suicide Hall, which O. Henry called McTurk's in his stories.

New York was a wide-open town, the degradation of which was ignored, year after year, by respectable New Yorkers. They reacted with outrage to Stephen Crane's realistic first novel, *Maggie, A Girl of the Streets,* which he published in 1893. Crane was inspired to write the novel after watching a young prostitute being beaten to her knees by a beefy policeman in the Broadway Gardens, a Tenderloin deadfall, while the patrons looked on without protest. His Maggie—and many of O. Henry's heroines—symbolized the thousands of tenement girls who turned from eight-dollar-a-week, twelve-hour-a-day jobs in the sweatshops to prostitution because "the sordid squabbles of a besotted tenement family become titanic struggles and mud puddles are magnified into measureless oceans."

Girls from all over the country, but particularly those daughters of the immigrant families on the West Side and the Lower East Side, those second-generation Americans who found the promise of America a lie, were recruited by the police-protected procurers of what was called the "slave system." The girl who took up prostitution had to indenture herself to a pimp or madam, who cut the police in on every dollar of her earnings. Hundreds of "cadets" roamed the city streets forcibly inducting young women into the system after drugging and beating them. One victim of the cadets was the daughter of a prominent rabbi. She was kidnaped in daylight and placed in a brothel. The daily papers kicked up a tremendous row, but "so strong were vice interests that no paper suggested the possibility of getting the girl out of the brothel in which she had been placed," a newspaper historian has written. "This was known to be utterly impossible, and the girl was left to her life of shame."[3]

Many of the streets which O. Henry walked daily were literally ruled by gangs which were almost private armies. Downtown, according to Alfred Henry Lewis (*The Apaches of New York*), Paul Kelly's Five Points Gang was able to muster 1,500 young thugs in an emergency. Adjoining his turf was Monk Eastman's Bowery Gang, a thousand strong, which often clashed in house-to-house fighting with Kelly and his followers. The Gas House Gang was supreme east of Third Avenue between Eleventh and Eighteenth streets, the Hudson Dusters on the West Side below Fourteenth Street. The ruling mob in Hell's Kitchen was the Gophers, led by the formidable One Lung Curran and augmented by a ladies auxiliary known as the Battle Row Ladies' Social and Athletic Club. All of them—Jewish, Irish, German and Italian—were a "stunted litter," according to the knowledgeable Lewis, and apt to flee if set upon by a determined outsider. "This is not perhaps from cowardice," Lewis observed, "but they dislike exertion, even the exertion of fighting, and unless it be to gain money or spoils . . . they back away from trouble."

O. Henry memorialized a number of the street fighters in his stories, particularly the Stovepipe Gang and its swaggering leader, Kid Brady, who was examined at some length in "Vanity and Some Sables." The Stovepipe Gang lounged around the streets of Hell's Kitchen with the primary objective of mugging an outsider who ventured into their territory. "Preferably," O. Henry wrote, "this was done by weird and singular tricks without noise or bloodshed; but whenever the citizen refused to impoverish himself gracefully his objections came to be spread finally upon some police station blotter or hospital register."

As a student of the sociology of the Stovepipe section, he wrote, "The chefs in 'Hell's Kitchen' are many, and the 'Stovepipe' gang wears the cordon blue. The members of this unchartered but widely known brotherhood appeared to pass their time on street corners arrayed like the lilies of the conservatory and busy with nail files and penknives. Thus displayed as a guarantee of good faith, they carried on an innocuous conversation in a 200-word vocabulary, to the casual observer as innocent and immaterial as that heard in the clubs seven blocks to the east.

"But off exhibition the 'Stovepipes' were not mere street corner ornaments addicted to posing and manicuring. Their serious occupation was the separating of citizens from their coin and valuables. . . . The police held the 'Stovepipe' gang in perpetual suspicion and respect. As the nightingale's note is heard in the deepest shadows, so along the 'Stovepipe's' dark and narrow confines the whistle for reserves punctures the dull ear of the night. Whenever there was smoke in the 'Stovepipe' the tasseled men in blue knew there was a fire in 'Hell's Kitchen.'"

Pre-eminent among all those bravoes of the tenement streets was Monk Eastman, the hetman of the Bowery, who always carried a blackjack, a set of brass knuckles and a bludgeon. He was regarded as the soul of chivalry because he always removed his brass knuckles before striking a woman. When he rushed to enlist in the army at the outset of American participation in World War I, the examining physician at the recruiting center counted up all his scars and was certain that Eastman had fought in every battle since Gettysburg. He asked Monk which formal military engagements had benefited from his services. "Oh," Monk replied, "a lot of little wars around New York."

In his stories O. Henry frequently matched the thugs and con-men of the New York underworld against his straight-shooting Westerners on a visit to the big city. Generally, in such stories as "Dougherty's Eye-Opener" and "The Poet and the Peasant," the Westerners outwitted or outfought the city slickers.

Two years before O. Henry came to New York a book titled *How the Other Half Lives* was published by a Danish-born reporter for the New York *Evening Sun.* Jacob Riis's celebrated work covered in a documentary way much of the territory O. Henry was to claim as his fictional domain. "The New York Ghetto," Riis wrote, "is not fit for men and women, much less children." He was outraged by the "overflow from the tenements of our home-heathen growing up in New York's streets today" and generally ignored while "tenderhearted men and women are busying themselves with the socks and the hereafter of well-fed little Hottentots thousands of miles away." He cited the statement of a prominent clergyman that 109 missionaries in Persia, Palestine, Arabia and Egypt "spent one year and sixty thousand dollars in converting one little heathen girl." Balanced against that picture of missionary overkill was an institution called the "baby farm," a brutal sort of pioneer child-care center, in which unwanted children were fed on sour milk and paregoric (a tincture of opium) to keep them quiet.

He also described a tenement packed with one-room sweatshops employing the labor of boys and girls in their early teens. In one room six adults and three children were working at their sewing machines in a room ankle-deep with half-sewn garments. "The faces, hands and arms to the elbows of everyone in the room are black with the color of the cloth on which they are working. The boy and the woman alone look up at our entrance. The girls shoot sidelong glances, but at a warning look from the man with the bundle, they tread their machines more energetically than ever." From such circumstances, Riis wrote, evolved the boy gangsters and girl prostitutes. "They reflect exactly the conditions of the tenements from which they sprang. Murder is as congenial to Battle Row as quiet and order to Murray Hill."

All these factors—the corruption of the children of the immigrants, the politically protected vice, the street gangs and the generations sentenced en masse to labor in the sweatshops—formed the background to O. Henry's work. He did not regard himself as a man with a message, or a writer of social significance, but one measure of how much of such elements seeped into his work is the fact that volumes of his stories are constantly republished in the Soviet Union along with those of the more predictable Jack London, Upton Sinclair and John Steinbeck.

Perhaps because of the time he spent in the Ohio State Penitentiary, O. Henry was also more sensitive than most of his literary contemporaries to the profound and striking changes just then taking place in American urban life; for example, the automobile. On the list of best-selling fiction in the spring of 1902 were A. Conan Doyle's *The Hound of the Baskervilles,* Gilbert Parker's *The Right of Way,* Mary Johnston's *Audrey,* Thomas Dixon's *The Leopard's Spots,* Charles Major's *Dorothy Vernon of Haddon Hall,* Gertrude Atherton's *The Conqueror,* Henry Harland's *The Lady Paramount* and Ellen Glasgow's *The Battle-ground.* All were writers on horseback; none mentioned an automobile, motorcar or horseless carriage.

To O. Henry, however, the lordly machines then thundering along Manhattan's streets—the Pope-Hartford, the Pope-Toledo, the Thomas Flyer and other pioneer models—were part of the city's magic. The automobile figured prominently in a number of his stories, and its speed, power and suggestions of affluence made it the centerpiece of "The Fifth Wheel." In "While the Auto Waits" a white car quickly establishes the hero as a man of wealth. A green car serves the same purpose in "The Third Ingredient." Quicker than anyone else O. Henry sensed the fact that the automobile would soon be used as a status symbol. Nancy, the street-wise heroine of "The Trimmed Lamp," is accused by her fellow shopgirls of making a play for a flashy fellow who has parked his car at the curb outside. "Him?" says Nancy scornfully. "Not for me. I saw him drive up outside. A 12 H. P. machine and an Irish chauffeur."

O. Henry's formal entrance on the New York literary scene came the first week of April 1902. Richard Duffy and Gilman Hall of *Ainslee's* had been eagerly awaiting his arrival after persuading their publisher to advance the necessary funds, not once but twice. They were beginning to wonder whether he really existed. Then late one afternoon at the magazine's offices downtown at Duane and Spring streets, as Duffy recalled, an office boy brought in the calling card of William Sydney Porter.

"I don't remember just when we found out that O. Henry was merely a pen name; but think it was during the correspondence arranging that he come to New York," Duffy related. "I do remember, however, that when we were preparing our yearly prospectus, we had written to him, asking that he tell us what the initial O. stood for, as we wished to use his photograph and preferred to have his name in full. It was the custom and would make his name stick faster in the minds of readers. With a courteous flourish of appreciation at the honor we were offering him in making him known to the world, he sent us 'Olivier,' and so he appeared as Olivier Henry in the first publisher's announcement in which his stories were heralded. Later he confided to us, smiling, what a lot of fun he had had in picking out a first name of sufficient advertising effectiveness that began with O."

Whatever impression they had formed of Olivier Henry from his letters, Duffy and Hall later admitted they were surprised by his actual appearance. "He wore a dark suit of clothes, I recall, and a four-in-hand tie of bright color. He carried a black derby, high-crowned, and walked with a springy, noiseless step. To meet him for the first time you felt his most notable quality to be reticence, not a reticence of social timidity, but a reticence of deliberateness. If you also were observing, you would soon understand that his reticence proceeded from the fact that civilly yet masterfully he was taking in every item of the 'you' being presented to him to the accompaniment of convention's phrases and ideas, together with the 'you' behind this presentation. It was because he was thus able to assemble and sift all the multifarious elements of a personality with sleight-of-hand swiftness that you find him characterizing a person or a neighborhood in a sentence or two; and once I heard him characterize a list of editors he knew each in a phrase."[4]

As O. Henry himself recalled that first meeting with the editors of *Ainslee's*, Duffy and Hall led him down the corridor to the office of the publisher. A certain trepidation was visible in their manner, perhaps because of the two advances they had wangled for him. "They escorted me with fear and trembling to the office of the publisher, Mr. S—, who abruptly dismissed them, closed his office door and motioned me to a chair. Fearing the worst was yet to come, I hastened to thank Mr. S—— for his generosity and assured him that his confidence was not misplaced. 'Don't mention it, my dear sir,' he rejoined. 'I was born and brought up in Pittsburgh, and was only too happy to assist in your escape.'"[5]

After a brief interview with the publisher, he accompanied Duffy and Hall on their customary homeward stroll up from Duane Street to Madison Square. They tried to discuss literary matters with him, but O. Henry was more interested in the sights and would not be distracted even by a glimpse of a passing titan of the publishing world. "Although he always humorously professed his sense of insecurity as an outsider," Duffy said later, "Gilman Hall and I tried to interest him in noticing Morgan Robertson, who was passing near the corner of Sixth Avenue and Twenty-third Street, princely dressed in a frock coat and top hat. It was our intention to have him meet fellow craftsmen from the beginning. In his own way he came to know Morgan Robertson later, but that day he had eyes only for the elevated railway, and gazing at it, inquired of us, so that we doubted his seriousness, why people were not afraid to ride on such trains, as they might so easily fall into the street. . . . In our many roamings about town he would always ride in a surface car or the subway, no matter what distance we had to go."[6]

Duffy, Hall and others who became his friends noted that he adopted a self-protective attitude. Strangers were always confronted not by O. Henry, literary man, but a drawling southern country boy. It served as his "barrier of initial reserve," noted C. Alphonso Smith, his first biographer. "Till this was penetrated —and he had to penetrate himself by sensing a potential friend in the casual acquaintance—there was no flow." He quoted a woman acquaintance, Mrs. Wilson Woodrow, on the subject of O. Henry's defensiveness, which he cloaked in a rural southern manner: "My first impression of O. Henry, and an impression that lasted during half the evening at least, was one of disappointment. This wonderful storyteller struck me as stolid and imperturbable in appearance and so unresponsive and reserved in manner that I had a miserable feeling that I was a failure as a guest, and nothing hurts a writer's vanity, a woman writer's anyway, so much as to have her work considered more interesting and attractive than herself. But presently Mr. Porter began to sparkle. He was unquestionably a great raconteur. I am sure that if his table-talk had ever been taken down in shorthand, it would have sounded very much like his written dialogue. . . . His wit was urban, sophisticated, individual; entirely free from tricks and the desire to secure effects."

One device that O. Henry used against potential invaders of his privacy, Smith wrote, was "a sort of pan-American dialect." This was particularly effective when anyone tried to lionize him. "O. Henry could not be prevailed upon to meet a man simply because the man was a celebrity nor, when he himself became a celebrity, would he permit himself to be visited as such if he could help it. . . . Thus a woman who had written to him about his stories and who insisted on bringing a friend to meet the great man said to him afterward: 'You mortified me nearly to death, you talked so ungrammatical.' Another method of evasion was to drop into a perfectly serious vein of Artemus Ward rusticity. There was fun in it for those who understood, but it was meant for those who did not and could not understand and it had the desired effect."[7]

Another southern habit of speech, noted by Bob Davis, one of his editors, was to address male acquaintances as "Mr. Man," "Colonel," "Major," or if he was seeking a favor, "General." His conversation was also sprinkled with you-alls. "He had the habit of bestowing military titles upon his intimates, seldom addressing anyone by his name," Davis recalled.

Richard Duffy also observed that "it was one of his whimsical amusements to speak in a kind of country style of English, as though the English language were an instrument he handled with hesitant unfamiliarity."

His colleague, Gilman Hall, who became the closest of O. Henry's professional friends, sensed that his provincial manner, his defensiveness on meeting new people, his guarded attitude toward strangers were rooted in something lurid in his background. "I was sure that he had a past, though he did not tell me of it and I did not inquire into it. It was not till after his death that I learned of the years spent in Columbus. I used to notice, however, that whenever we entered a restaurant or other public place together he would glance quickly around him as if expecting an attack. This did not last long, however. I thought that he had perhaps killed someone in a ranch fight, for he told me that he had lived on a ranch in Texas. This inference was strengthened by finding that he was a crack shot with a pistol, being very fond of shooting-galleries as well as bowling alleys. But when I found that he did not carry a pistol, I began to doubt the correctness of my theory."[8]

From the first, Richard Duffy also became aware of O. Henry's obsession with guarding his privacy. "Anyone who endeavored to question him about himself would learn very little, especially if he felt he was being examined as a 'literary' exhibit; although when he was in the humor he would give you glimpses of his life in Greensboro and on the ranch to which he had gone as a young man, because he had friends there and because he was said to be delicate in the chest. He would never, however, tell you the 'story of his life' as the saying is, but merely let you see someone or some happening in those days gone by that might fit in well with the present moment, for he always lived emphatically in the present, not looking back to yesterday, not very far ahead toward tomorrow."[9]

Bob Davis, who met O. Henry about a year after he came to New York, observed that any kind of public notice, aside from that given his stories, always caused him to vanish "like mist before a gale. He shrank from the extended hand of strangers; blushed at spoken approval and avoided conversations about himself. If alive today, and called upon to view a bookshelf containing the works of O. Henry, he would burst into Homeric laughter and leave the room."[10]

During his first months in New York, O. Henry roomed at the Marty, a small French hotel and restaurant on West Twenty-fourth Street between Broadway and Sixth Avenue, a short distance from Madison Square. His was a small room with a window looking out on an air shaft. He could probably have afforded something better, since he sold seventeen stories in 1902, but he was chronically broke, as his friends testified. Probably the most serious drain on his financial resources was his alcoholic intake. No one who knew him well denied that he was a steady toper who held his liquor well. Bob Davis estimated his average consumption at two quarts of whiskey a day; this in addition to wine and beer taken in large quantities with his meals. "His bibulous habits rarely affected his deportment, swayed his gait, or altered the tenor of his low, even voice."[11]

His alcoholic tendencies, of course, placed him firmly among the celebrated American writers who destroyed themselves through a combination of alcohol and the inability to handle the problems of success. The late Upton Sinclair, a fervent advocate of prohibition, listed among those whom he personally knew to have been maimed by "the claws of John Barleycorn" not only O. Henry but Ambrose Bierce, Jack London, Sinclair Lewis, Edna St. Vincent Millay, Eugene O'Neill, Scott Fitzgerald, William Faulkner, Ernest Hemingway, Finley Peter Dunne, Sherwood Anderson, Theodore Dreiser, Stephen Crane—practically a roll call of literary fame since the turn of the century. Liquor is apparently the occupational disease of writers, and the more talented seemingly are the worst afflicted.

A sketch of O. Henry during his early period in New York, when he was struggling for a foothold and living from one publisher's check to another, was provided by Witter Bynner, later a celebrated writer himself. Bynner had recently graduated from Harvard and was working at *McClure's* as a first reader when he came across a manuscript titled "Tobin's Palm" and signed by Olivier Henry. Bynner was excited by the story, but the head reader turned it down. Going over the head of his superior, Bynner took his case to S. S. McClure himself. McClure suggested that a letter be written to Olivier Henry asking for a second look at the manuscript. Bynner insisted that it should be retrieved in person and immediately, before it was snatched up by another magazine.

"Then go after it," McClure snapped. "We'll take it."

Young Bynner made a dash for the Hotel Marty and found O. Henry enveloped in gloom in his tiny room. It was furnished only with a bed, a chair and a trunk, the top of which O. Henry used as his writing desk. Bynner spotted the returned manuscript lying on top of the trunk and was so intent on recovering it that he ignored the amenities.

" 'Tobin's Palm'?" he asked the writer.

"Yes," O. Henry replied.

"It's sold," Bynner said.

"Good, I'm flat broke."

That laconic bit of dialogue was the beginning of a lasting friendship. Bynner convinced McClure that he should pay $100 for "Tobin's Palm," the most *McClure's* ever paid for the work of an uncelebrated writer. Until Bynner left the magazine in 1906, he obtained a number of O. Henry stories for *McClure's,* including one of the more famous, "The Trimmed Lamp." Though many years younger than the writer, he and O. Henry became such close friends that Bynner often stayed at the latter's apartment overnight when they dined late and Bynner didn't feel like going home to Brooklyn. Friendship, however, didn't exempt Bynner from the common experience of O. Henry's editors: waiting and fuming while O. Henry procrastinated over producing a story he had promised and on which he had often obtained an advance. "The magazine presses would be waiting and not a line of the promised tale. Then Bynner would hurry off in quest of the author," as a friend of Bynner's recalled.

" 'It's all written,' Porter would explain when finally cornered. 'Then let me have the copy.' 'Oh, I don't mean that it is down on paper; but it's all here.' The culprit would point to his head. Then, virtually to the last word, O. Henry would tell the story while Bynner listened. He had memorized it practically in its entirety before putting down the first word. 'Now write it down,' Bynner would say. So O. Henry would sadly turn to the irksome task with Bynner at his elbow gathering up the tale as it came sheet by sheet."[12]

He could conceive the idea of a story in a flash, but getting it down on paper was an anguished and laborious process. "He was one of the three or four in this generation—no more—who generate stories spontaneously," as Will Irwin, another of his protective and sympathetic editors, would recall, "who see life about them in story form. When the mood was on him he would look through a cafe window at a cab—and flash! would come a story. But composition was with him a fearful labor—a proof that easy writing is very hard reading.

"As an editor I was waiting for a story which he was under contract to deliver. On the last possible day I went down to his workshop to get it. . . . I waited all morning, reading a newspaper in a corner, while he finished it.

"The story seemed to come at the rate of about one short sentence in a quarter of an hour. He would run his hands through his hair, gaze at the ceiling, bite his pencil, put down three words, sit like a rock gazing at the wall, put down three more words . . .

"People have told me that Porter was lazy. Judging from the amount of stuff he published and the rate at which he turned it out, I should call him one of the most industrious literary workers of his time. Every man to his tools. Porter's conception was a flashing sabre, his execution a delving spade."[13]

Most of his earlier stories continued to appear in *Ainslee's*, which was his primary source of income. One issue (May 1903) contained three of his stories, one signed Olivier Henry, another under a different by-line, and "While the Auto Waits," which the New York *Times* and other newspapers singled out for the brisk modernity of its theme, under the name James L. Blish. Two of his more celebrated stories, "A Retrieved Reformation" and "Roads of Destiny," were published during his *Ainslee's* period.

He was becoming well known enough, in fact, to acquire one of the lesser camp followers of fame, an impostor. The story of O. Henry and the pretender was an O. Henry story in itself, though he never made use of it. The telling was left to Richard Duffy of *Ainslee's*. Few people were allowed to know that O. Henry was living at the Hotel Marty and they respected his passion for secrecy. "He was not unsociable, but a man that liked a few friends round him and dreaded and avoided a so-called party as he did a crowd in a subway," Duffy explained. "Thus it happened that while his name had become talked about in magazine circles, there were not many who knew him; and he had been living here for perhaps half a year when an editor came to see me, saying with some satisfaction that he had discovered who this elusive newcoming story-writer was and where he could be found.

"O. Henry was an undergraduate at a certain university, he said, naming it. The man was amazed when I told him that O. Henry had left my office only half an hour before, that he could be found at his room in West Twenty-fourth Street, and that to the best of our knowledge he had never laid eyes on the particular college mentioned. Later it transpired that when O. Henry's stories made their first stir at the college [Harvard], a young man foolishly took the credit of their authorship." Investigation showed that the young man involved was an orphan who had been sent to college by his uncle and aunt. When he was condemned by his uncle as an ingrate for falling behind in his studies, the youth happened to see a copy of *Ainslee's* with an O. Henry story advertised on the cover. He seized upon the inspiration of telling his uncle that his academic standing had suffered only because he was publishing short stories under the pen name O. Henry. "Before he could judge whither his prank or weakness would lead," Duffy related, "he received a letter from a magazine of the first rank asking him to contribute. The hoax, so to describe it, was promptly shattered."

On learning of the incident, O. Henry was more amused than

outraged. His only reaction, Duffy said, was to caution *Ainslee's*, "Just make sure you send all O. Henry checks to me."[14]

He did a little harmless posturing himself during a brief but warm correspondence with Mabel Wagnalls, the daughter of a book publisher (Funk & Wagnalls), in which he pictured himself as a breezy Westerner who had vaulted out of the saddle and into a literary career. The correspondence began when Miss Wagnalls wrote a letter praising one of his stories and asked for details of his previous career. "Since you have been so good as to speak nicely of my poor wares I will set down my autobiography. Here goes. Texas cowboy. Lazy. Thought writing stories might be easier than busting bronchos. Came to New York one year ago to earn bread, butter, jam, and possibly asparagus that way. I don't like to talk about literature. . . . I have much more respect for a man who brands cattle than for one who writes pieces for the printer. . . ."

He flattered the young lady by asking her opinion of several of his unpublished stories, which he sent her because he considered the "judgment of a normal, intelligent woman superior to that of an editor in a great many instances." But he still maintained his pose of the cowhand unwillingly conscripted in the service of American literature. "The whole business—life, literature, operas, philosophy, & shirtwaists—is a kind of joke, isn't it? I reckon that riding around on a pony on the Texas prairies thinking about the beans and barbecued beef we're going to have for supper is about as good as anything."[15]

There were times during that first year in New York when he barely had enough money to buy a five-cent glass of beer and edge his way toward the free-lunch counter of one of the neighborhood saloons. By the spring of 1903, however, his stories in *Ainslee's* and *McClure's* had attracted enough attention to cause editors to start seeking him out and solicit his stories. The reigning monarch of the daily newspapers down on Park Row then was the New York *Evening* and *Morning Worlds* published by Joseph Pulitzer. From Pulitzer's *Sunday World* came the offer of a cushy assignment; its bearer was the youthful Bob Davis, then a member of the Sunday paper's staff.

F. L. H. Noble, the crusty managing editor of the *Sunday World*, called Davis into his office on July 3, 1903—the latter would always remember the precise date—and instructed him to hunt down O. Henry and "make arrangements for him to write introductions to *Sunday World* specials." The writer would be supplied with the galley proofs of the articles and would be required to supply "whatever sort of a preface, whimsical, philosophical or serious, as he deems proper." Regarding payment, Noble added, "Offer him forty dollars a week. If he balks jump to fifty dollars. The third and last call is sixty dollars."

Davis found his quarry in Room 7 at the Marty, "a rather corpulent figure in his shirtsleeves and with his suspenders down, seated beside a washstand upon which reposed a huge bowl containing perhaps five pounds of cracked ice in which nestled a half dozen fine Bartlett pears." O. Henry bowed and asked his visitor to come in.

Davis announced that he had a proposition to make, noting that there was something about O. Henry's manner that "suggested the utter absurdity of bargaining."

"In fact," Davis blurted it out, "I have three propositions. I will make the last one first . . . The New York *World* authorizes me to offer you sixty dollars a week for introductions varying from three hundred to seven hundred words in length, as leads to special features appearing in the Sunday issue."

It didn't take long for O. Henry to decide that he was being offered a lovely little proposition. Turning out those prefaces would take no more than an hour or two a week, and he would be paid more than a first-rate reporter for six days of chasing fire engines or covering axe murders in Chinatown.

Gazing out the window with its bleak view of the air shaft, he replied, "If this last proposition is the best, you needn't make the other two. I accept your proposition. Moreover, mister, you can have the balance of the pears."

O. Henry and Davis then went down to the restaurant on the

ground floor and celebrated the occasion over a full-course French dinner and a quart of French wine.

The *World* assignment was so congenial, Davis said, that O. Henry always returned the proofs with the required introduction within twenty-four hours after receiving them.

The arrangement lasted for several months until Noble retired as editor of the *Sunday World* and was replaced by Caleb Van Hamm, who later became a Hearst executive feared from one end of that chain to the other. Hamm, a man of few, but caustic, words, asked Davis just why O. Henry was on the payroll for sixty a week. Davis explained.

"Can him," said Van Hamm.

Davis carried the word to O. Henry, who took the bad news calmly. During the following year Davis himself left the *World* and took over the post of fiction editor of the Frank Munsey Publications. One of his first moves was to sign a contract with O. Henry for first refusal on a number of his short stories.[16]

A few months after O. Henry had been "canned" so unceremoniously, Editor Van Hamm himself was replaced by Nelson Hersh, who immediately dispatched a young member of his staff, William Wash Williams, to search out O. Henry and arrange for him to come down to the Pulitzer Building because "I believe he can do a corking line of New York stories for us."

Williams, who became a friend, drinking companion and mini-Boswell like most of those emissaries sent to O. Henry from the newspapers and magazines, found an amiable man who looked a half-dozen years younger than he was (forty-one), "broadly built, possibly five feet seven inches tall and particularly heavy about the shoulders and chest. His head, which was large, round and well-covered with sandy brown hair, parted almost in the middle over a broad, high forehead, sat chunk down between his shouder blades on a thick and a very short neck. His features were not large but rather coarse and heavy; the nose short and fat, the lips thick, the cheeks broad and full, the undershot jaw ponderous, the chin firm and round, and when he pulled it back hard between the batwings of his collar—as was his habit—a roll

13. Will and Athol with their daughter Margaret, 1895. Athol died only two years later.

14. Will working as a teller in the First National Bank of Austin, from which he was later accused of embezzling funds. He was convicted and imprisoned.

15. O. Henry of New York.

NUMBER 55 IRVING PLACE

It was here, through the triple window, that O. Henry studied the heart of his City of Razzle Dazzle, his Little Old Bagdad on the Subway. Porter's rooms were immediately to the left of the entrance

16. Pete's Tavern

of fat swelled beneath it. His eyes, which looked out from under overhanging thin blond brows, were gray and small but keen, and at that time his upper lip was crossed by a light hair line of no consequence, which turned up slightly at each end and would, doubtlessly, be referred to as a mustache. . . . He was dressed in a well-fitting sack suit of dark gray pepper-and-salt material, white shirt, striped tie and black polished shoes."

Williams told him that his editor wanted an interview to arrange a contract for a series of short stories in the *Sunday World.* O. Henry immediately brought out two cigars and insisted that Williams join him in a smoke "so if there is anything the matter with the brand we will suffer together." He then announced that he was interested in the new Pulitzer proposal, adding that "I can write New York stories of my sort—short fiction, or semi-fiction yarns. It isn't a reporting proposition your editor has in mind, is it? I'm not much of a reporter."[17]

O. Henry agreed to meet Hersh the next day and then, in his best country-boy manner, asked Williams if he would "see me through" the interview because "I am not very thoroughly broken in yet to meeting New York editors." Next day he journeyed down to the gold-domed Pulitzer Building on Park Row and signed a contract to supply the Sunday edition with a story a week at $100 each. Not only was the price right, but he was supplied with an instant readership of perhaps a million New Yorkers every Sunday. From this point on, all his stories were signed O. Henry and all the other pen names were dropped.

There would be no more skipped meals, no more scrabbling at the free-lunch counters. He now had an assured income, though it would not have been enough even if it had been ten times as much. He gave money to anyone who expressed a need greater than his own, whether it was a friend or a panhandler. He was dispatching money to Pittsburgh for Margaret's support and soon would be sending her to one of the most expensive schools in the South. Liquor was cheap but his daily consumption, beginning at breakfast time, was also a constant drain on his income.

That O. Henry's intake was constant and considerable was determined by George MacAdam, the New York *Times* reporter who obtained the first and only formal interview with him. He talked to two bartenders in a saloon nearby whom O. Henry had rechristened "John Drew" and "Robert Lorraine" because he fancied they resembled those famous actors. The barkeep whom O. Henry called John Drew told MacAdam, "'He used to drop in pretty regularly about 10 o'clock every morning. Sazerac cocktail was his favorite drink. [O. Henry had probably acquired a fondness for that absinthe-flavored drink in New Orleans, where it was invented.] Some days the telephone bell would ring and he would tell me to send over to his rooms a bottle of Scotch. Then I knew he was writing. But I never saw him drink Scotch at the bar.

"'He was always very quiet; I never heard him make a joke or a funny crack. He was distant with strangers. With the exception of a few friends who occasionally came in with him, I never saw him get into conversation with anyone. But he was always listening and watching.

"'He had a heart like that'—the bartender indicated an organ the size of a pumpkin with his hands—'and if he had $10 he'd give it to you and then perhaps come over and borrow a half-dollar from me. He was always helping some of the boys out, and never a come-back. I've heard that from lots of people.'"[18]

There are two kinds of people who really love money, the sort who hoard it because to them money is power, the other, to whom it is to be spent as fast as it comes in. O. Henry was a worshiper of Mammon to the extent that he reveled in being a big spender. People who pretended to regard money as something evil in itself were either guilty of hypocrisy or self-deception. His own attitude was well defined in the words of Anthony Rockwell in "Mammon and the Archer":

"I bet my money on money every time. I've been through the encyclopedia down to Y looking for something you can't buy with it; and I expect to take up the appendix next week. I'm for money against the field. Tell me something that money won't buy."

For all his frank appetite for money, O. Henry could be ultra-discriminating about the source from which it came, no matter how great his current need. One thing he could not abide was an editor who offered him a "plot" and a cash advance to convert the outline into a story. It was his first principle that a story grew in the imagination and could not be produced through a mechanism. Gilman Hall remembered that "two things stirred his indignation: a salacious story and the proffer of a plot. 'Don't you know better,' he would say, 'than to offer me a plot?' It was a necessity of his nature to manufacture his products from the raw material."

He could also bear great resentments at his own expense against magazines which coldly rejected his work when he was struggling for publication. Clarence L. Cullen, a newspaperman like most of the people with whom he shared his off-duty hours, illustrated that cankered tendency in a recollection of O. Henry published in the New York *Sun* several years after his death. Cullen was sitting with him in his room one day when a batch of mail was brought up. Out of the handful of envelopes, he seized on one bearing the letterhead of one of the country's largest magazines (apparently the *Saturday Evening Post,* since Cullen identified it as the "most important" of "the leading fiction publications in all the world"). "Many times during the years when he had been struggling for a foothold as a writer of short stories he had submitted his tales, including the best of them, to the editor of this publication. Always they had come back with the conventional printed slip. When he reached the topmost rung of the ladder he meticulously refrained from submitting anything to that particular publication, the writers for which comprised the leading 'names' in the world of fiction.

"He ripped open this envelope which attracted his eye. There was a note and a check for $1,000. The note asked him briefly for something from his pen—anything—with that word underscored —check for which was therewith enclosed. If the thousand dollars was not deemed sufficient, the note went on, he had only to name what sum he considered fair and the additional amount would be remitted to him.

"Porter, who was probably the least vainglorious writer of equal fame that ever lived, smiled a sort of cherubic smile as he passed the note over to me. When I had finished reading it, without comment, he, saying never a word, slipped the check into the envelope, stamped the envelope and went out into the hall and deposited it in the drop. Not a word was passed between us."[19]

No doubt O. Henry, who effectively underplayed his frequent essays in self-dramatization and knew when a gesture spoke louder than words, enjoyed every moment of that little scene.

Chapter 5. The Quiet Man of 55 Irving Place

Like most writers O. Henry was a creature of sedentary habits. He was every bit as unathletic as his pudgy frame indicated. The exertion required to lift a heavy stone seidel of Würzburger provided all the exercise he needed. Thus his friend Bob Davis, by now the fiction editor at *Munsey's*, was considerably surprised one summer day when he strolled into Davis' office and suggested that they go fishing. Almost as much as physical exercise, he loathed talking about his work, anyone else's work, writing in general or writers in particular. That, and his distaste for the company of strangers, made him keep his distance from literary circles of all kinds, and the backbiting and back scratching that distinguished such gatherings. He was as determinedly unliterary as he was unathletic.

Yet on that summer's day, drifting along the noisome tidal flats off Long Island, Davis not only glimpsed O. Henry in one of his rare recreational moments but heard him philosophize about his work and the lasting power of the printed word. It is the only recorded instance of O. Henry talking about what his writing meant to him.

He and Davis went down to Port Washington and hired a boatman, rented his boat and bought bait for catching flounders. After several hours under the broiling sun, with the fair-skinned writer turning as red as a boiled lobster, they caught only two flounder and four sea robins. The boat had drifted close to the waterfront estate of Howard Gould, the playboy son of the late, piratical Jay Gould. O. Henry suggested that they beach the boat on Gould's property and have the lunch they brought in a picnic basket.

"Let's put the lugger on Mr. Gould's beach," was the way O. Henry put it, "and bask in the predatory atmosphere of inherited wealth. He can't do any more than ask us in to lunch. Do you reckon he would like to have both flounders, or do you want to keep yours?"

After picnicking on the Gould lawn near the boathouses, they sprawled in the grass and O. Henry, with the euphoria induced by food, wine, a cool sea breeze and the proximity of great wealth, began talking about his work and what it meant to him.

He showed Davis the notebook he always carried in a side pocket and reflected, "It contains a dozen pages of blank paper. With a lead pencil I write on these several sheets a tale three or four thousand words in length. You buy the story and print it in one of the magazines you edit. If it is a good tale it gets into a book, or perhaps is dramatized and put on the stage. Very well, that's the beginning that has to do with its earning power. I get royalties on the volume, the serial rights, the drama and maybe some day sell it for a motion picture. [The American film was still in its nickelodeon phase, but O. Henry apparently saw its market potential for a writer.] It goes on and on reaping profit and yet it is never anything but the figment of my imagination converted into words. . . .

"Now, I have a daughter, a child of my own flesh and blood, bone of my bone. She looks and acts like me. She is my most precious possession. She is a material, breathing entity; another me. In three score years and ten, according to the Biblical injunction, she will return to the earth, and that will be the absolute last of Margaret Porter, daughter of O. Henry. But my written words set down methodically, laboriously, on these sheets of white paper, fugitive reflections at best, live on. Queer, isn't it? Flesh: Mortal. Thought: Immortal."

The philosophical mood vanished when the sea breeze died down and the heat of the day returned, and O. Henry grumbled at the Port Washington station, "The thing I like most about this place is the railroad that runs out of it toward Manhattan."[1]

Only rarely and reluctantly he left his "Bagdad" reborn on the Hudson. In September 1903, he went back to Pittsburgh for a visit with his daughter and the Roaches, and soon hurried home to New York complaining of "smoke, soot, gloom, rain, hordes of Philistines and money-changers in all the temples."

Home now and for the next several years was Irving Place, one of the hundreds of villagelike sections that make up the metropolis. Many New Yorkers rattled around the city for years until they settled down in the neighborhood, self-contained with stores, restaurants, laundries and bars, that suited them. Irving Place, coincidentally named for another great storyteller, was the operating base that best fitted O. Henry's personality, and No. 55 is, of all the places he lived, the home of his restless spirit. He was recommended to that short street a block east of Fourth Avenue by William Wash Williams, who lived on it himself.

55 Irving Place was a narrow, four-story brownstone owned by a Hungarian couple named Jaffe. O. Henry rented the huge old parlor and an alcove opening off it, which he had refurnished as a bathroom at his own expense. "I like lots of room," he told Bill Williams as he showed the *World* man his new quarters, "lots of space to move about it, breathe in, stretch out in." He also admired the spacious fireplace with marble mantle, the wide bay window and the glass-beaded chandelier. Even in 1903 the apartment was a bit old-fashioned, but O. Henry himself was a bit old-fashioned, a relic of the frontier, of the post-bellum South. During the years of his residence, until 1907, he became one of the more famous (but still reclusive) citizens of New York City.

He was equally pleased by the fact that within a short walk were all the amenities he valued. Irving Place runs from Fourteenth Street on the south to the sedate elegance of Gramercy Park on the north, a distance of just six short blocks. It had a serene and secluded atmosphere which pleased him mightily. Even more necessary to his tranquillity was a good German *Brauhaus*. He loved to poke fun at German solemnity and German mutilation of the English language, as many of his stories testify, but one thing he shared with H. L. Mencken—who incidentally detested the trickiness of his stories and was a leader of the literary junta which pronounced anathema on them—was the almost spiritual necessity of unraveling himself in a beerhouse.

Knowing O. Henry's tastes, Bill Williams immediately led him to the nearest *Stube* with a classic reputation, Scheffel Hall, a high-vaulted beerhall at Seventeenth Street and Third Avenue, which had been converted from a church. It was "noted all over greater New York," as Williams later wrote, "for its German food and beer. It was a great family resort and drew its trade—largely German—from the four corners of the big city. Pigs' knuckles and sauerkraut went over its tables by the ton and Pilsener by the thousands of gallons. '*Gesundheit!*' chorused its length and breadth, was its spirit, and over and above, even more powerful and persistent than the fumes from the steaming dishes and clouds of tobacco smoke—the flavor of its atmosphere." O. Henry not only made Scheffel's his hangout but used it as the setting for "The Halberdier of the Little Rheinschloss"—"the big hall with its smoky rafters, rows of imported steins, a portrait of Goethe, and verses painted on the walls—translated into German from the orignial Cincinnati poets," which "seemed atmospherically correct when viewed through the bottom of a glass."[2]

Afterwards Williams acted as his guide on a tour of the neighborhood. At the corner of Seventeenth and Irving Place, about a block from No. 55, was the small yellow house with a tiny veranda which was reputed to have been the home of Washington Irving.

"A fellow kinda feels like wearing his hat in his hand when he stands here, doesn't he?" O. Henry said.

At Sixteenth and Irving Place was the sedate old Westminster Hotel, where Charles Dickens was said to have stayed on his American tour and became something of a local legend, as Williams related, by drinking a quart of whiskey every morning before breakfast.

O. Henry grinned at the story and said, "Well, whether he did or did not, a quart of liquor before breakfast is a lot of liquor." He asked Williams if there was a bar in the hotel and the reporter nodded. "Then I propose that we go in and have a smile where Charles had many a laugh." The Westminster bar was a tiny room with frescoed walls and ceiling, marble-top tables and a small patronage of quietly dedicated drinkers. O. Henry made the dark little nook his personal hideaway, Williams said, because "it offered escape and refuge from the hustle and bustle. . . . its atmosphere was heavy with old aristocracy."

He was equally though differently pleased with his first glimpse of the Hotel America on Fifteenth Street, which was converted in O. Henry's imagination to El Refugio as the setting for "The Gold That Glittered." The Hotel America was a gathering place for exiles from Central and South America, failed revolutionaries and hopeful conspirators. It naturally appealed at once to him as a link to his own Central American memories. Here congregated "the volatile exiles from the South . . . up from Chili [sic], Bolivia, Columbia [sic], the rolling republics of Central America and the ireful islands of the West Indies . . . scattered like burning lava by the political eruption of their several countries." At the Hotel America they schemed to return in glory. In the faded elegance of its lobby, under its glass portico, on the sidewalks outside—and at equally revolutionary Union Square only a short block away—the mustachioed hotheads gathered to "lay counterplots, to bide their time, to solicit funds, to enlist filibusters, to smuggle out arms and ammunitions, to play the game of long tow."

The southern end of Irving Place abutted on the tawdry fascinations of Fourteenth Street, with Billy McGlory's dive, Tony Pastor's vaudeville theater, Tammany Hall and Tom Sharkey's saloon among the leading attractions. O. Henry singled out Sharkey's saloon as the place he wanted to see close up. The man who fought Jim Jeffries presided over the cash register in person. Williams thought it a low-class place reeking of "squirrel whiskey" and "jingle gin" and observed that "the place was crowded with piker gamblers, ward politicians, cheap confidence men, sailors, pimps, pickpockets and gunmen of the shaved and bathed, East Side, snappily dressed variety," not to mention most of the district's prostitutes, "'cruisers,' old and young rigged out in the unmistakable cheap finery of their trade; hard-boiled petty 'gold-diggers' of the city's highways; sordid sisters of a sunken social stratum." One whole wall was covered by a "sign-painter's version of the great Sharkey-Jeffries fight at Coney Island; an awful thing, done in a thousand colors with every possible avoidance of art. . . ."

It was a disgusting place to a twenty-five-year-old outlander like young Williams, but he observed that Sharkey's absolutely delighted O. Henry, who was soaking up the merry atmosphere. For such places the latter had a collector's passion. "I could feel rather than see him taking it all in with an eager appetite," Williams recalled. "He was getting an element he wanted for his storehouse and getting it straight and good. . . . His quick, all-seeing and discerning eye was labeling each component of the variant mass. It was all good story stuff. Although I do not recall a word spoken as we stood there looking around while the brew in our glasses flattened, I knew he was missing nothing, but was appraising and filing away everything." More than a few grimy traces of Tom Sharkey's saloon found their way into "Past One at Rooney's" and "The Guilty Party."

They wound up their tour of the Irving Place neighborhood by walking around the block-square Gramercy Park with its iron fence and the gates to which only people living on the square have keys. It was and is one of the jewels of architectural New York, the epitome of whatever was graceful about the nineteenth century. Williams pointed out the old Edwin Booth residence, which had been converted into the Players Club, the homes of Robert Collier (*Collier's Weekly*), of Samuel Tilden ("the sage of Gramercy"), of Robert G. Ingersoll, Cyrus W. Field and Abram S. Hewitt. Mark Twain had once lived on the square, and David Graham Phillips, the novelist, not only lived there but died near one of the park's gates from an assassin's bullet.

Against the wrought-iron fence of Gramercy Park Nancy and

Lou of "The Trimmed Lamp" leaned and wept while a rookie patrolman passed by "pretending not to notice, for he was wise enough to know that these matters are beyond help so far as the power he represents is concerned, though he rap the pavement with his night-stick till the sound goes up to the furthermost stars."

Once established at 55 Irving Place, O. Henry settled into his routine, the steady production of short stories which brought him fame and carried him through the next several years until he married for a second time. Most of the day he worked at his desk or kept an occasional business appointment. The whiskey bottle kept a small alcoholic flame burning during the day—he was one of the very few writers capable of mixing alcohol and creative work—but at night he turned up the burner. It was a rare evening that didn't find O. Henry out on the town. Its streets and saloons, dance halls and vaudeville houses provided the raw material for his daytime labors.

Once night fell, he usually dropped in at Healy's Cafe, on the corner of Irving Place and Eighteenth Street, which everyone called "The Club." Irving Place was largely tenanted by bachelors, young men living in furnished rooms in the brownstones like O. Henry himself—newspapermen, doctors, lawyers, actors, musicians, artists—until success and/or marriage caused them to move to larger apartments and houses. Most of them gathered after work at Healy's for a few drinks. As Bill Williams described it, Healy's was a place for sedate drinking and quiet conversation. "It was a subdued, retiring and quiet place" on the ground floor of a five-story brownstone, and "the club members always tried to keep it so. It was not a burning flame attracting weak moths. The town drunkard could have missed it entirely on a dark night. . . . It was not until the curtain had been rung down on the workday and the dinner hour had passed, that the clubmen began to assemble in the canteen. There were doctors, lawyers, newspapermen, artists, freelance writers, actors, musicians, inventors, promoters, clerks, insurance men, salesmen, printers, politicians, bookkeepers, feather-dyers, with a detached fringe of Italian cobblers, valets, hostlers and night-hawk cabmen from the stable across the way."

The Club was a "gold mine of story material" for O. Henry, Williams said, and "how many of his little masterpieces he picked up from the characters he found and the yarns he heard in that place will never be known. He was long of ear and eye but short of tongue, and he would buy and listen and listen and buy until the last minute of the last hour many and many's the night."[3]

An autocratic Irishman named Cornelius Delaney was the night bartender, who would finally close up the saloon by shouting, "Not another drop! Out wit ye all! I got a home an' family to go to. Ain't youse guys got no homes a-tall?"

Delaney and his setting are described in "The Lost Blend," in which he became Con Langtry: "Con Langtry worked on the sober side of the bar in Kenealy's cafe. You and I stood one-legged like geese on the other side and went into voluntary liquidation of one week's wages. Opposite danced Con, clean, temperate, clear-headed, polite, white-jacketed, punctual, trustworthy, young and responsible and took our money.

"The saloon (whether blessed or cursed) stood in one of those 'little places' which are parallelograms instead of streets, and inhabited by laundries, decayed Knickerbocker families and Bohemians who have nothing to do with either."

It must have been a fascinating place for O. Henry to begin his nightly rounds, as alert for a picturesque character, an anecdote, an experience, as any latter-day Pepys. Odd characters drifted in, told their tales, drifted out and were never seen again. Their stories might have been true or mere boozy fancies. Occasionally they were performers on the perimeter of history, such as the Austrian count and ex-army officer who claimed to know the inside story of Mayerling. He had been present at the Crown Prince Rudolf's hunting lodge, he claimed, when Rudolf supposedly killed himself and his young mistress Marie Vetsera. Actually, the count told his audience at Healy's, the Crown Prince was bashed over the head with a champagne bottle during a wild party at the hunting lodge, and Baroness Vetsera was killed to prevent her from talking.

Another man wandered in from the streets and alleged that he was the person who inadvertently saved the life of Russell Sage, the miserly multimillionaire, when a lunatic came into Sage's office with a bomb. Sage grabbed the man and used him as a shield between himself and the exploding bomb. Although the man spent months in the hospital recovering from his injuries, he had never been able to get a dime's worth of compensation out of Russell Sage. Other storytellers at Healy's included an old newspaperman who had once interviewed Jesse James at his hideout; the former captain of a Mississippi riverboat; a reformed salesman of gold bricks; and the man who drove the twenty-two-horse team which drew the lead bandwagon in Barnum & Bailey's street parades.

Among the men to whom O. Henry listened with the greatest interest, according to Williams, were Jack Laden, who drove a hack nights and was probably the model for Jerry O'Donovan in "From the Cabby's Seat"; a Sicilian cobbler named Pietro Brisbano, with whom O. Henry discussed Italian wines and out-of-the-way Italian restaurants in Manhattan; and a quiet little German whom everyone called "The Professor," who earned his living teaching German to a private class and janitoring for a Lutheran church. They were the kind of people O. Henry could relax with, ordinary citizens who didn't much care that he wrote stories and was making a name for himself.

He was "not a good mixer," Williams said, but the regulars at Healy's accepted him and valued his company, taking him to be a reserved Southern gentleman (who held his liquor well) among the less inhibited, polyglot and diverse types who gathered there. "Repression, repression and more repression was the keynote of O. Henry's makeup," it seemed to Williams, who was writing, of course, long after O. Henry's past had been revealed and may have been influenced by a certain amount of hindsight. "Some of it was intrinsic and natural as rain; much of it was assumed and developed. He was born with a wall around him through which he himself was never able to break entirely and before which the world stopped. Experience had caused him to thicken that wall. I doubt if anyone O. Henry ever knew was able to penetrate fully the barrier which enclosed him, and feel just as certain that at no time in his life did he accomplish a full step outside it. He was a man who was alone whether by himself or in a crowd; and he both liked and disliked it. . . . I know that O. Henry often tried and tried hard to escape from himself but never succeeded in getting very far . . ."[4]

Aside from his explorations of Manhattan night life, O. Henry was also greatly, perhaps equally interested in what was happening to the modern woman, the New Woman as she was being called in newspapers and magazines, the grandmother or great-grandmother of today's miniskirted young rebel, career girl or flower child. Perhaps he sensed the changes that would be wrought in the structure of American life by the growing independence of women, and certainly he was one of the first writers, along with Frank Norris and Jack London, to gauge its importance. He became the working girl's popular biographer and defender, and particularly objected to the term "shop-girl" as being condescending or pejorative. In "The Trimmed Lamp," he wrote that "We often hear 'shop-girls' spoken of. No such persons exist. There are girls who work in shops. They make their living that way. But why turn their occupation into an adjective? Let us be fair. We do not refer to the girls who live on Fifth Avenue as 'marriage-girls.'"

His effort to observe the working girl and career woman as closely as possible led him to a long platonic friendship with Miss Anne Partlan, a thirty-year-old, tactful, attractive and intelligent woman who worked in an advertising agency and wrote short stories about working-class life as an avocation. She became one of the handful of persons who could claim to be close friends of O. Henry's.

His interest in her stories caused him to visit her shortly after coming to New York, and he then told her that "the hand-to-mouth life that girls led in New York interested him" and asked to meet her friends without letting them know he was a writer. "I used to have parties of my friends up to meet him and they never dreamed that this Mr. Porter, who fitted so well into our queer makeshift life, was a genius. He had absolutely no pose. 'An Unfinished Story' and 'The Third Ingredient' were taken straight from life. That is why there is never anything sordid in the little stories. We were poor enough in our dingy rooms but he saw the little pleasures and surprises that made life bearable to us."*[6]

As Alphonso Smith wrote, O. Henry was gripped most firmly by two sorts of people, "those who were under a strain of some sort and those who were under a delusion. The first stirred his sympathy; the second furnished him with unending entertainment. Both were abundantly represented in his stories. . . ."[7] The working girls he studied and wrote about, struggling to make their way in what was then indubitably a man's world, belonged in the first category.

"There was nothing of the brilliant wit about the great story writer when in the atmosphere of the shop-girl, clerk, or salesman," as Miss Partlan remembered his appearances at her gatherings. "Instead, there was a quiet, sympathetic attitude and, at times, a pre-occupied manner as if their remarks and chatter reminded him of his old days of bondage in the country drug store, and the perpetual pill-making which he was wont to describe with an amusing gesture, indicating the process of forming the cure-all.

"One evening a group of department store employes were hav-

* The plot for "The Third Ingredient" developed from personal experience during his first months in New York, he told Miss Partlan. One evening he didn't have enough money to buy dinner. "He became so hungry that he could not finish the story on which he was working, and he walked up and down the landing between the rooms. The odor of cooking in one of the rooms increased his pangs, and he was beside himself when the door opened and a young girl said to him, 'Have you had your supper? I've made hazlett stew and it's too much for me. It won't keep, so come in and help me eat it.' He was grateful for the invitation and partook of the stew which, she told him, was made from the liver, kidneys and heart of a calf. . . . A few days later he rapped at her door to ask her to a more substantial dinner, but he found that she had gone and left no address."[5]

ing dinner with me. Among them were sales-girls, an associate buyer, and one of the office force. I asked O. Henry to join us so that he might catch the spirit of their daily life. He leavened their shop-talk with genial, simple expressions of mirth as they told their tales of petty intrigue and strife for place amid the antagonism and pressure which pervades the atmosphere of every big organization. On leaving, he remarked to me: 'If Henry James had gone to work in one of those places, he would have turned out the great American novel.' "

Evidently O. Henry on the hunt for story material, satisfying his enormous curiosity about other people's occupations and the way things worked, was able to fling himself into the spirit of the occasion much easier than the standoffish O. Henry observed by his friends when he was off duty. Or perhaps he felt more at home among simpler people. At any rate, Miss Partlan provided a picture of O. Henry on an occasion when he was far from the aloof, withdrawn and reticent man his friends in the profession knew. She took him to a meeting of master craftsmen with her father, who was a mechanic and inventor of blacksmith's tools.

"Speeches were made by masters of their craft, filled with references to 'sidehill plows,' 'bolt cutters' and 'dressing chisels for rock use.' The speeches referred to the most humane make of horseshoes, bar iron, toe calks and hoof expanders. All of this fell on no more attentive ears than O. Henry's. A Scotchman presently arose and spoke on coach building. He told of a wood filling which he once made of the dust gathered from forges, mixed with a peculiar sort of clay. His enunciation was not clear and more than once O. Henry turned to me to ask me if I had caught the indistinct word.

"After the speeches came dancing of the Lancers and Virginia Reel. O. Henry threw himself into the spirit like a boy. He danced and whistled and called out numbers, laughing heartily when in the maze of a wrong turn. No one there dreamed he was other than an ordinary fellow working-man.

" 'Where do you keep shop, Mr. Porter?' asked the wife of a Missouri mechanic.

"'Mr. Porter is an author,' I replied impulsively.

"'Well, I can do other things,' he retorted with a note of defense as he continued, 'I can rope cows, and I tried raising sheep once.'"[8]

His fascination with the plight of the working girl—whom heaven, he believed, would not protect, contrary to the title of a popular song—began bearing artistic blossoms in the summer of 1904. That was when he wrote the first of a series of "shop-girl stories" which became so widely known that a critic would write, "Across the counter of every New York department store is the shadow of O. Henry," and the poet Vachel Lindsay would call him "the little shop-girl's knight."[9]

His first working-girl heroine was Masie, one of 3,000 saleswomen in a New York department store, who had "listened to the promulgated wisdom of the 2,999 other girls and had stored it in a brain that was as secretive and wary as that of a Maltese cat." Irving Carter, "painter, millionaire, traveler, poet, automobilist," falls in love with her across the glove counter where she works.

When Carter, a proper young man, asks if he can make a formal call on her and her family, she laughingly replies, "Oh, gee, no. If you could see our flat once! There's five of us in three rooms. I'd just like to see my ma's face if I was to bring a gentleman friend there!"

Carter, as the writer explains, had no understanding of the working-girl's life. "He did not know that her home is often either a scarcely habitable tiny room or a domicile filled to overflowing with kith and kin. The street-corner is her parlor, the park is her drawing-room, the avenue is her garden walk; yet for the most part she is as inviolate mistress of herself in them as is my lady inside her tapestried chamber."

The young millionaire is forced to court Masie in the streets and parks and soon urges her to marry him. Unaware that her world is bounded by the Jersey shore on the west, the Bronx to the north, Queens to the east and Coney Island to the south, he proposes to take her on a honeymoon to Europe and the Orient, "ride on elephants and see the wonderful temples of the Hindoos and the Brahmins and the Japanese gardens and the camel trains and the chariot races in Persia. . . ."

In a characteristic whiplash ending, Masie tells one of her friends that Carter "ain't in it any more. Say, Lu, what do you think that fellow wanted me to do? . . . He wanted to marry me and go down to Coney for a wedding tour!"

His other working-class heroines, in such stories as "The Guilty Party, An East Side Story," "An Unfinished Story," "Brickdust Row" and "The Trimmed Lamp," are more tragic than Masie, clearly the victims of the pressures of life in the tenement districts, of their yearnings for "better things," eventually (as the men who preside over the printing presses of Soviet Russia obviously discern) of a system dominated by a brutal materialism.

Liz of "The Guilty Party" is an East Side girl who drifts to her ruin, essentially because her father ignores her when she wants him to play checkers with her. Her mother begs the father to pay more attention to her so that she will not have to play in the street and "learn too much there that ain't good for 'em." But the situation isn't her father's fault, really, because, as he explains, he is dead tired from a long day's work. The story ends in a dream in which Liz kills the man who betrayed her and then commits suicide. A heavenly court acquits Liz and declares, "The guilty party you've got to look for in this case is a red-haired, unshaven, untidy man, sitting by the window reading in his stockinged feet, while his children play in the streets." Subconsciously, perhaps, O. Henry was also indicting himself as a guilty party for leaving his own daughter with her grandparents and rarely seeing her until she was grown.

In "An Unfinished Story," one of the most popular he ever wrote, O. Henry showed how his heroine, Dulcie, went to her ruin because her employer underpaid her. She received six dollars a week and the necessities of her life came to exactly $4.76. Dulcie wasn't starving for food but for a little luxury in her barren life; she particularly wanted more fashionable clothes, which led to her downfall. "I hold my pen poised in vain," says the narrator of the story, "when I would add to Dulcie's life some of those joys that belong to woman by virtue of all the unwritten, sacred, natural, inactive ordinances of the equity of heaven."

That story also ends in a dream sequence, with the narrator standing near a group of "prosperous-looking" angels. He asks a policeman who they are.

"Why, they are the men who hired working girls," the policeman replies, "and paid 'em five or six dollars a week to live on. Are you one of the bunch?"

"Not on your immortality," replies the narrator. "I'm only the fellow that set fire to an orphan asylum, and murdered a blind man for his pennies."

"Brickdust Row" was the tale of a slum landlord named Blinker who fell in love with a girl named Florence. He wants to see where she lives, but Florence tells him she lives on Brickdust Row. "They call it that because there's red dust from the bricks crumbling over everything. I've lived there for more than four years. There's no place to receive company. You can't have anybody come to your room. What else is there to do? A girl has got to meet the men, hasn't she? . . . The first time one spoke to me on the street, I ran home and cried all night. But you get used to it. I meet a good many nice fellows at church. I go on rainy days and stand in the vestibule until one comes up with an umbrella. I wish there was a parlour, so I could ask you to call, Mr. Blinker."

Blinker repents—what modern writer would dare invent a repentant slumlord?—and the next morning tells his lawyer, since he owns Brickdust Row, "Do what you please with it. Remodel it, burn it, raze it to the ground. But, man, I tell you it's too late. It's too late. It's too late. It's too late."

In "The Trimmed Lamp," one of the longest of his stories and one of the most carefully crafted, he tells the cautionary tale of two girls named Lou and Nancy, who live in a boarding house. Nancy works in a department store and is ambitious for a better (or more luxurious) life, while Lou is content to work in a laundry and go steady with her humble but faithful Dan. Nancy agrees to meet one of the "swell gentleman friends" of a coworker at the department store, a bald young man with diamond cuff links whose "tastes ran to shop-girls" and who is "the nephew of old Van Skittles himself." He proposes to Nancy but she rejects him, as she explains to Lou, because "his family only allows him $20,000 a year to spend." Lou is indignant and asks her friend, "Do you want to be a Mormon and marry Rockefeller and Gladstone Dowie and the King of Spain and the whole bunch?" To which Nancy coolly replies, "When I sell out it's not going to be on any bargain day."

Then, in a typical O. Henry switch, the two girls change their attitudes. Nancy has come to see that her values are all wrong and "Sometimes the dollar-mark grew blurred in her mind's eye, and shaped itself into letters that spelled such words as 'truth' and 'honor' and now and then 'just kindness,'" and she wondered "if Persian lamb was always quoted as its market value by the hearts that it covered." Lou, on the other hand, had decided that Nancy was right about looking for a flashier suitor than Dan. Dan wanted to marry her, she explained to Nancy, but "Why should I? I'm independent. I can do as I please with the money I earn. . . ." She ditches Dan, and Nancy, having come to her senses and valuing "Dan the constant, the immutable, the unchanging," takes up with her friend's castoff suitor.

Three months later the two girls meet by accident. Lou is adorned with furs and jewels, obviously having chosen the path of ruin. Nancy tells her that she is going to marry Dan. In the tear-drenched finale Lou, realizing the tragedy of her sellout, collapses against the iron fence of Gramercy Park "sobbing turbulently" while the "plainly dressed" Nancy tries to console her.

O. Henry was now beginning to produce the artistic distillate of his first two years in New York, the stories which made him accepted by the millions of ordinary people as their minnesinger and advocate. He considered himself a student of urban life at a time when the farm and small town were still regarded as the real

America, the James Whitcomb Riley heartland an Eden in contrast to the cruel inhumanity of the cities.

Something of his attitude toward New York was expressed in "The Making of a New Yorker," in which Raggles, "a tramp . . . but that was only an elliptical way of saying he was a philosopher, an artist, a traveler, a naturalist, and a discoverer," speaks for O. Henry himself.

His alter ego "studied cities as women study their reflections in mirrors; as children study the glue and sawdust of a dislocated doll; as the men who write about wild animals study the cages in the zoo. A city to Raggles was not merely a pile of bricks and mortar, peopled by a certain number of inhabitants; it was a thing with soul characteristic and distinct; an individual conglomeration of life, with its own peculiar essence, flavor, and feeling." Until he came to New York Raggles had wandered through many cities in search of one that would "engage and hold his critical fancy." Pittsburgh—and here the voice of Raggles' creator spoke most clearly—"impressed him as the play of 'Othello' performed in the Russian language in a railroad station by Dockstader's minstrels," a slattern "washing the dishes in a silk dress and white kid slippers, and bidding Raffles sit before the roaring fireplace and drink champagne with his pigs' feet and fried potatoes." New Orleans—more fondly recalled from his brief career as a fugitive—had "simply gazed down on him from a balcony. He could see her pensive, starry eyes and catch the flutter of her fan, and that was all."

But New York seemed "as cold, glittering, serene, impossible as a four-carat diamond in a window to a lover outside fingering damply in his pocket his ribbon-counter salary." Undoubtedly this was the way O. Henry himself felt about the city during his first months there: "This city of Manhattan gave him no clue; it was walled against him. Like a river of adamant it flowed past him in the streets. Never an eye was turned upon him; no voice spoke to him. . . . The houses were interminable ramparts loopholed for defence; the people were bright but bloodless spectres passing in sinister and selfish array."

What had particularly irked O. Henry-Raggles was the absolute and hardened egotism that "seemed to saturate the people as toys are saturated with paint. . . . Humanity was gone from them; they were toddling idols of stone and varnish, worshipping themselves and greedy for though oblivious of worship from their fellow graven images. Frozen, cruel, implacable, impervious, cut to an identical pattern, they hurried on their ways like statues brought by some miracle to motion, while soul and feeling lay unaroused in the reluctant marble." Raggles was convinced, in brief, that the city had no heart, it was a collection of humans without humanity.

Literally it was that most modern *deus ex machina,* the automobile, which made Raggles a New Yorker and brought him to the recognition that his fellow citizens were human after all. He was run down by a hit-and-run driver. When he came to, he found himself being ministered to by people he had seen only as detestable stereotypes—an elderly rich man, a goddesslike woman of privilege, a street-corner tough, all of them with eyes turned from steel and stone to something "soft and humid with human sympathy." Convalescing in the hospital a few days later, Raggles assaults a fellow patient because he was "runnin' down me town." "What town?" the nurse asks. "New York," Raggles replies.

It did not take an automobile accident to accomplish the "making of a New Yorker" in O. Henry's case. His was a case of love at first sight, first of all, perhaps, because it plucked at his imagination as no other place did and provided him with endless inspiration for his storytelling. "I would like to live a lifetime on each street in New York," he once told Gilman Hall. "Every house has a drama in it."[10]

New Yorkers saw themselves—still do—as hard-boiled cynics, but O. Henry was certain there were more gullible people in Manhattan than in Medicine Hat. "Catching suckers in New York is like dynamiting a Texas lake for bass," he observed in "Innocents of Broadway." "All you have to do anywhere between the North [Hudson] and East rivers is to stand in the street with an open bag marked 'Drop packages of money here. No checks or loose bills taken.'"

Such was the magic of O. Henry's New York that it even resolved a blood feud (in "Squaring the Circle") of forty years standing. Cal Harkness and Sam Folwell are each the sole surviving member of their families, wiped out to the last man by their vendetta in the Kentucky hills. Sam learns that Cal has moved to New York and, armed to the teeth, follows him. While searching for Cal, Sam is buffeted mercilessly by the hurrying crowds. At last Sam catches sight of Cal and is so glad to see a familiar face that he can only say, "Howdy, Cal! I'm durned glad to see you." And at Fifth Avenue and Twenty-third Street, the circle is squared, "the Cumberland feudists shook hands."

O. Henry never lost that feeling for the city's magic, the eagerness to "see what's around the corner."

Chapter 6. Fresh Out of Money

In 1904 and 1905 O. Henry was cranking out stories on almost an assembly line basis. To fulfill his contract with the *Sunday World* he had to produce a story a week, on deadline, and in addition he was working on a contractual arrangement with Bob Davis at *Munsey's* by which that magazine had first refusal on all his magazine stories with payment of ten cents a word for those it accepted. The stories *Munsey's* didn't want were published in *Ainslee's, Everybody's, Cosmopolitan, Smart Set* and other magazines. In 1904, the *World* published fifty-one of his stories —he missed one week's deadline—and fifteen others appeared in magazines.

Plot making is now regarded in low favor by critics and English professors, and O. Henry himself claimed he didn't plot out a story, that it grew out of his characters, but undoubtedly O. Henry at his peak was one of the quickest and most agile inventors of a story line ever to practice on New Grub Street. He could practically ad-lib a story if under the most intense editorial pressure. He was always spending advances more quickly than he could produce the stories for which they were obtained, and an atmosphere of incipient panic was the one in which he evidently functioned at his best.

He was completely candid in discussing the commerical aspects of writing with George MacAdam of the *Times,* or anyone else who bothered to ask him about such matters. "Editors are just like other merchants—they want to buy at lowest prices," he told MacAdam. "A few years ago I was selling stories to a certain magazine at the rate of five cents a word. I thought there was a chance that I might get more, so I boldly asked the editor for

17. The Sixth Avenue El, 1901.

18. Madison Square Garden bearing the statue of Golden Diana, a landmark of O. Henry's New York.

19. Union Square at the turn of the twentieth century.

20. Coney Island in the early 1900s.

ten cents. 'All right,' said he, 'I'll pay it.' He was just waiting to be asked. . . .

"I'll give you the whole secret of short-story writing. Here it is. Rule 1: Write stories that please yourself. There is no Rule 2. The technical points you can get from Bliss Perry [an academic expert on the short story]. If you can't write a story that pleases yourself you'll never please the public. But in writing the story forget the public.

"I get a story thoroughly in mind before I sit down at my writing table. Then I write it out quickly; and, without revising it, mail it to the editor. In this way I am able to judge my stories as the public judges them. I've seen stories of mine in print that I wouldn't recognize as my own.

"Yes, I get dry spells. Sometimes I can't turn out a thing for three months. When one of those spells comes on, I quit trying to work and go out and see something of life. You can't write a story that's got any life in it by sitting at a writing table and thinking. You've got to get out into the streets, into the crowds, talk with people, and feel the rush and throb of real life—that's the stimulant for a story writer. . . . I have never met any one but what I could learn something from him; he's had some experiences that I have not had; he sees the world from his own viewpoint. . . .

"People say I know New York well. Just change Twenty-third Street in one of my New York stories to Main Street, rub out the Flatiron Building and put in the Town Hall, and the story will fit just as truly in any up-State town. At least, I hope this can be said of my stories. So long as a story is true to human nature, all you need do is change the local color to make it fit any town. If you have the right kind of an eye—the kind that can disregard high hats, cutaway coats and trolley cars—you can see all the characters in the 'Arabian Nights' parading up and down Broadway at mid-day."[1]

The correspondence of most professional writers, taken in bulk, is something of a disappointment to anyone who expects it to be concerned with literature, with artistic aims, with revelations of how they conceive and execute their designs. Jack London's accumulated correspondence is dotted with more dollar signs than the files of any stockbroker. Money is what most writers write about. O. Henry's letters also offered sterling proof of the rule. A very large proportion of the correspondence gathered in his hometown library deals with the crasser aspects of his calling: O. Henry asking an editor for an advance, O. Henry asking for another advance, O. Henry promising to deliver the goods, O. Henry creatively explaining why he hasn't kept his promise, O. Henry driven to the wall and finally enclosing the story with the resentful air of a man giving his last quart of blood.

From 1904 to the end of his life, he waged a constant delaying action with the editors to whom he "owed" stories. When they became importunate, he would send them a few pages to keep their hopes alive.

Alexander Black, who for a time was editor-in-charge-of-O. Henry at the *Sunday World,* perhaps the paper's most exacting position next to that of the man who polished the Pulitzer Building's golden dome, called these "propitiatory fragments" which were "made on account." As Black described the exhausting process:

"The coming of the first fragment of an O. Henry story acknowledged the reasonableness of my official anxiety, for the weekly stories in the *World* had to be illustrated, and the illustrations needed a little more information about scenes and characters. Often this preliminary part (on the last day of grace) held no adequate hint for the draughtsman, but an accompanying line would wig-wag: 'The picture might be of a traffic cop holding open a pathway for a pretty girl.'

"The offender could awake to sparkling excuses. Sometimes they were not more original than those offered by an office boy with his eye on a ball game. Again, they would be ingenious. Always they would be joyfully colloquial. Promises had a like flavor. 'You can bet your variegated socks that I will send you an Easter story' was typical. Or the reassurance might run, 'May the ink in my bottle turn to Old Crow on the day that I hesitate to use it at the desire of you and the still dear *World*.'"[2]

Another unfortunate on the *World's* Sunday magazine staff who had the burden of coaxing stories out of O. Henry was William Johnston, who said he always started out his work week by sending a note to O. Henry demanding, "Where's this week's story?" Sometimes, Johnston said, O. Henry's reply had nothing to do with the case, as when he answered one of Johnston's demands with: "What do you say? Let's take an evening off and strike the Cafe Francis for a slight refection. I like to be waked up suddenly there by the music and look across at the red-haired woman eating smelts under an original by Glackens." Or as something of an excuse: "Being entirely out of tune with the muse, I went out and ameliorated the condition of a shop-girl as far as a planked steak could do so."

Late in 1905, as Johnston recalled, he experienced great difficulty in prying the story "The Guilty Party" out of the author. He sternly wrote O. Henry: "There was once a celebrated author who appeared before the judgment bar. A host of people were there saying nice things about him, when up spoke a weary editor and said, 'He never kept a promise in his life.'"

The riposte from O. Henry was prompt and overwhelming:

"Guilty, m'lud.

"And yet—

"Some time ago a magazine editor to whom I had promised a story at a certain minute (and strangely enough didn't get there with it) wrote to me: 'I am coming down tomorrow to kick you thoroughly with a pair of heavy-soled shoes. *I* never go back on *my* promises.' And I lifted my voice and said unto him: 'It's easy to keep promises that can be pulled off with your feet.'"[3]

Isaac Marcosson, the editor and writer, who made an O. Henry devotee of Sir James Barrie,* related how O. Henry once ob-

* Sir James wrote Marcosson in 1917 that ". . . I read all of O. Henry's books that I could find. I thank you for telling me about them." Marcosson in his *Adventures in Interviewing* added that "Barrie became such an O. Henry enthusiast that he presented a complete set of the American author's works to Mr. Asquith [the former Prime Minister]."

tained a large advance from a magazine, with an ironclad deadline set for delivery of the manuscript. Ten days before the deadline the harried editor, with white space yawning in the dummies for his next issue, began a telegraphic bombardment. On the day before the delivery date he telegraphed a couplet to O. Henry:

O. HENRY, IN YOUR HOUR OF EASE
SEND US THAT STORY, PLEASE.

And all the editor got in reply was another couplet:

WHEN CARE AND SORROW REND THE BROW
I CAN NOT SEND THAT STORY NOW.

John O'Hara Cosgrave of *Everybody's* was another editor who suffered along with O. Henry in his losing fights against deadlines and creditors and was evidently one of the softer touches when it came to helping the author out of his recurring predicaments. A typical O. Henry appeal, complete with the usual ramifications of borrowing from Peter to pay Paul, informed Cosgrave: "I owe Gilman Hall $175 (or mighty close to it) pussonally —so he tells me. I thought it was only about $30, but he has been keeping the account. He's just got to have it today. *McClure's* will pay me some money on the 15th of June, but I can't get any until then. I was expecting it before this—anyhow before Gilman left, but they stick to the letter. . . .

"I wonder if you could give me a check for that much to pay him today. If you will I'll hold up my right hand—thus: that I'll have you a *first-class story on your desk before the last of this week.* I reckon I'm pretty well overdrawn, but I've sure got to see that Hall gets his before he leaves. I don't want anything for myself. Please, sir, let me know right away, by return boy if you'll do it. If you can't, I'll have to make a quick dash at the three-ball magazines; and I do hate to tie up with them for a story."[4]

There is no reason to suspect that such maneuvers were part of a running confidence game on O. Henry's part. He always delivered and paid off—eventually. Fecklessness and procrastination were as much a part of his character as his constant, unhesitating and unquestioning readiness to help others. It would probably have been impossible for him to live any other way than hand to mouth. If he had suddenly become wealthy, he would probably have ceased to function as a writer; economic pressure was his necessary goad. There are many "compulsive" writers, but O. Henry was not one of them.

Although the constant guerrilla war with his editors, always conducted with a joshing amiability on his part and generally with a weary tolerance on his editors', would have sapped the talent and energy of most writers, it did not appear to affect him adversely. Debtors suffer less from ulcers than creditors, and O. Henry was a natural-born debtor. Judging from his correspondence, he surmounted several financial crises a week, but his situation was, like that of the Viennese, always critical but never serious.

All his capacity for worrying was diverted into another channel, that of concealing the fact that he had served a prison sentence. The possibility that he might be "exposed" gnawed at him constantly. All or most of his friends knew that his real name was William Sydney Porter, but none knew that he had served time. That secret he guarded with all the determination in his make-up. Occasionally there was the threat of disclosure, either by accident or, as he once confided to Al Jennings, through a blackmailer.

Early in 1904, when his writing career was just beginning to expand, came the first threat to his privacy on that score. The magazine *Critic* announced with a flourish that it had discovered the true name of O. Henry:

"Less than a year ago the readers of popular magazines began to be startled and delighted by certain fantastic and ingenious tales, mainly dealing with western life and bearing the strange device 'O. Henry' as a signature. In a short time people began to talk to each other about the stories, and very soon they began to ask who the author was. It was then that a new problem fell upon this over-puzzled age,—who is 'O. Henry'? No one seemed to know the author's real name, and immediately vague and weird rumors began to be afloat and the *nom de guerre* was soon invested with as much curiosity as surrounds an author after his decease.

"But, like most mysteries, when it was probed there was no mystery about it. 'O. Henry's' real name is Mr. Sydney Porter, a gentleman from Texas, who having seen a great deal of the world with the naked eye, happened to find himself in New York about two years ago and there discovered a market where people would buy stories of his experiences. Being of a lazy disposition he very naturally quitted active life and took to his desk. He signed the name 'O. Henry' merely because he did not take his real self seriously as a maker of fiction. He really does shun notoriety—a most unusual characteristic among present-day writers—and he disclaims any intention of having purposely created a mystery about his identity. But he is still not too old to become a professional."[5]

Equally as alarming was the fact that *Critic* published a photograph taken of him in his Austin years.

The *Critic* was not widely read, but it must have seemed inevitable to him that sooner or later O. Henry, Sydney Porter and the convicted embezzler known in Austin and Columbus as Will or Bill Porter would be linked together. Confirmation of that fear came later that year when he received a letter from Judge Robert Hill, the publisher of the Houston *Post*, who had loaned him $200 toward employing defense counsel.

The contents of Hill's letter are unknown but apparently it was phrased in friendly terms, judging from O. Henry's reply: "Your very kind letter was delivered to me by 'Everybody's Magazine.' . . . I haven't acquired success yet. . . . I am living here very quietly, not mixing with people much, and working hard. The picture of me that you saw in a magazine was inserted without my knowledge or consent." It must have been a worrisome mystery to O. Henry as to who did supply the photograph, and whether it was done with malicious intent.

"I am not advertising myself," he continued. "If I were I would not write over a pen name. I very much appreciate your generous letter, and I am glad to hear from you for another reason. I have reason to believe that my book [he was putting together the volume of short stories titled *Cabbages and Kings*] will bring me in some money, and with the first surplus over my living expenses I intend to settle up some old debts. Yours I have not by any means forgotten, and it comes among the first . . ."[6]

Bob Davis has recorded that O. Henry once seemed on the point of telling him about a certain shameful part of his past, then drew back as from a precipice. "The first and only intimation I ever received from him that there was a rift in his life came in the form of an unfinished sentence. We were discussing the trivialities that turn men from one occupation to another; accidents which influence destinies"—a favorite theme of O. Henry's, one he had encountered more than once in his own life. "Some day," O. Henry told the editor, "I'll tell you how I fell heir to enough spare time to take up fiction seriously. Perhaps it would be better to tell you now, so that . . ."

He stopped suddenly and stared out the window.

Davis urged him to finish what he started to say.

"No," O. Henry replied. "Let me write it to you. The story can be told in four lines. At least they will give you the idea."

About a week later, at the end of a note, O. Henry appended a curious signature which did indeed, though too cryptically for Davis to make sense of it at the time, tell his story: "Sydney Porter . . . X . . . his mark . . . O. Henry."[7]

According to another close friend, William Wash Williams, O. Henry's secret leaked out somehow, perhaps unknown to him. A man who pretended to be O. Henry's friend, Williams said, confided to him one day, "Say, Williams, you're keeping nice company! Do you know your pal, O. Henry, is an ex-convict?" Williams shook his head. "Well, he is," the other man said with malicious delight, "he served time in the pen at Columbus, Ohio, for embezzling the funds of a bank in Austin, Texas." Williams thought the man was lying. When the gossip was confirmed after O. Henry's death, Williams believed, as so many of his friends did, that O. Henry had taken the blame for someone else.

The constant tension of his professional life, the guilt he must have felt over not seeing his daughter more often than an annual summer visit to Pittsburgh or an infrequent visit from her, and other inner stresses linked to past and present, did not inhibit his literary output or stunt his consuming fascination with the folklore of Manhattan. Uptown may have been the preserve of Edith Wharton, but the streets of the West Side and lower Manhattan continued to be O. Henry Country. Wandering them at night, he felt himself slipping into the guise of Haroun-al-Raschid.

There was a sense of adventure, an expectation of romance about the meanest streets that he had never experienced on the Texas frontier or even in the French Quarter of New Orleans. Every corner he turned, every window he glanced up at seemed to promise a glimpse of tragedy or comedy. If he had been born a New Yorker, of course, he likely would have been blind to such possibilities, and without the fresh expectancy he brought to his nightly investigations his stories could never have been created.

In "The Green Door" he vibrantly explained that feeling of his for scenes that escaped more jaded eyes: "Without knowing why, we look up suddenly to see in a window a face that seems to belong to our gallery of intimate portraits; in a sleeping thoroughfare we hear a cry of agony and fear coming from an empty and shuttered house; instead of at our familiar curb a cab-driver deposits us before a strange door, which one, with a smile, opens for us and bids us enter; a slip of paper, written upon, flutters down to our feet from the high lattices of Chance; we exchange glances of instantaneous hate, affection, and fear with hurrying strangers in the passing crowds; a sudden souse of rain—and our umbrella may be sheltering the daughter of the Full Moon and first cousin of the Sidereal System; at every corner handkerchiefs drop, fingers beckon, eyes besiege, and the lost, the lonely, the rapturous, the mysterious, the perilous changing clues of adventure are slipped into our fingers. But few of us are willing to hold and follow them. We are grown stiff with the ramrod of convention down our backs. We pass on; and some day we come, at the end of a very dull life, to reflect that our romance has been a pallid thing of a marriage or two, a satin rosette kept in a safe-deposit drawer, and a lifelong feud with a steam radiator."

For himself O. Henry was determined to "hold and follow" whatever "clues of adventure" came his way.

There were times, of course, when his openness, his receptivity made a sucker out of him. The women he associated with, except for a few platonic friends like Anne Partlan, were of what contemporary writers referred to delicately as the demimonde. Some were working girls out for a bit of fun, but many were living by their wits or free-lancing in prostitution. O. Henry was generous but like any man who considered himself a worldly fellow he hated to be conned.

One of the few times William Wash Williams ever saw him really angry was one night when O. Henry appeared in the doorway of Healy's Cafe and beckoned to him. He wanted young Williams to walk around Gramercy Park with him while he let off steam.

"Don't you hate deceit?" he burst out. "It simply makes me wild. I can stand any kind of a human except a downright liar. I despise a liar. . . . What has me riled up tonight is this . . . Sometime ago—a month or six weeks ago—a girl I've known for some little time came to me with a story about her mother, down in Pennsylvania, being seriously ill, not expected to live, might die any time and all that, and asked me for fifty dollars so she could go home and see the old lady once more before she passed away.

"Well, that's always a good story, you know, thousands of dollars have changed hands on it and, of course, I gave her the money, with many words of sympathy and expressions of hope that she would find conditions better than they had been reported. . . . And now I find out that the whole yarn was a fabrication; that her mother had been dead several years and didn't live in Pennsylvania anyway.

"I don't give a rap about the fifty dollars, but what makes me sore is that she lied to me to get it—lied to me when she didn't have to, the little devil. Here she goes ahead and works her picayune set of brains overtime, maybe, getting together that cock-and-bull story about her dying mother when she didn't have to have a story at all. . . . Anybody can have my money any time; they don't have to lie to get it; just say they want it. I'm an easy mark and I know it, but that's my own business."

To Williams it seemed that O. Henry's attitude toward women, while he always behaved toward them with a southern courtliness, no matter what their class, was one of "deep-seated distrust."

Apparently that outer layer of cynicism could easily enough be peeled off by an attractive young woman, at least until she proved herself fickle or deceitful. One night, he told Williams on another rueful occasion, he took a girl to the elegant and expensive Shanley's, one of the uptown "lobster palaces." Shortly after they sat down he began to suspect that she was flirting with a man at another table.

"Then I began watching her covertly but closely and finally satisfied myself that she was making signs to someone behind me. I said something about 'Where's our waiter?' and began looking around as though in search of him, and discovered a fellow eating alone at the table next to ours and back of me. She didn't suspect that I was on to the racket and I waited awhile until I was certain of what she was doing, beyond possibility of mistake. Then I got up, asked her to excuse me, went to the desk, paid my check, got my hat, walked out and left her sitting there. And that's the way to treat them, Bill. No need making a fuss; just quit them cold and cut them out forever after."[8]

O. Henry was not likely to meet many pure, innocent homebodies on his rounds. In his nightly rambles, often with Williams or some other friend as a companion, he remained drawn to the all-night cafes, the saloons, the vaudeville theaters, the dance halls and dives that contained the lowest social strata of the metropolis. The "tougher they were the more attraction they held for him," Williams observed.

One favorite observation post was Koster's and Bial's Cafe at Sixth Avenue and Twenty-fourth Street, the heart of the Tenderloin, where streetwalkers, pimps, procurers and prospective customers congregated. A ragtime piano player pounded away in the rathskellar in the basement; there were singing waiters and can-can girls.

Once settled at a table, O. Henry proceeded to glean story material in a businesslike fashion. He invited four or five of the girls to join him and ordered drinks. In his soft-voiced and courteous way, he then encouraged the girls to talk about themselves. He was always tactful, receptive, never prying.

The girls who hung around Koster's and Bial's couldn't figure him out, couldn't understand why a man would merely want to talk to them and buy them drinks without any other motive. One night Williams went to the cafe alone, and one of the girls asked him, "Where's your nut friend this evening?" It developed that she meant O. Henry. Williams indignantly denied that his friend was a nut and asked the girl why she thought he was.

"Well, you know he never offers to take one of us girls out—simply wants to talk to us here and buy us drinks—but he pays us just the same. He always slips each girl around the table a bill before he leaves—a couple of them as a rule. . . . He's a queer bird. What's his idea? The first time he slipped me a bill I didn't know I had it until I went to get up. I found it in my lap. And that's the way he'd give it to the other girls, too."[9]

Also on his regular rounds were the Cairo, the Bohemia and the Berlin on Twenty-ninth Street. They were the kind of places about which a New York *Sun* reporter wrote: "It was a motley crowd with a few good suckers mixed in for the easy picking of the thieves."

Another pit stop on his list was that huge old deadfall, the Haymarket, at Sixth Avenue and Thirtieth Street, where out-of-town marks were trimmed by the scores every night. Nevertheless the establishment was operated under strict rules, the first of which was, "Catch your goose in our yard, but pluck it somewhere else." To weed out the cheaper sort of tough, the Haymarket charged a twenty-five-cent admission for men, but women were admitted free. Decorum was required on the dance floor, and anyone essaying the bunny hug, the grizzly bear or any of the more shocking new dances was heaved out by a gigantic bouncer. The girls who came there were mostly prostitutes and jack-rollers (familiar with the uses of chloral hydrate to soften up a victim), but they had to behave themselves while on the premises.

One veteran habitué wrote that they had to pass a sort of civil-service examination before they were allowed to hang out at the Haymarket. They also had to abide by the rules, couldn't smoke, drink too much or pick anyone's pocket. "Rule No. 1 was that no man who fell for them was to be robbed on the premises. Rule No. 2 was that if they stole from a patron after taking him somewhere else, and the man put in a rap against them with the police, then they had to pay the money back to calm down the patron and save the police from undue embarrassment." The girls who worked the place regularly received a percentage on the drinks they persuaded men to buy. For a girl to turn a decent profit on her night's work she had to encourage her companion for the night to buy champagne and spend from $50 to $100. Little wonder that when Eddie Corey, the owner-manager, sold out he was able to retire to an estate on Long Island and buy a ninety-two-ton yacht.[10]

The Haymarket's process of separating a man from his money without actually robbing him was a matter of continuing fascination to O. Henry. Occasionally he took an out-of-towner with him while he researched the sociology of the place and the people who made their living there. His companion, however, was required to mind his manners and not ask direct questions of the girls. O. Henry's method was to draw them out indirectly, let them tell their own stories if they were in the mood. One night he and Williams took a young Middle Westerner to the Haymarket. The latter was a naive, priggish fellow and annoyed O. Henry, first of all, by ordering lemonade for himself.

O. Henry asked several of the girls to sit with them, and the visiting young man made his second mistake by bluntly saying, "You don't look like the kind of girl who belongs in a place like this. Have you been coming here long?"

The girl bristled. "Kid," she replied, "they wanted to put me in the cornerstone of this place but I wouldn't let 'em."

O. Henry listened to that exchange with disgust, leaned over to Williams and whispered, "Let's get out of this, Bill. The fellow is not only a simpleton, but an ass."

The tourist was hustled off protesting that he was only trying to help his host dig out a typical O. Henry story.

Other ports of call O. Henry visited frequently in his ceaseless search for the raw material of his stories included the "clean" vaudeville theaters, Tony Pastor's and Keith's on Union Square, and the Academy of Music on Irving Place, where George M. Cohan opened some of his earlier comedies. On a lower level, but no less worthy of study from O. Henry's viewpoint, was the Dewey Theater opposite Tony Pastor's. The Dewey's painted curtain depicted the old admiral himself on the bridge of his flagship at the battle of Manila Bay. When the curtain was raised, however, the proceedings were shockingly unhistorical; "even the Fourteenth Street women," Williams noted, "wouldn't go to the Dewey." The centerpiece of the program was a girl who swung out over the audience on a trapeze and stripped down to her tights, meanwhile tossing her garters to the men below.

From soaking in the atmosphere of the Dewey, O. Henry probably got the idea for the story titled "The Memento" and its heroine, Rosalie Ray, who similarly performed on a swing and with a "graceful, strong kick . . . sent flying, high and far, the yellow silk garter that each evening spun from her agile limb and descended upon the delighted audience below."

Rosalie decides to quit the tawdry fringe of show business, as she explains to her friend Miss Lynnette D'Armande, and rusticate in a Long Island village because she can't stand the men—"the men leering and blathering at you across the tables, trying to buy you Wurzburger or Extra Dry, according to their estimate of your price. And the men in the audiences, clapping, yelling, snarling, crowding, writhing, gloating—like a lot of wild beasts, with their eyes fixed on you, ready to eat you up if you come in reach of their claws. Oh, how I hate 'em!"

One of O. Henry's outdoor research centers was the so-called bed line in Madison Square Park, where an itinerant preacher implored his listeners to contribute fifteen cents for each of the homeless men ranked around him and waiting for a place to sleep that night.

He described the scene in "The Fifth Wheel," most of the earnings from which he contributed, from time to time, to the evangelist and his outdoor mission.

"The ranks of the bed line moved closer together: for it was cold, cold. They were alluvial deposit of the stream of life lodged in the delta of Fifth Avenue and Broadway. The bed liners stamped their freezing feet, looked at the empty benches in Madison Square whence Jack Frost had evicted them, and muttered to one another in a confusion of tongues. . . . Standing on a pine box a head higher than his flock of goats, the Preacher exhorted whatever transient and shifting audience the north wind doled out to him. It was a slave market. Fifteen cents bought you a man. You deeded him to Morpheus; and the recording angel gave you credit.

"The Preacher was incredibly earnest and unwearied. He had looked over the list of things one may do for one's fellow man, and has assumed for himself the task of putting to bed all who might apply at his soap box on the nights of Wednesday and Saturday. . . . The hour of eight was but a little while past; sightseers in a small, dark mass of pay ore were gathered in the shadow of General Worth's monument. Now and then, shyly, ostentatiously, carelessly, or with conscientious exactness one would step forward and bestow upon the Preacher small bills or silver. Then a lieutenant of Scandinavian coloring and enthusiasm would march away to a lodging house with a squad of the redeemed. All the while the Preacher exhorted the crowd in terms beautifully devoid of eloquence—splendid with the deadly, accusative monotony of truth. . . ."

He told a companion one night that the bed line was "quite a study" with "a little of everything in it this side of the feminine gender." He was always fascinated by one particular phase of the human condition, people's response to the pressure of poverty and/or bad luck, the way they confronted inexorable destiny.

"Some of those poor devils," he observed, "are fellows who are down for the first time, in hard luck, out of a job and broke temporarily. That's the outfit you and I and our kind would line up with. They won't be in that line long—maybe a night or two." The others were what a later generation would call hard-core unemployed, many of them defeated from the first by the circumstances of birth and breeding—"those who have had the ten counted over them," as he put it, "who have even forgotten how to think about coming back."[11] There was nothing ideological about his observations, except in the implications which could be drawn from them. He had no prescriptions for the alleviation of such conditions as the bed line, and his political views—if he had any—are nowhere recorded.

Evidently he regarded it as an obligation to help those who unwittingly supplied him with the material for his stories. Aside from cash handouts, he made a habit of slipping his visiting card to those needing medical attention of some kind and unable to afford it, with a line scrawled on it, such as "Please take care of this poor soul and chalk it up to me" or "This unfortunate is in need of your assistance; see that she gets it and bill me." The messages were addressed to Dr. Collin L. Begg, who practiced in the Irving Place neighborhood.

"I never kept books on Porter's patients," Dr. Begg related after O. Henry's death. "He would send them around to my office with his card, on which was written a request that I take care of them, in that whimsical style of his, and I would do it and forget it. Then every once in a while he would appear and hand me ten or twenty dollars without a question as to how our account stood, and I couldn't have given him a statement to save my soul if he had asked for it. I saw him only a short time before his death and he handed me twenty dollars. I told him, at the time, that I didn't believe he owed me anything and was loath to take the money. 'Never mind, Doctor,' he said, 'if I don't owe it to you now, I will.' "[12]

. . . . Further uptown on the O. Henry beat were the bowling alleys and shooting galleries where he occasionally found an hour's recreation. A newspaperman named Roy Norton, who lived a few blocks from O. Henry's rooms, testified that he was a crack shot with a revolver. One night O. Henry showed up at his apartment, Norton said, and announced that he had read in a newspaper that Norton had won a rifle competition. "Come on around to a gallery I know on Seventh Avenue," O. Henry suggested. "I'll see whether all that newspapers publish is lies." He took Norton to a target-shooting range, made him demonstrate his skill and then displayed his own prowess with a revolver. Firing at a moving target suspended by a piece of twine, he proved to be a "dead-center shot," as Norton put it. The proprietor of the range told Norton that O. Henry was "one of the best revolver shots at a moving target that he had ever seen." Later O. Henry begged Norton not to tell anyone about his skill with a six-shooter because "My reputation is bad enough as it is and besides somebody might try to get me on the police force."[13]

Other night haunts favored by O. Henry included Huber's Museum, with its standard snake charmers, living skeleton, tattooed man, fat lady and strong man, where he was engrossed not by the freak show but the patter of the lecturer, and a celebrated Bohemian resort on the fringe of Greenwich Village, Joe Schmidt's, where "The Face on the Barroom Floor" was supposed to have been composed. He also liked to mingle with the bums, malcontents and political agitators who thronged Union Square at night.

But it was the anonymous crowds of the parks, sidewalks and

saloons that he sought out; he could rarely be lured into social occasions of the slightest formality. The Lotus Club wanted to honor him on one of its celebrity nights, and Lindsey Denison, a *World* reporter with whom he was friendly, was assigned to persuade him to attend.

O. Henry shook his head and said, "More than three faces to study."

"Is that supposed to be an alibi?" Denison demanded.

"I never want to be anywhere where I have more than three faces to watch," O. Henry explained. "I can keep track of those three faces, study them, and guess what is going on in the minds behind. I am willing to be one of four at a dinner table, but there never must be more than four."[14]

O. Henry's restiveness on social occasions became so notorious among his friends that they called him "The Elusive Pimpernel." Some of his fade-outs from festive scenes were regarded as classic vanishing acts. His friends at the *World* once badgered him into promising to attend the annual picnic of the Sunday magazine staff on Long Island. O. Henry showed up late and disappeared early. A few days later Alexander Black, the associate editor of the supplement, asked him what had happened to him. All that O. Henry would reveal was that he had wandered away from the picnic grounds and "found a wonderful road." Undoubtedly the road was the Long Island Railroad, which bore him swiftly back to Irving Place and more familiar scenes.[15]

He was distinctly uneasy in the role of a guest under any but the most accidental circumstances, and even then a fondness for appearing incognito often asserted itself. One night Lindsey Denison accompanied him on an extensive pub crawl, at the end of which they found themselves at the door to the Denison apartment. Denison urged him to come in.

"Who's there?" O. Henry warily asked.

"Only my wife and a couple of girls."

"And who are the girls?"

"Oh, they're the right sort," Denison assured him. "Not upstage or anything like that. Of course, they're lion-hunters, especially when the lions happen to be authors, and they're particularly interested in your work."

"Nothing doing," O. Henry snapped, starting to walk away.

"Listen," Denison said. "There's no reason I should introduce you under your own name. I'll tell you what I'll do. I'll say that you are your own old friend Arthur Williams of Texas, of whom you've told me so much. Then I'll mention that you know O. Henry very well. In that way you may have a chance to get the real lowdown on yourself."

That approach intrigued the author. He was introduced to the girls as Arthur Williams, and Mrs. Denison did not give the game away. The girls sat at his feet and implored him to tell them all about his friend O. Henry.

He startled the girls by denouncing O. Henry as a scoundrel who stole all his plots, lived by cadging money from all his acquaintances and even extorting funds from the shopgirls he wrote about with such sympathy.

"And to think," said one of the girls sadly, "that a man like that could write such a beautiful thing as 'An Unfinished Story.'"

"I'll tell you about that, too. He wrote that story for the sole purpose of revenging himself on a shop-girl in Wanamaker's who had turned him down."

After the girls left, he sat around with the Denisons and laughed with them over the success of the impersonation. Then, suddenly, a sober and rueful look came on his face. "In all that rigamarole," he said, "there was just one bit of truth. The real Dulcie *was* a shop-girl in Wanamaker's and she did turn Piggy down. And Piggy—I was Piggy."[16]

Chapter 7. Fame If Not Fortune

The year 1904, O. Henry's forty-first on earth, was easily the busiest and most productive of his career. As the price for his stories went up, he simply produced less. But that vintage year of his life as a writer, with sixty-six stories published in the *World* and various magazines, saw him at the peak of his creative power. In addition to turning out more than a story a week, on the average, he was preparing his first book for the press. The volume was to be titled *Cabbages and Kings*, the publisher, S. S. McClure. Its substance was the Central American tales he had published, somewhat synthetically woven into a pseudo-novel.

Gilman Hall and other editors had been urging him to try his hand at a novel, but that was one project he would never quite get around to. Then one of his editorial wranglers, Witter Bynner, was seized with the inspiration of taking his Central American tales, with Anchuria (Honduras in reality) as their locale, and supplying them with the connective tissue to produce a book which might loosely be called a novel and sold as such. Then as now, collections of short stories weren't selling too well.

The project was Bynner's conception and it probably would never have been completed without his virtual collaboration. Bynner's idea, an ingenious one testifying to the first-rate inventive mind he later demonstrated as a writer on his own, was to take the long story titled "Money Maze," which supplied the rudimentary plot, break it up and scatter it among the other stories. The plot revolved around the theft of Anchuria's national treasury and a case of mistaken identity involving President Miraflores and an American embezzler hiding out in Anchuria, President Wahrfield of the Republic Insurance Company.

Under Bynner's constant prodding, verging on a necessary harassment, O. Henry turned out several new stories ("Fox-in-the-Morning," "The Vitagraphoscope," "Remnants of the Code") to form narrative bridges and a number of passages in the stories were spread around to link up a loose and episodic story line.

After a hard summer's work, during which *Cabbages and Kings* was written, pasted together and edited by Bynner in his spare time and by O. Henry in whatever hours he could spare from his story-a-week grind, the book was published in November 1904.

Helter-skelter as its composition was, there were descriptive passages that briefly revealed a different, more poetic O. Henry: "The mountains," he began his mural of a Caribbean sunset, "reached up their bulky shoulders to receive the level gallop of Apollo's homing steeds, the day died in the lagoons and in the shadowed banana groves and in the mangrove swamps, where the great blue crabs were beginning to crawl to land for their nightly ramble. And it died, at last, upon the highest peaks. Then the brief twilight, ephemeral as the flight of a moth, came and went; the Southern Cross peeped with its topmost eye above a row of palms, and the fireflies heralded with their torches the approach of soft-footed night."

Perhaps it was flourishes like that which caught the eye of some of the more respectable literary critics. *Cabbages and Kings* was not a commercial success and hardly repaid the efforts of Bynner and the author, but it was very well received by the reviewers. The *Critic* praised it as the most amusing book about Central America; not, on reflection, the most outrageous compliment. *The Independent* heralded it as a "delight," and *The Bookman's* reviewer asserted that O. Henry was "seriously threatening the supremacy of Richard Harding Davis in a field in which for several years that most widely known writer has been absolutely alone" and congratulated him on "that wonderful background of white beach and weaving palms and sunshine and flowers and fruit and dirt and discomfort . . ."[1]

Even more flatteringly, the eminent Harry Thurston Peck discerned in *Cabbages and Kings*, despite its scissors-and-paste composition, a classical architecture—a discovery that surely must have amazed the architect and undoubtedly brought forth his loudest guffaws. "It represents," Peck declared, "a type of story which is nearly two thousand years old—the second step in the evolution of the novel. Mr. Porter finds his ancient prototype in Apuleius of Madaura, that African novelist who wrote in Latin as strange as some of Mr. Porter's English, his romance entitled *The Golden Ass.* Apuleius at the very beginning of his book says: 'I shall weave together for you in this tale various stories in the Milesian manner.' This is precisely what Mr. Porter has done about seventeen hundred years later. Without knowing it he has constructed a series of Milesian tales which have no relation to each other, but which are artfully made to hang upon another Milesian tale which serves as a thread to bind the whole together. Thus in *Cabbages and Kings* there are told the stories of 'The Shamrock and the Palm,' the plot by which Billy Keough and Johnny Atwood discomfit the astute Pink Dawson, 'The Flag Paramount,' 'The Admiral,' 'Dicky,' and 'Rouge et Noir.' These are all Milesian stories—that is to say, short stories with no immediate relation to the principal story, which in itself is another Milesian, mechanically wedded to them."[2]

With such learned dissections being performed, O. Henry, through the publication of *Cabbages and Kings,* now came to the serious attention of the literary world. It was no affectation on his part to shun that attention, and cling to his preference for praise from a police reporter rather than a Yale professor of American literature. It represented no pose when he was irritated by being compared to Maupassant or some other old master (but especially Maupassant, comparison to whom brought the O. Henry protest, "I never wrote a filthy word in my life and I don't like being compared to a filthy writer").

He heartily disliked and avoided large gatherings where he might be cornered by persons more curious about him than his work, or might be placed on display. "On the surface," Will Irwin related, "he was a silent, a shy man. His favorite diversion, he used to say, was to sit around a table where three or four pleasant people were gathered together, and be free of any worry about food and drink, and just listen. He had the faculty of sitting perfectly silent and yet of stimulating the talk rather than deadening it. And about once in ten minutes he would throw in a remark, delivered in a low, apologetic Southern voice, which went straight to the heart of the thing."

Once Irwin persuaded O. Henry to accompany him to a chafing-dish party at an artist's studio. Among their fellow guests was Gelett Burgess, the author of the famous ode to a purple cow. "Burgess, much to his disgust, was always pointed out and spoken of as the author of A Purple Cow. . . . He got to hate those lines, and I only saw him laugh once at any reference to them. It happened on the evening I'm telling you of. O. Henry had been put to work beating eggs. For ten minutes he beat, patiently, silently. Then he began:

> "I never beat a rotten egg,
> I never hope to beat one.
> But I can tell you anyhow,
> I'd rather beat than eat one."[3]

For most critics, academicians, poetasters and writers who wrote or talked about writing, he had nothing but the scorn of the working professional for the amateur and dilettante. In person or in their commentary they left a bad taste in his mouth. Occasionally he found himself trapped with what he called a "literary gent," when he lunched with an editor, for example, or dined with someone in the publishing world.

Once he returned to Irving Place from a sortie uptown and looked up Bill Williams, saying, "Let's go over and sit in Union Square with the bums awhile, I want to get out of a fog."

Williams asked what was bothering him.

"Oh, I've been to a dinner with some literary people," he said, "listening to a discussion of stuff I don't know anything about until my mind's in a funk. They're nice enough people, you know, and would be interesting, no doubt, to one of their kind, but when it comes to spending a whole evening discussing literature I'm stopped, flabbergasted and ruled off the field. I can't chip in a sentence and have to sit there like a dummy with everything going over my head like a Sixth Avenue elevated train. What do I know about literature, or care!"

On another occasion he complained that other writers also "bore me stiff," and told Williams: "I wonder why it is that writers feel they must forever talk about their work and nothing else. They're always talking shop and I'm not the least bit interested. I don't enjoy a minute of the gab. It only tires and bores me. You know how it is—or maybe you don't, because you newspapermen can get out and have a good time and forget shop. But these magazine writers never seem to forget they are writers. A little of that stuff goes a long way with me."[4]

If he had a pose, it was to pretend that he was really just a newspaperman himself, one who happened to mix a little fiction with fact. Actually he detested straight journalism, chafed under the tyranny of fact. He simply wasn't the newspaper type, which in its more successful forms was likely to run to strong legs and a thick skin. The *World* once persuaded him, after much argument from the top echelon, to try a little straight reporting. Big Bill Devery, a former police chief who had distinguished himself by running the Tenderloin as a personal fief and enriching himself in the process, had become something of a town character with his crude philosophy. The newspapers had attacked him mercilessly when he lorded it over the police department and issued such dictums to his constabulary as:

> "Hear, see and say nothin',
> "Eat, drink and pay nothin'."

Somehow the *World* editors convinced themselves that Devery was actually a sort of O. Henry character, now that he was harmlessly in retirement, and that O. Henry was just the man to extract a good long feature from him. The experiment was a resounding failure. "I tried to tell them downtown that I was no interviewer," he related to a friend. "So I went up and met the old fellow at his home—after chasing him all over the west side of town—and I didn't know what to ask him, and he didn't have brains enough to lead out on my line, so the whole thing was a fizzle from start to finish. I was embarrassed to death and never felt more like an ass in my life. They'll never get me to try the stunt again."[5]

The *World* executives regarded him as mulishly unco-operative when they decided to publicize the prestige he had attained through publication of *Cabbages and Kings* and capitalize on the growing reputation he had won in the *Sunday World* magazine section. A promotional campaign was ordained. Bill Williams, known around the city room as a close friend of the writer's, was detailed to obtain a needed photograph of him or to bring O. Henry down to the *World* building to have his picture taken by one of the newspaper's photographers. Williams knew he was in for a tussle, and that he might need the "famous Borax twenty-mule team to drag him down to the office."

At the time Williams did not know the reasons for O. Henry's determination to stay out of the spotlight, only that he was exceedingly wary of personal publicity. He had dinner with his friend that night and made certain it was "setting well," before bringing up the matter of the publicity photo. O. Henry said he had only one picture of himself and that had been taken some years ago, and as a compromise suggested that the *World* have one of their artists draw a sketch of him. From then on Williams was in the middle of a tug of war. The editors insisted that he pry a picture out of O. Henry; the latter refused to change his position on having a new photograph taken.

Williams would have to settle for the old photograph, O. Henry declared. "I'm going to lend you that picture," he added, "with the understanding that you are free to do whatever you damn please with it. I'll ask you no questions providing you return the original to me when you are through with it. I don't want it to get into any other hands. Is that satisfactory?"[6]

Williams had no choice but to agree. He almost wept, he said,

21. The Flatiron Building, Broadway and Fifth Avenue,
The Skyscraper of O. Henry's era in New York.

22. Tony Pastor's, a popular theatrical spot in the 1900s.

23. The Men's Dining Room at Delmonico's, where editors would frequently take O. Henry to dine.

24. The Haymarket, Thirtieth Street and Sixth Avenue, the more unformal kind of tavern where O. Henry sought his pleasure and company.

25. Sara Lindsay Coleman, who became O. Henry's second wife in November 1907. She returned to Asheville, North Carolina, not long after the marriage.

26. O. Henry playing cards at home in Asheville on one of his infrequent return visits.

27. Margaret Porter, O. Henry's daughter as a young woman. As when she was younger, she and her father spent little time together.

28. The renowned Chelsea, where O. Henry lived in the last few years of his life.

29. Drawing from an interview with O. Henry in the New York *Times,* April 1909. Always afraid of having his past uncovered and broadcasted, he refused to be photographed for the paper. © 1909 by the New York Times Company

30. O. Henry back home in North Carolina shortly before his death in 1910.

when O. Henry dug out of his trunk a faded photograph, at least ten or twelve years old, showing him with a long mustache and a cravat with a huge knot. The *World* had to use that picture in its advertising of the star of its Sunday section.

The *World* had almost as much difficulty in extracting "The Gift of the Magi" from O. Henry as it did any material for its publicity promotion. That most famous of his stories—the one invariably included in high-school reading programs—was produced under even more hectic circumstances than usual. His story, reflecting a bachelor's sentimental view of marriage in the extreme devotion of the young husband and wife, but certainly not his own experiences with the complexities of married love, was scheduled for the *Sunday World*'s Christmas issue. It had to have something to do with Christmas, something at least faintly religious, though O. Henry himself was what one of his acquaintances called a sterling example of the "modern world pagan." He wasn't against religion, he simply ignored it.

The *World* decided that O. Henry's Christmas story would form the centerpiece of its magazine section with its illustrations in color. Running the magazine section through the color presses meant that the illustrations had to be ready well in advance of the usual deadline, and that the text of the story also had to be set in type before the rest of the section. A long struggle between the editors under the golden dome on Park Row and O. Henry in Irving Place then ensued. The deadline came and went. Editors agonized and O. Henry comforted them with the usual bland excuses.

Finally Dan Smith, the illustrator assigned to the project, was sent sloshing through the snow to interview O. Henry in his rooms at 55 Irving Place.

Unperturbed, O. Henry admitted to Smith that not a line of the story had been written; worse yet that he hadn't the glimmering of an idea for it.

"I've got to work on the drawings at once," Smith said despairingly. "Can't you tell me something to draw and then fit your story to it?"

O. Henry stared out the window for a few moments and finally told the artist in his Carolinian drawl that he might be able to ad-lib something. "I'll tell you what you do, Colonel," he said, conferring the usual military title on someone he didn't know very well. "Just draw a picture of a poorly furnished room, the kind you find in a boarding house or rooming house over on the West Side. In the room there is only a chair or two, a chest of drawers, a bed, and a trunk. On the bed, a man and a girl are sitting side by side. They are talking about Christmas. The man has a watch fob in his hand. He is playing with it while he is thinking. The girl's principal feature is the long beautiful hair that is hanging down her back. That's all I can think of now. But the story is coming."

Several days passed without any copy coming from 55 Irving Place. The betting on Park Row was that O. Henry, for once, would miss the deadline and the Sunday section would be left with a gorgeous illustration in color and blank space all around. Men known to be friendly with the writer were rounded up in the *World's* city room and sent up to Irving Place to plead for copy, at least a few pages. One of them was Bill Williams, to whom O. Henry confessed he was "empty as a bass drum."

On the day that the story positively had to be produced, Lindsey Denison was assigned to determine whether there was the faintest possibility that the Sunday magazine would be saved from disaster at the last moment.

O. Henry, now having reached the last moment of the deadline, at last was ready to apply himself to the story which he titled "The Gift of the Magi." He went to the cupboard and brought out a bottle of scotch, poured drinks for himself and Denison, and then pointed to the sofa near his desk.

"Lie down there," he directed the reporter, shoving aside the manuscript of another story on which he had been working. "I've got to forget this story and write another one. Have to have it done this afternoon and not a line written. I've thought of an idea but I need a living model. I'm going to write a story about you and your wife. . . . I think that you two are the kind who would make sacrifices for each other. Now stay on the sofa and don't interrupt."

Three hours later, using Denison as a model for the hero of his story, he wrote the last paragraph of "The Gift of the Magi." Denison rushed the copy downtown, it was set in type that evening, and Christmas 1905 was a memorable one for faithful readers of the *Sunday World*.[7]

Through all his time in New York, O. Henry tried to grow closer to his adolescent daughter. It was no lack of paternal love that kept them apart. He simply didn't feel that he was capable of raising a young girl in New York City, on Irving Place, amid the uncertainties, the untidiness and irregularity of a free-lance writer's existence. She was better off with her grandparents for the time being. Meanwhile he dedicated himself to seeing to it that she received the best possible education, and in 1905 she was sent to the exclusive and expensive Ward-Belmont finishing school, in Nashville, Tennessee, at an annual cost of $1,000.

It couldn't replace family affection, of course, as her unhappy life proved. The children of writers—especially the more famous ones—fare poorly. Writers are of necessity too self-centered, too engrossed in the struggle of bringing life to the people of their imagination to spare much thought for the people of their flesh, the people to whom they are morally obligated. If O. Henry had been willing to change his way of life, give up a semi-Bohemian existence that suited him down to the last hazard and unpaid bill, rent an apartment and hire a housekeeper, he undoubtedly could have brought Margaret to New York to live with him.

Instead, he contented himself with summer visits to Pittsburgh and writing jolly little letters, such as: "Here it is summertime, and the bees are blooming and the flowers are singing and the birds making honey, and we haven't gone fishing yet. Well, there's only one month till July, and then we'll go, and no mistake. I thought you would write and tell me about the high water around Pittsburgh some time ago, and whether it came up to where you live, or not. And I haven't heard a thing about Easter, and about rabbit's eggs—but I suppose you have learned by this time that eggs grow on eggplants and are not laid by rabbits.

"I would like very much to hear from you oftener; it has been more than a month since you wrote. Write soon and tell me how you are, and when school will be out, for we want plenty of holidays in July, so we can have a good time. I am going to send you something nice the last of this week. What do you guess it will be?"[8]

He wrote to her in that playful, patronizing tone just at a time when an adolescent girl is viewing adults, especially her parents, with a sharp, undeceived and critical eye. No doubt Margaret was also dismayed by the fact that her father always called her "Jim" or "Pete" or some other boy's name, which would naturally give her the impression that he had wanted a son and was disappointed in having to put up with a daughter.

She must also have perceived that a more normal and natural father would have brought her up himself, no matter what excuses were offered to the contrary. Even such a firm friend of O. Henry's as Bob Davis observed that "destiny" kept father and daughter "too much apart" in the nine years between his release from the penitentiary and his premature death, but that O. Henry perhaps "had a share in helping to mold that destiny."

Davis believed that O. Henry kept his daughter away from him out of the omnipresent fear that his stay in prison would be revealed through a "chance encounter . . . the man out of the past who might be lurking around the corner." And O. Henry may also have feared that greater intimacy with his daughter "might bring Margaret to the realization, or even the suspicion of the secret which he thought to keep from all the world."

When she did come once to New York, O. Henry announced to Bill Williams and other friends in the neighborhood that he would be dropping out of his nocturnal rounds for a few days and occupying himself with showing Margaret the big city. After the girl returned to her grandparents, O. Henry somewhat sheepishly explained the photograph of himself and his daughter taken in a "rubberneck coach" used to convey tourists around the city. Ordinarily, regarding himself by now as a sophisticated New Yorker, he would not have ventured within audible range of the barkers who rounded up the outlanders and escorted them on tours of Chinatown, the Bowery and Grant's Tomb.

On examining the photograph, Williams grinned and jokingly exclaimed, "Welcome to our city!"

"Now, Bill," O. Henry replied, "I can explain to your entire satisfaction. You see my daughter's visit was a very short one, and being anxious that she see as much of New York as possible, I figured we could cover more interesting points on the rubberneck coach than any other way in the time we had to do it. So I showed her the town that way, and as having a picture taken of the outfit before starting on the trip seemed to be a part of the program, we went the whole hog. I bought the print you have in your hand to send to her. Do I look like an ass in it?"

"Not exactly," Williams said with reservations.

"I felt like one, but what could I do about it? You know, you have to conform once in a while, even when it makes you feel ridiculous . . ."

Even from that rare attempt at conformity, he managed to extract the material for a short story, "Sisters of the Golden Veil," most of the action of which takes place on a rubberneck bus, describing how "the inside of the great automobile began to thump and throb, like the heart of a coffee drinker" and how the "top riders nervously clung to their seats."

Perhaps his gradually increased efforts to draw his young daughter closer to him were prompted by a certain premature intimation of mortality. He had always been haunted by the possibility of succumbing to tuberculosis, which had struck down so many of his antecedents as well as his wife. The same possibility must have caused him to fear for his daughter, who had inherited the fatal tendency from both sides of her parentage.

Aside from the tubercular threat, which was only enhanced by his drinking, his lack of fresh air and exercise and his irregular habits, he had other reasons to believe that his health might be deteriorating: insomnia and pains in his back and abdomen. A typical appeal for an advance from *Munsey's* included in his note to Bob Davis the information that he had consulted an uptown specialist and was "taking two kinds of dope out of two boxes" which had been prescribed for him. He added that he was "getting some good sleep of nights" as a result. Attached to the promise that he would be sending a story in "a very few days" was the usual hook: "Got $50 more up there you want to advance to a hypochondriac? Let it be in cash if so. I must sell a little part of my soul to buy some bread. . . ." And attached to the hook was the customary additional barb about having to hack out stories for the cheaper magazines for quick money if Davis didn't come through: "If you ain't got the money let me know, and will tackle the Philistines."

Apparently there was more than hypochondria behind those internal disturbances, because shortly after that his friendly neighborhood physician, Dr. Collin L. Begg, received a rather panicky night call from him.

"About two o'clock one morning, during one of those times when Porter locked himself in his rooms and strained every force in him in an effort to catch up with orders," Dr. Begg would recall, "my telephone rang and when I got up and answered it, Porter was on the wire. 'Hello! Is this you, Doctor?' he said. 'I don't like to bother you at this time of night, but I wish you would come over. I believe there is something serious the matter with me.'"

Dr. Begg questioned him about symptoms in the hope that he might be able to prescribe some treatment over the phone and save himself a trip over to Irving Place at that hour. "No," O. Henry replied, "I'm afraid you'll have to come over. I can't describe the symptoms well enough over the phone to give you any kind of a basis for diagnosis and I will regard it as a great favor if you will run over and see me."

Dr. Begg dressed and hurried over to 55 Irving Place. "I found Porter stripped to his underclothes," he related, "and pacing up and down the room in a highly nervous state. 'Doctor,' he said, before I had hardly had time to take off my hat and set my medicine case down, 'I believe I have kidney trouble.'" Dr. Begg asked him what grounds he had for the self-diagnosis. "'Well, I just feel that way,' he said. 'I wouldn't be surprised if I have Bright's disease.'

"I laughed that off and told him I thought he was unduly alarmed but I couldn't make any sort of diagnosis on the spot and he would have to give the necessary specimen for analysis before I could really tell anything about it. Then I began to question him . . . all the time he kept pacing up and down and rubbing his hands together. 'You've just been working too hard,' I suggested. 'I don't believe there is anything seriously wrong with you but I will go into your case more fully. . . .' I gave him a sedative.

"With that I reached for my medicine case and hat and got up to go. In an instant he was at my side with a hand on my arm. 'I can't tell you, Doctor, how much good it has done me to have you come over and I want you to know that I appreciate your doing it. I hope I'm as all right as you seem to think I am. But now that you're here can't you kind-a stay a little bit? Have a smoke and kind-a get myself together before you leave.' So I sat down and smoked a cigar with him and we talked along about little or nothing for an hour. He quieted down after a while and when I left he said he believed he could sleep."

After a complete examination the next day, Dr. Begg was pleased to report to the patient that "there wasn't anything the matter with his kidneys. It was just a plain case of over-wrought nerves."[9]

Despite that assurance, O. Henry continued to suspect that there was something physically wrong with him and in at least one letter to an editor friend mentioned his belief that he was suffering from Bright's disease. It turned out, unfortunately, that he read the signals of his physiology better than any doctor, and that his premonitions were correct.

Fame continued to come quite rapidly to O. Henry but fortune refused to keep step. Even after the price scale for his stories rose considerably above the *World's* hundred a week, his income never totaled more than $14,000 a year at the most. That hardly placed him in the financial company of a steel magnate, or even of a Jack London, who was building a castle in northern California, or the lordlier company of Richard Harding Davis, Edith Wharton and David Graham Phillips, each of whom received $1,000 for a short story.

The additional income from collections of his stories published as books did not add greatly to his income, though their popularity was growing. His estate made more money from their posthumous publication than O. Henry did during his lifetime. His own recompense was largely in the form of flattering reviews, such as those which greeted his second volume, *The Four Million,* in 1906. The publisher's preface was largely justified when it claimed that "Not very long ago someone invented the assertion that there were only 'Four Hundred' people in New York City who were really worth noticing. But a wiser man has arisen—the census taker—and his larger estimate of human interest has been preferred in marking out the field of these little stories of the 'Four Million.'" That volume, in fact, contained some of the O. Henry stories which have passed the test of time and are often included in anthologies: "The Gift of the Magi," "The Cop and the Anthem," "An Unfinished Story" and "The Furnished Room." It was praised by most of the literary magazines and even the *Atlantic Monthly* approved of it, with the reviewer observing that his stories were "pervaded by gentleness. In symbolism and color his slang need not yield to that of Mr. George Ade; he knows his world as well, but he sees it with an eye for its beauty as well as its absurdity. There is imagination as well as vision, and beyond his expert knowledge of our colloquial tongue he possesses in the background, to be used when needed, a real style."[10]

His growing acceptance as a literary figure as well as an entertainer of the subway-riding masses was also indicated by the tendency of reviewers to compare him with other masters of the short story, particularly Bret Harte, in the deft use of local color. The flattery, from all accounts, did not turn his head; his attitude toward his work remained earthbound. An aspiring writer who asked his advice on how to write short stories received this reply: "The first step is to get a kitchen table, a wooden chair, a wad of yellow foolscap writing paper, one lead pencil and a drinking glass. They are the props. Then you secure a flask of Scotch whiskey and a few oranges, which I will describe as the sustenance. We now come to the plot, frequently styled the inspiration. Combining a little orange juice with a little Scotch, the author drinks the health of all magazine editors, sharpens his pencil and begins to write. When the oranges are empty and the flask is dry, a saleable piece of fiction is ready for mailing."

And he still directed roguish messages to editorial offices to bail him out of his financial crises, though now he could afford to make them less elaborate, more to the point. William Griffeth, who had succeeded Theodore Dreiser as editor of the *Broadway Magazine* and was trying to enlist him as a regular contributor, received a note from O. Henry briefly stating his predicament: "Please send me $25. I've invited a friend to dinner. From the looks of him, he isn't going to pay for it; and I can't."

When Al Jennings, his old friend of Honduras and Ohio State Penitentiary days, came to New York on the first of several visits, he found no evidence of the stuffed shirt, the swelled head, or the inflated self-esteem which might reasonably have been expected of a successful author. Jennings had reformed completely. With the agility formerly devoted to holding up trains and banks, the little Oklahoman had himself restored to citizenship by President Theodore Roosevelt, the number one western buff of all time, who boyishly adored outlaws and town-taming marshals alike. Jennings came to New York shortly after being admitted to the Oklahoma bar.

O. Henry met him at Grand Central and then escorted him on a rubberneck bus tour of the city. That evening they set out again. "Where are we going?" Jennings asked. "Everywhere and anywhere," his friend replied. "We may land in Hell's Kitchen or we may find ourselves in Heaven's Vestibule."

Most nights they rambled around the city and Jennings observed with interest the writer's methods of research, of keeping himself in constant touch with the kind of people he wrote about. One night they picked up a streetwalker, "a little, thin, white creature," and took her to dine with them at Mouquin's, which catered to the more expensive and knowledgeable palates of pre-Prohibition New York. Jennings was puzzled by O. Henry's choice of a dinner companion. "There was nothing remarkable about her. I couldn't see a story there. The only spark she showed was when dinner came and then a look of inspired joyousness lighted her face. It seemed to be that Porter must surely be disappointed."

Jennings questioned him about it after the girl left them. " 'When I see a shipwreck,' he said, 'I like to know what caused the disaster.' 'Well,' I said, 'what did you make of that investigation?' 'Nothing but the glow that wrapped her face when the soup came. That's the story.' "[11]

Another night O. Henry took Jennings to dinner at the Hoffman House to meet Gilman Hall and Richard Duffy. With O. Henry's encouragement, Jennings dominated the table talk with recollections of his years as the terror of the Indian Territory.

After they'd parted from Hall and Duffy, O. Henry ruefully remarked to Jennings, "Colonel, I stood in your shadow tonight."

"What do you mean?"

"I was some pumpkins with Hall and Duffy until you came along," O. Henry replied. "Would you mind the next time we are together telling them I held the horses for you? I think it would add to my prestige."[12]

During his three-week stay in New York, Jennings found his friend a moody fellow much of the time, often worried about the past and the threat of exposure. "Bill," Jennings told him, "you've got a feminine streak in you; you're so unreliable," referring to his alternations between melancholy and high spirits. "Sometimes," O. Henry explained, "things look so black I don't see much use in anything. I can't bet on myself. Sometimes I want to have nothing to do with anyone."

According to Jennings, O. Henry confided in him more than anyone else, a trust evidently based on their mutual prison experience and adventures in Honduras. Once Jennings asked him bluntly how it came about that he [O. Henry] was sent to prison. "I borrowed four [thousand dollars] from the bank on a tip that cotton would go up," Jennings quoted him as replying. "It went down and I got five [years in prison]." Jennings added that he believed his friend was being humorous, that he was personally convinced that O. Henry "took the fall" for someone else in the bank.[13]

One night O. Henry showed Jennings a photograph of his daughter, mentioned forebodings about the state of his health and remarked, "If anything should happen to me, I think I'd feel happy if you would look after her."

Either on that visit or a subsequent one, Jennings wrote, O. Henry brought up the subject of blackmail. According to Bob Davis and other New York friends, it later came to be generally believed that the writer's constant need for fresh funds stemmed from the fact that he was being blackmailed by someone who knew he was an ex-convict.

Jennings in his memoir *Through the Shadows with O. Henry,* on which Will Irwin collaborated, recalled that O. Henry told him one night, either on his first or second trip to New York, that the blackmailer was a woman. He quoted O. Henry: "I can't stand it much longer. She comes after me regularly and she's the wife of a big broker here, at that. Tonight I told her to go hang. She'll get no more from me."

Jennings questioned him about the woman's background and how she happened to get O. Henry in her clutches.

"We used to sing under her window [in Austin], once in a while," O. Henry recalled. "She came to me months ago. She knew my whole history.

"She was in terrible straits," he continued in a half-choked voice. "Her southern pride wouldn't let her ask any of her circle.

She wanted a thousand. I had $150 Gilman Hall had sent me. I let her have it. She has been to see me regularly ever since. I've emptied my pockets on that table for her. Now I'm through. I could have killed her."

"You should have called her bluff the first time," Jennings said.

"I have much to lose," said O. Henry in a low voice. "I don't look at things as you do."[14]

It was one experience that he never managed to convert into one of his ironic little tales, but it would have made a good one.

Chapter 8. "Train's Late for Happiness"

Many of O. Henry's heroines were girls he met in his nightly wanderings, and his study of their characters and personalities was often extended to a more intimate knowledge than that acquired across a cafe table. Bob Davis, his editor and later his biographer, observed that O. Henry was a "full-blooded" man with entirely heterosexual instincts; another friend saw him as a complete "pagan," without any of the puritanical hangovers that afflicted and inhibited many men of his generation. That the New York of his time was abundant with young females available for seduction was made startlingly clear at the trial of Harry K. Thaw for the murder of free-swinging Stanford White, the great metropolitan shocker of the Edwardian years.

The moral attitude of the Edwardians, of course, was much more relaxed than that of the Victorians, which itself was not (from certain accounts now being more closely evaluated) all it was supposed to be. The shocking thing about the revelations of the Thaw trial—girls being seduced on pink velvet swings, nude girls popping out of papier-mâché cakes, champagne suppers in private dining rooms—was that all the naughtiness came out in the open. Until then the free-swingers at least could be counted upon to be discreet, to continue "providing an example" for the lower classes.

O. Henry was not a member of the high-living Stanford White circle; he could not have afforded the initiation fee or the dues, and besides, he did not care for hunting in packs. For him sexual adventure was a means of alleviating his loneliness, dispelling the melancholia of returning alone to the rooms in Irving Place.

Some of that feeling was transmitted in his story "The Furnished Room," which "received its latest guest with a first glow of pseudo-hospitality, a hectic, haggard, perfunctory welcome like the specious smile of a demirep. The sophistical comfort came in reflected gleams from the decayed furniture, the ragged brocade upholstery of a couch and two chairs, a foot-wide cheap pier-glass between the two windows, from one or two gilt picture frames and a brass bedstead in a corner. . . . Each plank in the floor owned its particular cant and shriek as from a separate and individual agony. It seemed incredible that all this malice and injury had been wrought upon the room by those who had called it for a time their home; and yet it may have been the cheated home instinct surviving blindly, the resentful rage at false household gods that had kindled their wrath. A hut that is our own we can sweep and adorn and cherish."

There was no doubt in Bob Davis' mind that before his second marriage O. Henry was what then was called a "womanizer" or "skirt-chaser." For recreation, Davis said, that was "his most natural pursuit" and "he had his light affairs, many of them, and his conquests were more or less easy. Many of his heroines were drawn direct from life, being polished up and whitewashed for the purposes of fiction."[1]

Even such tolerant friends as Davis must have been a little shocked, however, when they learned several years after O. Henry's death of his search for romance, and/or sex, through the personals column of the New York *Herald.* Until the postal authorities ordered the publisher to cease and desist, the personals column of the *Herald,* running to half a dozen pages daily, was popularly known as the "Whores' Daily Guide and Compendium." Many of the ads were for "massage parlors," Turkish baths, houses of assignation and other pitfalls; others were the invitations of "chic Parisian ladies with cozy suites" and "witty affectionate ladies possessing beautiful figures" craving the company of "jolly sports," or such appeals as "Refined young woman seeks immediate loan" and "Lady, loyal, loving, lovable, with famished heart craves devotion of but one man financially worthwhile."[2]

On September 10, 1905, this saturnalia in agate type included the following appeal:

"Two neighborly 'literary fellows,' 35 and 30, seek social acquaintance of two intelligent, attractive and unconventional young ladies interested in artistic ideas with a view to mutual improvement and entertainment. Omar. 116 Herald."

"Omar" was O. Henry. Who the other literary fellow was—if he existed—was never revealed.

At least one young woman answered the ad, as she herself revealed in a magazine article published in 1914. She was Ethel Patterson, who was living in a furnished room in Harlem.

"Indeed," she wrote "Omar," "I am awfully lonesome. You can't understand, for there's two of you. There's only one of me. Take my word for it that it is not nice to be a girl working all alone in a city where you scarcely know a human soul. I am at a point where I talk to elevator boys and car conductors. That is why—and because I am also a bit of a gambler—I thought I would write to you. I have been brought up to believe 'gentlemen do not do that sort of thing' *you* are doing. But I have been brought up to believe 'ladies do not' either. And as I am unwilling to admit I am not 'a lady,' that gives *you* just the one chance on which I propose to gamble.

"Who *are* you? Out of space you have spoken a name I love [she meant his signature "Omar," being an admirer of the *Rubaiyat of Omar Khayyam*]. Out of space I am answering you. Will you come within signalling distance, you ships that, perhaps, shall not pass in the night?

"Pardon me that I do not give you my own name and address. You might, you know, be—well—almost anything. An entire matrimonial agency, for example. . . ."

She signed herself "A Woman."

The wit and candor, as well as the wistfulness of her reply touched O. Henry, and he answered Miss Patterson with a playfulness that indicated he had abandoned any purely lecherous intentions:

". . . Not by our 'Personal' shall you fall; we hope it will be a dirigible balloon in which you may soar into the more pleasant strata of clouds and ether.

"My brother 'Omar' and I are not connected by any more binding tie than that of similar tastes and well-established mutual friendship. Weary of the counterfeit Bohemia into which people who 'write' are dragged, we sent forth the 'Personal' into space in the hope of winging some wild, free creature of the aerial regions above who might prove congenial company in search of the (genuinely) romantic and the (reasonably) adventurous.

"I came from the saddle of a Texas bronco four years ago to New York. The conventionalities and the routine of the little circle I have been revolving in have about caused me to stampede. The more 'people' I meet the 'lonesomer' I get. I can well sympathize with a woman who is lonely in the Big City. . . .

"You—'a bit of a gambler at heart'? Let's see if you are. You made a very careful lead with your 'A Woman' signature. Well, I must admit you were right to do that. But I'm playing a trump—here's my picture (which you won't recognize) and here's my card and address. You won't recognize the name, for I write over a *nom de guerre.*

"I trust you thus because you say you are a 'literary fellow' and I have confidence in 'the gang.' If you would care to come within speaking distance and give us a hope that we may gather 'beneath the bough' with you we would be glad to hear from you again."

O. Henry signed it "Yours to the bottom of the jug, The Two Omars."

Five days later, on September 22, Miss Patterson replied: "Shake hands. Six years ago *I* 'came from the saddle of a Texas bronco.' 'Stampede!!!' Sometimes I feel as though I just naturally can't stick it out. You know the feel. You *must.* . . . And I have two more years than you of pent-up loneliness. . . . Well, anyway, I feel better now. I know that somewhere else in this jungle of houses there is another human whose eyes and heart turn backward toward 'Home.'

"It was decent of you, Mr. Porter, to send me your card and address. Your confidence in this infinitesimal portion of 'the gang' will not be misplaced. I don't know whether or not I should show my appreciation by being equally frank. I'm afraid I can't. . . . Will you let me be unknown to you a little longer?

"I *want* to accept your invitation to 'come within speaking distance' but I do not know how. Of course the simplest method is to tell you where I will meet you. But how in the name of Heaven am I to know you when I get there? Shall I wear a red rose? Isn't that the proper thing under such circumstances?"

She closed by describing herself as a brunette and "not pretty."

Obviously intrigued, O. Henry replied by return mail that she "should know that you are always safe in approaching the campfire of a Texan" and thanking her for sparing him the awkward formality of a formal call. "Why should I add to the awful tedium of your life is sitting on a slippery couch in your 'parlor,' hitching up my trousers an inch at the knees to preserve the crease (when you weren't looking) and drinking a cup of English breakfast tea (which is no good—always get uncolored Japan), and asking you whether you like 'Man and Superman' or the Hippodrome the better."

He could behave like a "perfect gent," he added, but he was "tired of the New York bluff" and favored instead "unconspicuous unconventionality." His own life was full of color and variety but he was often "bored, disgusted, angry, dissatisfied—why?—because I haven't got a 'Pal' to help me enjoy these things." He pictured himself as a rough and ready fellow who "slept on the ground for three years in the cattle and sheep camps, and I don't care for society phrases."

That she was a brunette didn't dismay him because "I have admired blondes all my life, and my judgment and taste have been proven faulty." The other Omar, he said, was the editor of a magazine and "you would run no risk if you should see him standing on a corner with a red rose in one hand and a corkscrew in the other for purposes of identification." As for himself, "I resemble more than anything else a retail butcher who is worried about his bills."

He facetiously suggested that at their proposed rendezvous he could "walk up Broadway at 7:45 with one shoe off and a fur boa around my neck screaming 'Murder!' every thirty seconds. You could come down the street singing 'Hiawatha' in a pink kimono and your hair cut short."

Or more properly they might meet in the subway station at 125th Street and Lenox Avenue with Omar No. 1, the possibly fictitious magazine editor, as their chaperone. They could "run out somewhere for a quiet little dinner, and discuss Shakespeare and musical glasses." He was willing to "lay my hand on the cigars in my upper left hand pocket" and swear that they would meet under the most decorous circumstances.

For some reason which Miss Patterson did not explain in her magazine confession, she did not answer that letter. The tentative romance by mail ended, but that wasn't quite the end of the story. Two years later, when O. Henry was again a married man, they met at a party. A mutual friend introduced them, no doubt confirming O. Henry's theory that New York was just one gigantic village, and Miss Patterson identified herself as "A Woman." Whenever they met after that, she said, he playfully, punningly called her "Miss Terry."[3]

Most of his transitory romances were conducted with the secretiveness that marked his aptitude for living like an espionage agent in enemy territory. His friends, in their recollections, rarely mention seeing O. Henry with a young woman. He surfaced with a female companion only occasionally, and then with an utterly respectable young lady; the others, presumably, were spirited in and out of 55 Irving Place by the dark of the moon. Bill Williams did recall one occasion on which he and O. Henry went over to the Chelsea apartment of a nice young woman whom the latter evidently had known for some time. They had dinner at her apartment, with O. Henry revealing himself as an expert amateur chef and broiling a large porterhouse steak. O. Henry was in high spirits and disclosed an "aptitude for real sociability" with women when he was in the mood.

About the time O. Henry was posing as "Omar" the jovial "literary fellow," he was also renewing by correspondence his boyhood friendship with a woman of approximately his own age, Miss Sara Lindsay Coleman, who was still living with her mother in the family home near Asheville, North Carolina. They had met when O. Henry was twelve or thirteen while Miss Coleman was visiting kinfolk in Greensboro. They were distantly related, O. Henry's uncle having married her second cousin. She was now an attractive, though not beautiful, woman, whose firmness of character is strikingly evident in photographs; the type whom other women would pay the left-handed compliment of calling "handsome."

A tentative and intermittent postal romance began. It was initiated by Miss Coleman, who taught school and occasionally published magazine stories about the life of a mountain boy.

"If you are the boy who once liked a small girl in a green-sprigged muslin dress, and I think you are," she wrote him on learning from her mother that the famous O. Henry was really the Will Porter who had hung around her gate when she visited Greensboro, "when you come to Asheville don't stop there. Ride through the town and keep on riding until you reach a lane to the left. At the end of the lane you'll find a big pine tree, a white house, and me."

It was exactly the right, deft approach to an O. Henry who had reached the age when he began to book back and find an unsuspected, somewhat sentimental value in the years long past.

With a burst of nostalgia for the days of his innocent youth, O. Henry replied immediately that he was "gladder to get your little note than the biggest editor's check I ever saw." He enclosed a photograph of himself, and demanded, "Does it look anything like the moon-struck little shrimp that used to hang around and bother you so much? I can remember what an awkward, bashful, sentimental, ugly, uninteresting nuisance I was then. No wonder I couldn't make any impression on you! I've improved a good deal since then. In fact, it seems to me that the older I grow, the better looking and more fascinating I become." He said he was also sending her a copy of *Cabbages and Kings* with the suggestion that "It's just the thing to prop the kitchen door when the wind is in the east."[4]

In the long-distance courtship that followed, both seemed to be playing the role they thought was expected of them. Miss Coleman, a trifle coquettish, once sent her photograph, then demanded that it be returned immediately. O. Henry was roguish, boyish, impetuous, headlong romantic.

"Kick the mountains over," he implored in one letter, "and pack a kimono and a lead-pencil in a suitcase and hurry to New York. Get a little studio three stories up with mission furniture and portieres, a guitar and a chafing-dish and laugh at fate and the gods. There are lots of lovely women here leading beautiful and happy lives in the midst of the greatest things in this hemisphere of art and music and literature on tiny little incomes. You meet the big people in every branch of art, you drink deep of the Pierian spring, you get the benefit of the earth's best . . ."

That was the wrong tack to take with Sara Lindsay Coleman, a sensible and strong-willed southern lady, to whom guitar strumming and midnight welsh rarebits in a Greenwich Village studio had little or no appeal, and she ignored the suggestion. Instead, she asked him if he could find her a literary agent to handle her stories. He hunted up a woman agent who succeeded in selling some of Miss Coleman's stories, but he preferred to think of her as a "Dear Lady of Lavender-Scented Memories," as he addressed her in one letter, rather than as an ink-stained colleague.

He pictured himself as a big-city beachcomber needing the love of a good woman. "I need a boss. For the last month I've been so no-account and lazy I haven't turned out a line. I've felt kind of melancholy and dreary and lonesome." This was the period when he suspected he had Bright's disease and had consulted several doctors. "But none of them knew that what I needed was just somebody to fix a cushion for me and tell the gas-bill man I wasn't in."[5]

Miss Coleman was weary of spinsterhood, and during the two years of their correspondence began to imagine herself as the wife and taskmaster of a world-famous author. In a story titled "Wind of Destiny," which told the story of her romance with O. Henry in fictional terms, her heroine confesses, "I am sick for a bigger life. . . . Teaching is routine after twelve years." In another passage she sees herself admirably suited to the keeper-of-the-flame role, the motivation, often misconceived, of women who marry what they consider to be genius.

In her story O. Henry was Bobby, and she wrote, "Bobby's wife must give. The hands that take into their keeping that precious thing—his genius—what tender, comprehending hands they must be."

They finally met on September 11, 1907—his forty-fifth birthday—when Miss Coleman visited friends in Boston, then stopped in New York on her way back home. During her several days in the city, O. Henry courted her intensely, and the climax of her brief stay in New York was a proposal. Miss Coleman didn't accept and didn't refuse. There was a codicil to the proposal.

In a letter which has since been lost or destroyed, a copy of which was made by O. Henry's first biographer and has been preserved by the Greensboro Public Library, Miss Coleman related that on her last night in New York O. Henry started to unburden himself about certain "lost" years in his life. Face to face, however, he was unable to tell her specifically about the prison sentence. He said he would write out his confession and send it to her in North Carolina. Then she could decide whether or not she wanted to accept his proposal.

O. Henry kept his promise and sent her a long letter detailing his conviction for embezzlement and his three years in the Ohio State Penitentiary, but maintained that he was innocent of the charge. She believed his protestations and wrote that she was willing to marry him.

In reply, he urged her to consider the matter carefully. Perhaps he was having second thoughts about marriage and wondered whether he was committing himself once again to an institution which, as his conversation with Bob Davis several years before showed, he found something less than perfect. He must also have divined that Sara would insist that he live a fairly regular, sedate, conventional and therefore non-Bohemian life as her husband; his night wanderings and his attendance at the saloons would be sharply curtailed. Bachelorhood, except for its lonely moments, was for O. Henry a fairly comfortable estate. He had moved from 55 Irving Place when his landlady gave up the house, lived for a short time on East Twenty-fourth Street between Madison and Fourth avenues, then established himself at the Caledonia Hotel on West Twenty-sixth Street between Broadway and Sixth Avenue, where the staff was drilled to keep out unwanted callers. Then, too, there was the fact that he told several persons that the only woman he ever loved was his first wife.

There were still other inhibiting factors which may have made him hope that Sara would reconsider and reject him. By 1907 his health indubitably was failing and the symptoms could not be laid to hypochondria. In addition, he was finding his work harder and harder to produce. Visiting him at the Caledonia, Bill Williams, his friend on the *World* staff, noted that "the effort seemed to grow greater and the rate slower and slower. . . . it was taxing him to the limit to make the grade. He never complained. When I would ask him how he felt he usually answered, 'Oh, pretty good. How's yourself?' But I knew he wasn't well; I could see it and feel it when I was with him. . . ."[6]

But Sara was tenacious, and the wedding date was set for November 27, 1907. In the words of the heroine of "Wind of Destiny"—Sara herself—"Luxuriously I dive again into the most wonderful box of candy I ever dreamed of; luxuriously I sniff the perfume of the most exquisite flowers I ever saw. Tomorrow when I wear my flowers to church I'll feel like a real princess. . . ."

O. Henry arrived about a week before the wedding in Asheville, and a letter to Gilman Hall, who was to be his best man, was about equally divided between discussion of the mechanics of the wedding ceremony and more practical considerations. The prospective bridegroom apparently had not become any less haphazard in his handling of financial affairs.

"I wired you today 'MS mailed today, please rush one century by wire.' That will exhaust the Reader check—if it isn't too exhausted itself to come. You, of course, will keep the check when it arrives—I don't think they will fall down on it surely. I wrote Howland a pretty sharp letter and ordered him to send it at once care of *Everybody's*. . . . When this story reaches you it will cut down the overdraft 'right smart,' but if the house is willing I'd mighty well like to run it up to the limit again, because cash is sure scarce, and I'll have to have something like $300 more to see me through. The story I am sending is a new one; I still have another partly written for you, which I shall finish and turn in before I get back to New York and then we'll begin to clear up all debts. . . . Please look over the story and arrange for bringing the $300 when you come—it will still keep me below the allowed limit and thereafter I will cut down instead of raising it."

Gilman Hall's duties as a best man were more than ordinarily rigorous. In the same letter O. Henry instructed him:

"(1) Please go to Tiffany's and get a wedding ring, size 5⅛. Sara says the bands worn now are quite narrow—and that's the kind she wants.

"(2) And bring me a couple of dress collars, size 16½. I have ties.

"(3) And go to a florist's—there is one named Macintosh (or something like that) on Broadway, East side of street five or six doors north of 26th St., where I used to buy a good many times. He told me he could ship flowers in good shape to Asheville—you might remind him that I used to send flowers to 36 West 17th Street some time ago. I am told by the mistress of ceremonies that I am to furnish two bouquets—one of lilies of the valley and one of pale pink roses. Get plenty of each—say enough lilies to make a large bunch to be carried in the hand and say three or four dozen of the roses."

He was also anxious that Hall should understand that marriage would change and regularize his former way of life. A new O. Henry, or Sydney Porter, would emerge from the church with the wedding party. "I note what you say about hard times and will take heed," he assured Hall. "I'm not going into any extravagances at all, and I'm going to pitch into hard work just as soon as I get the rice grains out of my ear. . . .

"I'm right with you on the question of the 'home-like' system of having fun. I think we'll all agree beautifully on that. I've had all of the cheap bohemia that I want. I can tell you, none of the 'climbers' and the cocktail crowd are going to bring their *vaporings* into my home. It's for the clean, merry life, with your best friends in the game and a general concentration of energies and aims. I am having a cedar-wood club cut from the mountains with knots on it, and I am going to stand in my hallway (when I have one) and edit with it the cards of all callers. You and Mrs. Hall have latch-keys, of course."[7]

The marriage, before a Presbyterian minister, went off smoothly and the middle-aged couple honeymooned at a resort hotel in Hot Springs, North Carolina. They stayed several weeks, longer than they expected, because O. Henry fell ill. He got out of the sickbed, despite Sara's pleas, and finished a story in answer to a telegraphed plea from the publisher who had advanced him money on it. There were other worries, too. His latest collection, *Heart of the West,* did not greatly appeal to the reviewers, who generally reported that it was second-rate compared to the earlier volumes. The stories were too full of Texas badmen and other ingredients of the despised Western to satisfy the eastern critics. Hollywood eventually looked upon one of the characters in his *Heart of the West* stories and found him admirably suited to a series of mediocre but moneymaking films. That character was the Cisco Kid in "The Caballero's Way."

Almost immediately upon the Porters' return to New York in December 1907, O. Henry seemed to forget his pledge to Gilman Hall that henceforth he would settle down to a quiet domestic life. Instead of establishing a home, as Sara undoubtedly would have wished, the couple moved into the Chelsea Hotel on West Twenty-third Street, which was and still is a home away from home for the literary, musical and artistic world. At the same time he kept his room at the Caledonia, where he did his writing. Maintaining two establishments was a continual financial drain and kept O. Henry constantly at work to produce twenty-nine stories during 1908. Gerald Langford (*Alias O. Henry*) in analyzing his income believed that he netted about $14,000 that year—a lot of money for 1908—but it all slipped quickly through his fingers. The income from his books was of little help, because he sold the rights to them for a few hundred dollars.

Only when he signed a contract with Doubleday the following year did he start realizing a decent return on his collected stories. That publisher bought up as well the copyrights on his earlier volumes and became O. Henry's guardian, guide and protector to a greater extent, perhaps, than any of the magazines to which he contributed. Faithful to his memory, that house established annual O. Henry short-story awards and yearly publishes a volume of prize stories in his name.

Sara tried to keep her husband from driving himself so hard, particularly after he told her that the doctors had diagnosed his illness as diabetes and warned him that he had only two years to live unless he took better care of himself. The first thing they proscribed, of course, was alcohol, but he continued his steady consumption of whiskey and beer.

In the summer his personal and professional friends rallied around and insisted that he, Sara and his daughter Margaret, who came up from Nashville to live with them on graduating from Ward-Belmont, move out to Long Island during the hot months. They believed that he would be able to work better in the cottage they had found at Good Ground, about forty miles from New York, and undoubtedly believed that the peaceful surroundings and the fresh sea air would tranquilize him and keep him away from the bottle. Gilman Hall and others not only found the house for him but took over the job of furnishing it and hiring two servants. Then that little circle of editors leaned back and waited for a stream of first-rate stories to flow in from Good Ground, Long Island.

They waited in vain, particularly Gilman Hall, now editor of *Everybody's*, where O. Henry was especially "overdrawn."

Furthermore, Hall learned that O. Henry wasn't even staying at the cottage. He assigned an associate editor, George Barr Baker, to find the author and try to extract a story from him. By now Baker was experienced in the difficult process of locating and pinning down O. Henry. He reasoned that the writer had always functioned at his best in the city, no matter how hot and noisy. Breaking through the ring of bellhops and elevator operators who guarded his privacy at the Caledonia, Baker found O. Henry in his hideaway, working at his desk, apparently unconscious of the din raised by the clanging trolleys on Broadway and the roar of the Sixth Avenue Elevated. Smoke and soot and the heat of the summer's day came in from the open windows.

O. Henry finished the sentence he was working on and then told young Baker, "Here's your story, not quite done, but you will have it on Monday morning."

"That's good," Baker said. "But I certainly didn't expect to find you here. I thought you were supposed to be down in the country."

"The country," O. Henry said bitterly, shaking his head. "Couldn't stand it. It drove me to distraction."

"What did?"

"Why, the noise, the terrible noise. Do you know there is a bird, a malignant little bird, that comes to my window and calls to me most annoyingly. Calls to me? That bird howls at me from morning to night. Does so deliberately just to disturb me. Then those cows, those two cows! They are forever mooing. And then the water, continually plashing, plashing. Couldn't stand it any longer. The noise was driving me mad. Prevented me from even thinking of work. Had to come up here for peace and quiet."

"Quite true," Baker sighed, realizing that the O. Henry Protective Society had miscalculated again. "And now that the story's done—"

"Not quite," O. Henry broke in, raising his hand as though to ward off an attempt to snatch it from under his nose. *"Nearly* done. And while we are on that subject let me suggest that if I were a different kind of a man, which of course I am not, I would hint that with a starving wife and daughter, and one or two servants who are also starving, as well as a hungry dog, an advance of saying one hundred and fifty dollars would be exceedingly welcome. But, as you understand, I am not that kind of man. . . ."[8]

Marriage had indeed reformed him in few visible ways; his fiscal waywardness was unchanged, and his editors continued to be bombarded with high-handed appeals, such as the one that landed on Bob Davis' desk at *Munsey's*, which was signed "Bill the Bedouin" and read, "I am a man of dam few words. I want $125 (don't read that a dollar and a quarter). That, in addition to the $150 that I screwed out of the high-browed and esteemed B. Merwin during your absence will make a total of $275 which will be more than covered by the moral and entertaining tale that I agree to have finished and delivered to you all by 10:30 A.M., Monday, August 27 or perhaps earlier. Pursue the liberal policy and get the best stuff." Or again to Davis: "Say—a fool and his money, etc. Is there anything doing for about $49.98 today for the purpose of purchasing things offered for sale in the marts? I had to send most all of that stuff abroad that you gimme the other day. Don't press the matter if it seems out of order. I'll be even and ahead of the game pretty soon. There will come to you on Monday a new story . . ."

O. Henry's ability to make and spend money was a thing of awe to his new wife. One night they discovered that, having just invited guests down from New York for the weekend, there wasn't enough food in the house to feed them. O. Henry got up at six the next morning, slaved away at his desk until noon, produced a new story of several thousand words and sold it by telephone an hour later.

Perhaps the most satisfying part of that summer was his reunion with his daughter. Whatever resentment Margaret may have felt over being kept for the past years in a finishing school and before that with her grandparents seemed to have been dissolved. Judging from her photograph, she was a pretty girl with large wistful eyes and an appealing smile. At seventeen she had decided to be a writer, and did in fact try but without any signal success. In one of the few pieces she had published, a reminiscence of her father, she recalled that he never ordered her to do anything and "never did I fail to follow his advice or try to fulfill his expressed wish." There was at least one exception to this. O. Henry was considerably annoyed with the girl when she refused to continue her schooling. He wanted her to attend Smith. If she must be a writer, well and good, but he wanted her to be grounded firmly in the classics, forgetting that his own career had thrived on very little formal education.[9]

Meanwhile, Sara was finding him an increasingly difficult husband, quick-tempered and impatient with her as he rarely was with anyone else. His wives, it seemed, not unnaturally saw a facet of his personality never glimpsed by his friends, who considered him the most easy-going of men. His willfulness came to full flower in the presence of women with an emotional claim on him, which he obviously resented. "No one could manage that man," Sara sighed in the course of a 1934 newspaper interview. "He was a law unto himself and had a deep dislike for anything that resembled nagging or fussing."[10] That his wife would "fuss" over his reckless consumption of food or liquor for his own good did not excuse what he regarded as a breach of good marital relations.

It often seemed to her that he relieved the tensions of his work by picking a quarrel with her. Once he came home to the Chelsea from the workroom at the Caledonia and noticed a vase full of roses. One orchid peeped out of the mass of roses, and he asked her about it. The florist, Sara explained, had given it to her as a goodwill gesture.

"And didn't you know better than to take it?" he demanded. "Didn't your instinct tell you not to take it?"

Challenging a southern lady's sense of propriety was going too far; Sara was so upset that she ran from the room, flung herself on their bed and wept.

A short time later a contrite O. Henry came in and apologized. "You don't know this big town as I do," he said. "I'm trying to protect you, to take care of you."[11]

Another time they quarreled so bitterly when she rebuked him for his lack of consideration that he packed her off to Asheville and her mother for a cooling-off period. Sara was certain that the marriage was finished, but in a few days he wrote a letter full of contrition and asked her to return immediately, which she did.

"If only," she wrote in a magazine article in 1912, "I could have been more sensible; if only he could have been tenderer."

She recalled that he once told her he could not endure marriage if the "door to the cage" wasn't left open so he could slip in and out at his pleasure.[12]

On the other hand, from several accounts, he always dutifully defended his second marriage against the doubts of some of his friends who believed that he was a born bachelor. One of the doubters was Al Jennings, who arrived in New York on a visit soon after O. Henry's marriage. He and Richard Duffy picked up O. Henry at the Caledonia for a night on the town. O. Henry seemed depressed, Jennings noted, but his spirits picked up after a few convivial hours at Mouquin's. It had occurred to Jennings that it would have been more in line with the traditions of southern hospitality if they had dined at the writer's home, and he suspected his friend might have been wary of introducing a fellow ex-convict to his wife.

O. Henry surprised him by suggesting that they drop around at his apartment. "I'd like you to meet my wife," he told Jennings.

Sara greeted them with "great cordiality" and "chatted with pleasant ease," as Jennings recalled. About midnight he and Duffy got up to leave. Somewhat to his surprise, O. Henry picked up his hat and prepared to join them.

Also surprised, Sara asked, "Why, you're not going too, are you, Mr. Porter?"

O. Henry stayed behind to talk to Sara for a moment while Jennings and Duffy took their departure.

Jennings was just asking Duffy why O. Henry had remarried and "put an end to his liberty" when O. Henry caught up with his friends on the sidewalk outside the Chelsea.

O. Henry had overheard the remark, was not affronted, but asked, "You're dissatisfied with my matrimonial venture?"

Bluntly Jennings replied that he thought it was the "silliest" thing his friend could have done.

"She is a most estimable young lady," O. Henry said.

Estimable or not, Jennings said, it seemed to him ridiculous for O. Henry to have married again.

"I loved her," O. Henry said in a rather dutiful tone.

"Oh, my God! That covers a multitude of sins!"

If there was any injured party to the marriage, O. Henry retorted, it was Sara. "I've married a high-bred woman," he added, "and brought all my troubles upon her. Was it right?"[13]

The question remained suspended in the crisp night air.

Bill Williams, who had been O. Henry's almost constant companion before the marriage, could never bring himself to visit O. Henry's new home, though "I have never been able to explain it to myself satisfactorily." Sara was a "most excellent lady" and a "charming hostess," but there must have been something slightly chilling about the "high-bred" southern lady that kept away O. Henry's old friends from his semi-Bohemian bachelor days—except, of course, for the most sedate members of the circle, the Gilman Halls and others who believed marriage would be "good" for O. Henry.

Williams was invited for dinner "time and again," he recalled, but "constantly evaded setting a definite date. 'Bill,' O. Henry would say, 'how about that dinner engagement. I want to get that fixed up because I'm anxious to have you come over . . .' But I stalled it along and never went. Each time I was brought to the edge of it I balked at the jump. . . ."

Once he encountered O. Henry, in a melancholy and possibly rueful mood, wandering around the old Irving Place neighborhood. After strolling around for a time, Williams walked back to the Chelsea with him and in answer to his question O. Henry said that "he was finding married life all right and had 'no kicks to register.'"[14]

After the summer on Long Island the Porters took a lease on an apartment at 88 Washington Place for seven months. It was a large and comfortable apartment, renting for the then considerable price of $100 a month. Early that winter of 1908–9, however, Sara went back to North Carolina and her mother's home, where O. Henry visited her from time to time. His daughter Margaret was persuaded to enter a school in Englewood, New Jersey, for the winter term, and her father resumed the careless, unfettered ways of bachelorhood.

Perhaps he summed it up best when he said to a friend, "Train's late for happiness, Colonel."

Chapter 9. A Reach for the Laurel

Perhaps O. Henry and his wife had decided to separate temporarily not because of any emotional disturbances but to allow him to concentrate on his career. There is no doubt that he found being both a husband and a writer a great strain at times. Just when a story started moving forward under his pen, in the workroom at the Caledonia, he would have to abandon it and return to the Chelsea for dinner.

There were the distractions necessarily attendant on marriage, the constant requirement to "consider" Sara. Though writing was her avocation, she was not a professional who lived or starved on what she could produce. She could not be expected to understand that when he lashed out over a trifle, such as the orchid in the bouquet of roses, he was actually venting his rage and frustration over a story that refused to let itself be written. Quarreling, making up, trying to explain himself simply took too much time and effort.

He was forty-six years old and probably he believed that it was high time he made the big attempt for recognition, for a lasting reputation. Until now he had regarded himself as a humble storyteller in the marketplace, grinding out his stories to pay the bills. Their literary content seemed negligible to their author. But now important people were saying that O. Henry was more than a highly productive hack. Publication of *The Voice of the City*, the third collection of his New York stories, restored him to the esteem of the critics. It included such first-class work as the title story, "A Lickpenny Lover," "Dougherty's Eye-Opener," "While the Auto Waits," "The City of Dreadful Night," "The Memento" and "The Fool Killer."

About that time, too, a well-known commentator had considered O. Henry's career at appreciative length in one of the leading literary reviews and declared that he was a writer to be taken seriously, a worthy successor to Rudyard Kipling in making the short story respectable. Short stories collected in a book had become a drug on the market, he noted, but O. Henry's were rehabilitating the genre. "The facility, the light touch of O. Henry, his mastery of the vernacular, his insight into the life of the disinherited, make it needless for him to resort to such inventions as Stevenson's learned Arabian." Furthermore, he wrote, O. Henry was an original, who could not be compared with anyone else. "The combination of technical excellence with whimsical, sparkling wit, abundant humor and a fertile invention is so rare that the reader is content without comparisons."[1]

O. Henry followed up *The Voice of the City* with publication of *The Gentle Grafter* later the same year, and it also was generally well received. Included in that volume were most of his underworld stories. Much of the material evidently was culled from his three years in prison. Dr. John M. Thomas, the chief physician at the prison, stated that "*The Gentle Grafter* portrays the stories told him on his night rounds. I remember having heard him recount many of them. . . ." The New York *Times* reviewer praised the volume as "something vital, warm and human that commands your liking." *Current Literature* proclaimed him as "A Yankee Maupassant."

It was evident that he had sufficient reason now to believe that he was more than a hard-driven hack producing stories on the demand of editors and creditors. The magazine and book publishers, too, were demonstrating their faith in the increasing promise of his career. He had begun preliminary work, mostly in his head, on a novel for Doubleday, Page & Co., now established as the publishers of his collected stories, and was planning a series of stories on life in the contemporary South, an interest apparently awakened by his trips to visit his wife.

In 1909, living alone on Washington Place, his ambitions spurred by the new plans and projects, he wrote one of his most celebrated short stories, "A Municipal Report." Four years after his death, in a symposium conducted by the New York *Times*, it was selected by readers as the greatest American short story. Needless to add, its literary rating has since depreciated considerably.

There were two versions of the way in which he got the idea for "A Municipal Report." One was that he was annoyed by the assertion of the late Frank Norris that most American cities were so stodgy that they couldn't serve as the background for notable literature. "Fancy a novel," Norris had written, "about Chicago or Buffalo, let us say, or Nashville, Tennessee. There are just three big cities in the United States that are 'story cities'—New York, of course, New Orleans, and, best of the lot, San Francisco."

O. Henry not only quoted Norris at the beginning of "A Municipal Report" but ended it with the italicized punch line, "*I wonder what's doing in Buffalo.*" He admitted at the outset that glamorizing Nashville was a difficult proposition, describing as its atmosphere, "Take of London fog 30 parts; malaria 10 parts; gas leaks 20 parts; dew drops gathered in a brickyard at sunset, 25 parts; odor of honeysuckle, 15 parts. Mix."

Another account of the story's conception, cited by Bob Davis, was that O. Henry and a visitor were discussing how a writer found the materials for his stories during an afternoon chat in his workroom at the Caledonia. O. Henry maintained—it was one of his few theories about writing—that an able writer could build a story around the most trivial object if his imagination was in working order.

"I've got some of my best yarns," O. Henry is said to have remarked, "from park benches, lampposts and newsstands."

His companion, happening to have a Rand & McNally booklet on Nashville in his pocket, mostly a compilation of statistics, tossed it over to O. Henry and challenged him, "Write a story based on that."

"I'll do it," O. Henry snapped.[2]

However the story was conceived, O. Henry apparently valued the idea so highly that (rare occurrence) he outlined it in a letter to William Griffeth of *Broadway Magazine;* it served as the basis for a cash advance. As O. Henry outlined the story:

"The old nigger hack-driver is a relic of the old South. [As, of course, was O. Henry when he used the term "nigger."] He is a night-hawk and a ruffian (probably) but his piratical depredations upon travelers and transients are for the sole purpose of supporting an old lady (the poetess) who is the last of the family to which he once belonged. All his small earnings are contributed to that end.

"Major Caswell, a type of the degraded Southerner, is living off the slender income of his relative (Azalea Adair). He is the rat thoroughly despicable.

"Azalea Adair is a type of the tenderly nursed lady of the old regime, but she is drained of her resources (furnished by the old negro) by her impossible relative.

"In the end there is a dramatic and mysterious murder, the victim being Major Caswell. The 'snapper' comes in the last paragraph, revealing the slayer by a bare intimation. The whole scheme is to show that an absolutely prosaic and conventional town (such as Nashville) can equal San Francisco, Bagdad, or Paris when it comes to a human story.

"The beginning of this story is not written yet—there will be 2 or 3 pages containing references to Frank Norris's lines in which the words occur 'think of anything happening in Nashville, Tennessee.' I have to look this up in Putnam's Magazine.

"It will work out all right."

Just in case Editor Griffeth hoped that he had changed his ways, O. Henry disenchanted him by adding two postscripts: "P.S. Your money back if you want it. P.S.S. Send the dough to the Caledonia." Whatever Griffeth's subsequent travail in obtaining the story, it must have been worth it.

The labors of those who believed, and paid for their belief, that O. Henry was capable of converting himself into a novelist (Jack London had just turned the trick with great success), were much less fruitful. O. Henry had finally given in to the urgings of those who thought he had the artistic and physical stamina to write a novel after resisting the idea for several years. Once he complained to Bill Williams, his future Boswell, about people who pressed the project on him. He had just come from a gathering where, he said, he had been "given more advice than an only child." He added:

"Now, tonight, one of the outfit suggested that I ought to write a novel—yes, why didn't I try my hand at a novel?—thought I could put over something big. The idiot! I didn't say anything but I'll tell you, Bill, why I have never undertaken to write a novel and probably never will.

"It's as simple as 'Mary had a little lamb.' It was never intended that I should write novels. I wasn't cut out on that pattern. I was designed, created and set going to write short stories, and as long as I stick to that I will have my measure of success; but if I wander off into some other field I'll get lost just as sure as we two are sitting here. . . . I couldn't write a novel anyway; I would lose interest in the story before I could finish it. I have to do stories which can be wound up and disposed of quickly, at one sitting if possible."[3]

His conversion may have come about because of the $1,500 advance which Doubleday dangled in front of him for a novel. He never could turn down a cash advance. And momentarily, according to Sara, he got excited about the idea. With the projected novel, she later told an interviewer, "he planned to do something better than he had ever done before, which was the story of his own life as only he could tell it."[4]

The only work he ever did on the project, however, was a long letter on the nature of autobiographical fiction (quoted below) and the selection of a title, *The Rat Trap,* which apparently conveyed his feelings on the human condition.

His novelistic ambitions had been placed in the care of Harry Peyton Steger, a Doubleday executive with extraordinary sympathy for his literary ward. A native Texan and a Rhodes scholar, Steger occupied an apartment across the hall from O.

Henry's room at the Caledonia. He became such a close personal friend that he acted as Margaret's guardian for a time after her father's death.

A considerable part of Steger's energy was devoted to promoting O. Henry's career during the last two years of the latter's life; he persuaded O. Henry to sit for his first and only photographic portrait, and even cajoled him into being interviewed by the New York *Times*.

George MacAdam, then the *Times*'s top cityside reporter, later recalled that it took six weeks to track down and corner O. Henry even with Steger's blessing, with "O. Henry using as the old dodges—'out,' 'previous engagement,' 'up to the ears in work,' etc. Despairing of making an engagement, Mr. Steger, one afternoon, first ascertaining over the telephone that the quarry was in his apartment at the Caledonia, led me thither, pointed out the door, and revealed the countersign, one loud knock followed by two quick taps. This was the author's appointed signal that Desirables were without."[5]

In the story published April 4, 1909, MacAdam wrote that "I can heartily subscribe to the adjective but not to the noun in O. Henry's phrase of self-portraiture. [He had described himself more than once as looking like a 'healthy butcher.'] He surely does look 'healthy'—short, stocky, broad-shouldered, ruddy-faced, clear-eyed, and none of his hair missing. He has none of the wan intellectuality, none of the pale aestheticisms that are conventional parts of the makeup of literary lions that disport themselves at afternoon tea parties. One can readily see that he is the natural father of 'the moral reflection that life is made up of sobs, sniffles, and smiles, with sniffles predominating,' which moral reflection is culled from 'The Gift of the Magi' and is the thread upon which most of his stories are strung.

"One more 'aside.' O. Henry has a way of smiling with both mouth and eyes when he says something that you are quite sure is the truth, and of looking solemnly straight-faced when he says something that you more than half suspect is josh. This is offered as a possible key to the interview. . . ."[6]

O. Henry must have been looking "solemnly straight-faced" during much of that session with the *Times* reporter.

First off, he cut five years off his age and gave MacAdam his birth date as 1867. Similar inaccuracies and significant omissions marked the entire accounting O. Henry gave of his life to date. He blandly informed MacAdam that he started his career on the Houston *Post,* then published *The Rolling Stone,* instead of the other way around. His weeks as a fugitive in New Orleans and later in Honduras and his stay in the Ohio Penitentiary were all jauntily concealed, with dates and facts purposely misstated; his account was not entirely a fabrication, merely a biographical mélange. It is quoted largely because it shows a professional storyteller's ability to create a fairly plausible blend of fact and fiction.

After *The Rolling Stone* folded, O. Henry said, "a friend of mine who had a little money—wonderful thing that, isn't it, a friend with a little money—suggested that I join him in a trip to Central America, whither he was going with the intention of entering the fruit business. Well, it takes a long time and costs a lot of money to learn how the little banana grows. We didn't have quite enough of the latter, and so never did learn the whole secret of the banana's development.

"See any revolutions? No, but I discovered plenty of the finest rum you ever tasted. Most of the time I spent knocking around among the Consuls and the refugees.

"The banana plantation faded into nothing; I drifted back to Texas. In Austin I got a job in a drug store. That was a rotten two weeks. They made me draw soda water, and I gave up.

"Let me see: after the soda water I think there came the highball stage. I went to New Orleans and took up literary work in earnest. . . . It was during these New Orleans days that I adopted my pen name. I said to a friend: 'I am going to send out some stuff. I don't know if it amounts to much, so I want to get a literary alias. Help me pick out a good one.' He suggested that we get a newspaper and pick a name from the first list of notables that we found in it. In the society columns we found the account of a fashionable ball. We looked down the list and my eye lighted on the name Henry. 'That'll do for a last name,' said I. 'Now for a first name. I want something short. None of your three-syllable names for me.' 'Why don't you use a plain initial, then?' asked my friend. 'Good,' said I; 'O is about the easiest letter written and O it is.'"

After that, he said, he "drifted around the country" and finally wound up in New York.

He was extremely modest on the subject of his work and said he considered himself a failure as a writer. "I always have the feeling that I want to get back somewhere, but I don't know just where it is.

"My stories? No, they don't satisfy me. I see them in print and I wonder why people like them. I wait till they come out in book form, hoping that they may look better to me then. But they don't. It depresses me to have people point me out or introduce me as 'a celebrated author.' It seems like such a big label for such picayune goods.

"Sometimes I feel that I'd like to get into some business; perhaps some clerkship; some place where I could see that I was doing something tangible, something worth while."

At the end of the interview, however, his ego had revived sufficiently for him to announce somewhat grandly, and certainly with excessive optimism considering that he hadn't written a line, that his first novel was being published "in the fall." Furthermore, "you may quote me as saying that it is going to be a good one. I've always had a desire for style. In this novel I'm going to give particular attention to style, also to character and plot. These really are the essential things in a novel. Tell the world that this novel will be worth a dollar and a half of any man's money."[7]

Presumably this was happy news for Harry Steger. In an article for *World's Work* written during his publicity campaign of the spring of 1909, the Doubleday executive declared that the body of O. Henry's work constituted a sort of American version of Balzac's *Human Comedy,* that his stories were written in ragtime tempo, in the language of the streets, but when viewed as a whole gave the effect of grand opera. He also asserted that O. Henry was now the "most popular short-story writer in America."[8]

It was to this enthusiast that O. Henry directed a long letter detailing his plans for the novel, which from the evidence of that letter would have been the most serious, exhaustive effort of his writing career.

"My idea," he wrote Steger, "is to write the story of a man—an individual, not a type—but a man who, at the same time, I want to represent a 'human nature type,' if such a person could exist. The story will teach no lesson, inculcate no moral, advance no theory.

"I want it to be something that it won't or can't be—but as near as I can make it—the *true* record of a man's thoughts, his description of his misadventures and adventures, his *true* opinions of life as he has seen it and his *absolutely honest* deductions, comments, and views upon the different phases of life that he passes through.

"I do not remember ever to have read an autobiography, a biography, or a piece of fiction that told the *truth.* Of course, I have read stuff such as Rousseau and Zola and George Moore; and various memoirs that were supposed to be window panes in their respective breasts; but, mostly, all of them were either liars, actors or posers. (Of course, I'm not trying to belittle the greatness of their literary expression.)

"All of us have to be prevaricators, hypocrites and liars every day of our lives; otherwise the social structure would fall into pieces the first day. We must act in one another's presence just as we must wear clothes. It is for the best.

"The trouble about writing the truth has been that the writers have kept in their minds one or another or all three thoughts that made a handicap—they were trying either to do a piece of immortal literature, or to shock the public or to please editors. Some of them succeeded in all three, but they did not write the *truth.* Most autobiographies are insincere from beginning to end. About the only chance for the truth to be told is in fiction.

"It is well understood that 'all the truth' cannot be told in print—but how about 'nothing but the truth'? That's what I want to do.

"I want the man who is telling the story to tell it—not as he would to a reading public or a confessor—but something in this way: Suppose he were marooned on an island in mid-ocean with no hope of ever being rescued; and, in order to pass away some of the time he should tell a story *to himself* embodying his adventure and experiences and opinions. Having a certain respect for himself (let us hope) he would leave out the 'realism' that he would have no chance of selling in the market; he would omit the lies and self-conscious poses, and would turn out to his one auditor something real and true.

"So, as truth is not to be found in history, autobiography, press reports (nor at the bottom of an H. G. Wells), let us hope that fiction may be the means of bringing out a few grains of it.

"The 'hero' of the story will be a man born and 'raised' in a somnolent Southern town. His education is about a common school one, but he learns afterward from reading and life. I'm going to try to give him a 'style' in narrative and speech—the best I've got in the shop. I'm going to take him through the main phases of life—wild adventure, city, society, something of the 'underworld' and among many characteristic planes of the phases. I want him to acquire all the sophistication, that experience can give him, and always preserve his individual honest *human* view, and have him tell the *truth* about everything.

"It is time to say now that by the 'truth' I don't mean the objectionable stuff that so often masquerades under the name. I mean true opinions, a true estimate of all things as they seem to the 'hero.' If you find a word or suggestive line or sentence in any of my copy, you cut it out and deduct it from the royalties.

"I want this man to be a man of natural intelligence, of individual character, absolutely open and broad minded; and show how the Creator of the earth has got him in a rat trap—put him there 'willy nilly' (you know the Omar phrase): and then I want to show what he does about it. There is always the eternal question from the Primal Source—'What are you going to do about it?'

"Please don't think for the half of a moment that the story is going to be anything of an autobiography. I have a distinct character in my mind for the part. . . ."[9]

Despite the disavowal, it was apparent that the novel would be autobiographical. The letter is quoted at length because it is perhaps the most self-revealing prose O. Henry ever wrote. It is also one of the few of his surviving letters in which the facetious tone, the voice of the performer, the self-deprecatory and self-conscious joshing of the comedian, are entirely absent.

It seems obvious that O. Henry was deadly earnest about writing such a novel, about creating something that was lasting and would speak for him, he thought, as none of his short stories could. Some of his friends and one or two of his biographers indicated a belief that he was using the projected novel as bait for advances from the publisher. The tone of the letter to Steger, however, conveys a deeply felt ambition, the desire to abandon the role of troubadour to the sidewalks of New York and the byways of the Southwest, to strip away O. Henry and reveal the William Sydney Porter underneath.

If his health had not started to decline, he would undoubtedly have made the effort. But in trying to break out of the "rat trap" he considered his own life to have been, he might well have fallen into another trap, the same one that snared Mark Twain when he wanted to be serious. The public was conditioned to accept him as an entertainer; O. Henry as a philosopher would have bewildered and vexed a readership that asked only a simple but well-told tale from him. And it would have required a tremendous psychological effort from him, obviously, to face himself and his life squarely and pitilessly. A lifetime of evasion and covering up was poor preparation for ruthless self-examination, though it might have seemed to him a welcome opportunity for purging himself.

As to the deterioration of his health, he continued to display himself to the world as a heedless optimist, despite occasional complaints about feeling badly and sleeping poorly. He also continued drinking at the old steady rate, though it was the worst possible thing for a man in his condition. He overworked himself, turning out eight short stories, working on a musical comedy with a collaborator, and collecting the volume published as *Roads of Destiny*. By his own account, and that of others, he refused to take his doctors' warnings seriously. Few people, including his wife and possibly even himself, had any idea how ill he was. He was inclined to evade the truth by blaming his troubles on neurasthenia and hypochondria. But, tragically, he was a false hypochondriac.

His attitude toward the matter was delineated by a first-person story titled "Let Me Feel Your Pulse," which ironically was published a month after his death. In the story, he tells of going to a new doctor for treatment:

"'How long has it been since you took any alcohol into your system?' he asked.

"Turning my head sidewise, I answered, 'Oh, quite a while.'

"He was a young doctor, somewhere between twenty and forty. He wore heliotrope socks, but he looked like Napoleon. I liked him immensely.

"'Now,' said he, 'I am going to show you the effect of alcohol upon your circulation.' I think it was 'circulation' he said; though it may have been 'advertising.'

"He bared my left arm to the elbow, brought out a bottle of whiskey, and gave me a drink. He began to look more like Napoleon. I began to like him better.

"Then he put a tight compress on my upper arm, stopped my pulse with his fingers, and squeezed a rubber bulb connected with an apparatus on a stand that looked like a thermometer. The mercury jumped up and down without seeming to stop anywhere; but the doctor said it registered two hundred and thirty-seven or one hundred and sixty-five or some such number.

"'Now,' said he, 'you see what alcohol does to the blood-pressure.'

"'It's marvelous,' said I, 'but do you think it a sufficient test? Have one on me, and let's try the other arm.'" But no!

"Then he grasped my hand. I thought I was doomed and he

was saying goodbye. But all he wanted to do was to jab a needle into the end of a finger and compare the red drop with a lot of fifty-cent poker chips that he had fastened to a card.

" 'It's the haemoglobin test,' he explained. 'The color of your blood is wrong.'

" 'Well,' said I, 'I know it should be blue; but this is a country of mixups. Some of my ancestors were cavaliers; but they got thick with some people on Nantucket Island, so—'

" 'I mean,' said the doctor, 'that the shade of red is too light.'

" 'Oh,' I said, 'it's a case of matching instead of matches.'

"The doctor pounded me severely in the region of the chest. . . . Then he looked grave and mentioned a string of grievances that the flesh is heir to—mostly ending in 'itis.' I immediately paid him fifteen dollars on account."

Amid all the hilarity at the expense of himself and his diseased organs there is a distinctly autobiographical flavor; likewise the account of what happens next to the narrator, whom the doctor bundles off to "a madhouse in the Catskills," actually, perhaps, what was then known as a "milk farm," or drying-out place for alcoholics. He grimly describes the menu: "phosphoglycerate of lime hash, dog-bread, bromo-seltzer pancakes and nux vomica tea." Later he is placed under the command of a physical therapist "so tall that I was not sure he had a face," and meets a lady novelist named Lulu Lulington, author of *Why Love Loves,* who is making mud pies. Other patients include "architects playing with Noah's arks, ministers reading Darwin's 'Theory of Evolution,' lawyers sawing wood, tired out society ladies talking Ibsen . . . a neurotic millionaire lying asleep on the floor, and a prominent artist drawing a little red wagon around the room." His physician begins to look "a little less like Napoleon," but the narrator obeys his instructions and next is packed off to the Long Island shore, then to a mountain resort, where a country doctor cures him by tricking him into taking long walks.

The solution to his own problems wasn't quite that simple. At the urging of Steger and other friends he was finally coaxed into returning to North Carolina for a long rest cure to be supervised by his wife and daughter. Sara later wrote that she was shocked by his pale and haggard appearance and swore they wouldn't be separated again. Taking long walks in the wooded mountains together, she would recall, "we came very close in the days that followed." One day, she said, "he threw his arms around me and said, 'It's just like old times, isn't it?' "[10]

After a few weeks of a more regular, outdoor life it seemed to his wife and daughter that O. Henry was recovering. Margaret would remember moments, as she wrote, "when he seemed miraculously freed from the hovering shadow of ill health that clouded the last few years. I have known him to sit at the piano and strum the accompaniment to a gay darky song, singing in dialect, with only me as audience."

Possibly as a jab at her stepmother, Margaret added, "The intrusion of another person would precipitate a hollow silence."

"In one of these lighter moods," she continued, "he brought a mandolin and a guitar home. He had taught me guitar accompaniment, so we spent many an hour reviving half-forgotten tunes."

There were other times when he succumbed to the melancholia that dogged his post-prison years and only increased with the onset of his internal disorders. Then, as Margaret Porter recorded, "a shadow would descend and he would be plunged into silence, black silences, the portent of which he alone could know; for, although there is understanding, it is not humanly possible to accompany one of those dark journeyings."

One such occasion, she poignantly remembered, was "toward the close of the last year," on an evening when "he had been particularly gay during dinner . . . and afterward had entertained the household with impersonations of well known people. From the elevation of the first landing of the stairs in the great living room [of Sara's mother's home] he called out celebrities: 'Buffalo Bill.' His make-up for this was the index of one hand held across his upper lip, the forefinger of the other meeting it at right angles, bisecting his chin. Down the list he went. Never was his mood lighter.

"Then, suddenly, someone entered or left the room, attention was momentarily taken from him, and when it returned he was not there.

"I found him sitting in the far corner of the dark porch overlooking the mountains. There was no moon and the night was black. I felt that it was no less dark than the sudden depression that had seized him. A strong wind blew steadily from the mountains. The night seemed filled with premonition. I felt that he sensed it too. I could not—and knew that he would not have me—speak. I sat on the steps near him. After a long time, still without words, we got up and went together into the house."[11]

After a month or two of recuperation O. Henry felt strong enough to start writing again. To his Doubleday editor, Steger, he wrote that he felt so much better that he would "be able to write a novel with each hand simultaneously in a short time." He had taken an office in downtown Asheville, about six miles from the Coleman home, in the Legal Building. Down the hall was the office of Judge Thomas A. Jones, Sr., an elderly and jovial lawyer with a fondness for telling and listening to stories. Jones became O. Henry's closest friend in Asheville and also acted as his legal consultant; the only fee he would accept was a pair of gold cuff buttons.

"There wasn't a day," Judge Jones later reminisced, "when he wouldn't come into my quarters and talk about what was on his mind. He never seemed to understand his popularity. Just couldn't account for it and looked upon literature as a meal ticket."

One day O. Henry expressed his vexation with the medical profession, telling Judge Jones, "Recently the doctors have been fixing me out with a number of complications that cost money. There doesn't seem to be in the pathological record a single within-the-reach-of-all disorder that fits my case. . . . I made application for a cheap symptom, but the medical sharks cannot supply any in the present market.

"On that table by the window you will find the first pages of a story entitled 'An Experiment in Neurasthenia'"—apparently the one he retitled "Let Me Feel Your Pulse"—"and as my legal adviser you are entitled to know the stuff is biographical. With the returns from that story I propose to pay my doctor bills."

Aside from the subject of doctors, Judge Jones said, "there was nothing harsh about his humor. I never heard him utter a joke that would wound." The judge quoted one of O. Henry's favorite stories: One weekend he visited a friend who had a manor house up in the hills back of New England. The room in which he slept was unduly spacious and contained at one end a large fireplace. At breakfast the host asked his distinguished guest how he liked the sleeping accommodations. 'Extremely,' answered Porter. 'The open fire was so damned hot that I was blistered and the bed was so far north that my breath formed icicles. A man occupying a revolving chair in the middle of the room could be fairly comfortable. Never before have I met a barbecue and a blizzard under the same roof.' "[12]

In all, however, the return to his native mountains was a depressing experience. He was finding, like Thomas Wolfe, then a nine-year-old boy growing up in the streets of Asheville, that "you can't go home again."

Often Sara or Margaret would enter his office and find him, not working, only staring out the window at the mountains which circle Asheville.

In his boredom he even resumed an old boyhood pastime of chicken watching. He considered himself, in fact, something of a chicken expert or chicken sociologist. The structure of the chicken social system, the ramifications of the pecking order, the haremlike groupings around the rooster, were all worthy of the most intensive study in O. Henry's opinion.

Henry Steger came down on a visit and joined him one evening in observing the nightly rituals of the hen-roost. "See those old sisters fussing and fuming about who is to sit next to the rooster," he pointed out with the delight most of his contemporaries would reserve for the Floradora Sextette. "Listen at 'em quarrel and watch 'em peck each other. Old Chanticleer is right in the middle of them, with a long row of worshipful sisters on either side. Lots more fun than to watch a bunch of people go to bed."[13]

During the autumn of 1909 he spent more time tramping through the mountain woods with Margaret, each with a gun under the arm, but hunters in appearance only. They shot, Margaret wrote, "only at inanimate targets, though troops of rabbits scurried through the dry leaves and squirrels were busy storing away nuts. It was almost as though he felt that life was too precious a thing to steal from any creature. He had never joined in the so-called sports that involve killing."

The "reverence for life" apparently had increased as O. Henry seemed to sense the approach of his own death. One cold late-autumn afternoon she met him as he returned from a walk in the woods carrying something in his left hand. "It was a dead bird, warm and limp," Margaret recalled. "His expression was rueful, and his laugh short and not quite steady as he said that he had aimed at a cornstalk and killed a songbird. We were near the house. He stooped quickly, made a hollow in the moist earth, laid the bird on a bed of leaves, covered it with earth and leaves. To the other member of the household"—a backhander aimed at Sara, of whom Margaret was somewhat jealous—"who joined us, he replied that he had had a 'fine walk.' But I knew that the joy of the day, for him, was buried beneath the leaves at his feet."[14]

After several months O. Henry felt he had recovered sufficiently to return to New York and take up a new phase of his career. There was a touching moment of parting with his daughter, as she described it: "For a few short minutes on the day of his departure we found ourselves unexpectedly alone. 'Bill,' he began—he had always called me 'Bill,' 'Jim,' or 'Pete,' seldom Margaret—'Bill.' It was an attempt to put into words all the unspoken things of the past.

"In it I sensed his realization of the futility of attempting to express the emotions that crowd the moment of parting. Also I felt, as I believe he did, that this parting was going to be different from all the others. Words are such impotent things in the face of parting. 'I have seen,' I managed to tell him, 'and understood.' There flashed across his face an expression of inestimable relief and one of his rare smiles. We did not meet again."[15]

Margaret's own life was brief and tragic. After her father's death an attempt was made to launch her as "Miss O. Henry," until the editors eager to capitalize on the relationship realized that she had not inherited her father's talent. There was an unhappy first marriage to a newspaper cartoonist named Oscar Cesare. After less than a year, she left Cesare and went to Reno for a divorce.

From Reno she proceeded to Hollywood, where she entered negotiations with a motion picture studio for the film rights to O. Henry's stories. In the middle of the negotiations she fell seriously ill, a victim of tuberculosis like her mother, her paternal grandmother and her maternal grandfather. On the urging of friends she went out to live in the California desert, near the town of Banning, where she bought a few acres and had a bungalow built. She was befriended by a young English writer named Guy Sartin, who came over to her home and read to her day after day while she struggled against the disease.

In the spring of 1927, Margaret suffered a severe attack of coughing and knew she wouldn't last much longer. She and Sartin were married in her bungalow, and three days later she died, but not before leaving all the proceeds of her father's literary estate to the bridegroom-widower. She was thirty-eight years old when she died.

His daughter and only child was not the most successful of O. Henry's creations, and no doubt he was conscious of his failures as a father when they parted on the station platform in Asheville. Vain regrets were not uppermost, however, as he renewed his pursuit of a more substantial livelihood in New York. He was glowing with optimism at the moment. There was a seemingly bright possibility that his name would now grace the marquees of Broadway; the brief career of O. Henry, playwright, was under way.

Chapter 10. A Dalliance with Broadway

The theory that a novelist or short-story writer could convert himself overnight, and with little additional effort, to writing directly for the theater was a long time dying. It did not seem to occur to theatrical producers that there was a sizable difference between writing for the printed page and composing scenes and dialogue to be spoken on the stage. Mark Twain and Bret Harte had been coaxed into collaborating on a stage play which collapsed behind the footlights and under a barrage from the drama critics. Jack London had also taken the plunge, which turned out badly. Ambrose Bierce was briefly recruited and quickly disillusioned. Henry James was tried and found wanting.

Even so, O. Henry became the willing victim of Broadway's professional optimists. In the first place, writing plays was ten times as lucrative as writing short stories or novels. The author received a share of the ticket price for every person who entered the theater. Secondly, there was something alluring about working in the theater: the herd warmth of collaboration. Instead of the lonely struggle to create stories in a hotel room, there was the team effort of writing and producing a play and the necessary association with amusing and glamorous people. Thirdly, there was the prospective thrill of having one's words spoken, one's characters literally brought to life and fleshed out. And not least, there were the generous advances dangled by producers searching feverishly for plays at a time when the theater was booming and every marquee on Broadway was lighted the year round.

One of those talent hunters was George Tyler, a top producer whose fixation for several years was the dramatist potential in O. Henry. "His ardor," Alexander Woollcott, the owlish critic of the New York *World,* observed, "has always been addressed to growing a dramatist where only a novelist grew before." Tyler kept pestering O. Henry to write a play whenever they met and through a constant barrage of notes. "Every O. Henry story naturally prompted such a hope. Every one of them fairly tingled with the stuff of which plays are made, and much of that stuff, rented or borrowed or blandly stolen, has since found its way into theaters all over the world."[1]

O. Henry's flirtation with the theater began, however, under the auspices of another producer. It came about in the spring of 1909 while O. Henry was living alone in New York and was supposedly concentrating on the novel which he announced would be published that fall. Perhaps it came as a welcome relief from that unshouldered task when Harry Askin, the head of the theatrical trust in Chicago, the theater then being carved up into regional fiefdoms, proposed that a musical comedy be fashioned from one of O. Henry's stories, "To Him Who Waits," which had been published in January in *Collier's Weekly.*

Askin proposed that the musical be written in collaboration by O. Henry and Franklin P. Adams (better known as F.P.A.), who conducted a column in the *World's* celebrated page opposite editorial. Adams was a droll but meticulous craftsman, with a Yankee face and a Yankee acerbity, who was later renowned as one of the wits of the Algonquin Round Table.

A friend told O. Henry, "Adams says he got the idea for his share of the play from a check for advance royalties. Where did you get your idea for your share?"

"From the *hope* for a check for advance royalties," O. Henry replied with a grin.[2]

As Adams later related in a magazine article ("Lo, the Poor Musical Comedy," which oddly enough appeared in *Success Magazine,* October 1910), he and his collaborator were set to their task with little guidance from Producer Askin except that he required a lead role for an actor who was "a fast talker, dances very well and sings excellently." Askin further instructed Adams, "You're inexperienced and you don't know. I've been in this business twenty-seven years. We need comedy here. Laughs is what we want all the time."

A composer named A. Baldwin Sloane was engaged to write the music, but O. Henry and Adams would be expected to supply the lyrics, an exacting minor art form which could be expected to confound the inexperienced.

The idea of the collaboration was first presented to Adams, who was then nominated to persuade O. Henry to join in the project. The fact that Askin sent the latter a check for $500 was really the only persuasion O. Henry needed, especially since he told a friend that he had noticed "some suspicious tracks outside the door that closely resembled those made by Lupus Americanus." Put less facetiously, O. Henry, as usual, was broke. The thought of a quick killing on Broadway was delectable.

"I called on O. Henry," Adams recalled in his memoir on the collaboration, "and we discussed it at length. His other pseudonym was Barkis. We agreed to collaborate, both of us to work on the dialogue and both on the lyrics. And as it happened it was almost a complete collaboration. Hardly an independent line was written."

Neither, Adams said, was inclined to slough off the job as unworthy of their talents. "We were interested in the piece and anxious to please the manager, who had gone out of his way to get us. . . . O. Henry and I would convene nearly every afternoon and talk the thing over, outlining scenes, making notes of lines of dialogue, tentative ideas for lyrics, etc. . . . We enjoyed working at this time. It was fun blocking the plans and O. Henry was simply shedding whimsical ideas for lines and situations. . . ."[3]

In the first flush of inspiration, they were also tossing off the words for such forgettable tunes as "In Yucatan," "Let Us Sing," "Love Is All That Matters," "Caramba," "Dear Yankee Maid," "Little Old Main Street" and "You Will Always Be My Sweetheart."

As everyone knows who has survived the bear-pit process of turning out a play, the preparatory stages are the easiest. Ideas flow, situations seem to spring to life, and putting the words on paper seems a cinch. The collaborators love each other like brothers and guffaw at each other's jokes. Getting the play all written down, scene by scene, and then having it approved by a producer who may or may not be semi-literate is the hard part. And O. Henry was not strikingly well equipped for an essay in dramaturgy. His tastes in the theater ran to vaudeville and the burlesque house.

The first thing the collaborators did was to completely discard the plot of "To Him Who Waits" and start from scratch. They decided to base their comedy on an anthropological expedition to Central America which was investigating the theory that American Indians were descended from the Aztecs. O. Henry wanted to call the comedy *The Enthusiastics,* to which the producers objected as sounding like a high-school production. Finally he came up with the suggestion that it be titled *Lo!*—from Pope's "Lo, the poor Indian" couplet—which was certainly short enough to fit any marquee. The producers accepted that idea.

O. Henry and Adams worked separately in the mornings and met in the afternoons either at Adams' apartment at 16 Manhattan Place or O. Henry's room at the Caledonia. Then they put the play together, scene by scene, lyric by lyric, and sent it along to Askins' office.

One early difficulty arose from their mistaken belief about the way musical comedy tunes were concocted. They thought the libretto came first, and that the composer wrote the music to fit the words. Instead, as Adams recalled, "most of our songs were constructed to fit tunes the composer had already written"—which was at least twice as difficult, especially for a pair of tyros.

Adams believed that O. Henry was "fairly lazy" by nature—perhaps he did not realize that his collaborator was also a very sick man—but credited him with pouring all his available energy into the project. "O. Henry never worked harder or more conscientiously in his life. He lost weight. He worried."

They began working nights as well as days on *Lo!* when the producers rejected the first three scripts submitted and they had to grind away on a fourth version. O. Henry memorialized their exasperations and frustrations in a bit of verse:

"Dramatization is vexation;
Revision is as bad;
This comedy perplexes me
And managers drive me mad."

All the time, they were working under intense pressure, since the producers wanted to take the show on a tryout tour of various middle western towns that summer, then bring it to New York for the 1909–10 season.

Thanks to Adams, some of the lyrics of *Lo!* survive, and compared to some of the torrential slush that appeared on Broadway they indicated a certain wry, witty talent. One recitative went as follows:

GIRL: Little drops of water, little grains of sand,
Make the mighty ocean and the pleasant land.
BOY: Little drops of seltzer, little drops of rye,
Make the pleasant highball, when a man is dry.
BOTH: It's the little things that count, everywhere you go;
Trifles make a large amount. Don't you find it so?
GIRL: Little deeds of kindness, little words of love,
Make our life an Eden, like the heaven above.
BOY: Little drops of promise, made to little wives,
Make us little fibbers all our little lives.

The script was finally made satisfactory to the producers by mid-summer, and it was sent into rehearsal in Chicago. Adams went out to provide whatever show-doctoring was necessary while O. Henry stayed in New York hopeful of word that they had struck a bonanza. *Lo!* opened obscurely in Aurora, Illinois, on the night of August 25, 1909, and found a receptive but hardly enthusiastic audience. Adams tinkered a bit with the script, and the *Lo!* company then departed for a fourteen-week tour of the Middle West. On its journey it played one-night stands in Waukegan, Illinois, Janesville, Wisconsin, and St. Joseph, Missouri, among other places classified as "tank towns" by theatrical producers. In Milwaukee it settled down for a whole week's stay. *Lo!* finally expired somewhere in the wilds of Missouri on December 5, and plans for bringing it to Broadway were abandoned.[4]

Little of the effort survived except for the lyrics of a song titled "Snap Shots," which excited a little attention on Tin Pan Alley, and for which Adams credited (or blamed) O. Henry for composing in their entirety:

> Watch out, lovers, when you promenade;
> When you kiss and coo, in the deep moon shade.
> When you're close together in the grape-vine swing,
> When you are a-courting or philandering.
> Mabel, Maud and Ann, Nelli, May and Fan,
> Keep your eyes open for the Snap Shot Man!
> Snap! Shots! Hear the shutter close!
> What a world of roguishness the little snapper shows!
> Click! Click! Caught you unaware—
> Snap Shot Man'll get you if you don't care!

At least O. Henry, in his first theatrical venture, could claim to have invented the shortest title for a show in musical comedy history.

Even while *Lo!* was being rehearsed in Chicago, George Tyler in New York was trying to persuade O. Henry to write a dramatic play on his own. "A Retrieved Reformation," the story of the safe-cracker which he wrote in the Ohio State Penitentiary, would make the basis of an excellent play, Tyler believed.

The clincher for O. Henry, as usual, was the $500 which Tyler was willing to advance on the project.

As with the never-to-be-written novel, he struggled in vain. The O. Henry of his prime, of 1904 instead of 1909, might well have succeeded, particularly since he had acquired some knowledge of the mechanics of theater from collaborating on *Lo!* Alexander Woollcott, who examined O. Henry's brief theatrical career at length and with the insights afforded by his friendship with Franklin P. Adams, believed that O. Henry simply could not initiate such a project by himself. "O. Henry was a little brother to that forlorn fellow who figures in Augustus Thomas's reminiscences and whose successive lodgings in New York were always traceable by stray bits of mss. which never progressed beyond the brave beginning: 'Act I. Scene I. A Ruined Garden.' To that family of dramatists O. Henry belonged. It was a large family. It still is."

Even while he grappled with the problems of turning the hapless Jimmy Valentine into a stage hero, O. Henry was, all unknowing, and all but unrecompensed, on the outer fringes of the discovery of a theatrical gold mine. That little story of his, "A Retrieved Reformation," was the beginning of a Mother Lode stretching from New York to Hollywood and all the tributary centers of the entertainment business. It was the genesis of what become known as the "crook play," the underworld drama, and eventually the gangster picture. Such plays and films have made millions of dollars in the past half-century, but only $500 for the man who unwittingly tapped the bonanza. His particular contribution was to take a humanistic view of the outlaw, show that even a criminal was capable of good works and self-sacrifice, and thereby make him a merchandisable item in the theatrical market.

He had gone to Asheville for his rest cure by the time George Tyler decided that "A Retrieved Reformation" would never be converted into a stage play, at least not by O. Henry. Tyler offered O. Henry a small flat payment for the dramatic rights to the story, which would then be turned over to a professional playwright.

O. Henry took the offer to his new legal adviser, Judge Jones, who recalled that "I advised him not to sell the dramatic rights without a percentage of the royalties. He said the yarn was not worth a nickel more than $250 and that he was satisfied."[5]

But even while surrendering the project to other hands, O. Henry would not abandon his hopes of writing for the theater. It was really his last hope, presuming that he realized he no longer had the vitality to turn out enough stories to make a living for himself and his family. One hit on Broadway would be his annuity. So he wrote Tyler:

"I hereby transfer to you the entire dramatic rights etc. of the story you write me about—the title is 'A Retrieved Reformation.' I am glad to be able to hand over anything you might be able to use. But I want you to let the $500 that I owe you still remain owing, for I'm going to write that play yet and soon.

"I've been in bad shape for a long time both as to writing and refunding. I'm wrestling with a bad case of neurasthenia (so the doctor says) but I'm getting back into shape again. I am living about six miles out of Asheville and spend most of the time climbing hills and living out of doors. I have knocked off twenty pounds weight. I eat like a drayman and don't know what booze tastes like. In fact I'll be better than ever in a week or two. I got out the scenario of 'The World and the Door' [a short story of his he was proposing to dramatize] some days ago and began to plan out the acts and scenes. I'll surprise you with it as soon as I get down to hard work.

"I deeply appreciate your leniency and kindness and intend to 'come up to scratch' yet with the goods. So the dramatic rights to 'Retrieved Reformation' are yours and if you strike another story you like take it too. In the meantime I owe you $500 and am going to pay it. . . ."[6]

With the rights to "A Retrieved Reformation" secured, Tyler moved swiftly to bring it to the stage. He contracted for Paul Armstrong, known along Broadway as "the Hair-Trigger Playwright," a sound and experienced craftsman, to write the adaptation. Armstrong, a tall, broad-shouldered, ruddy-faced man who wore a wide-brimmed black hat on his rambles around Times

Square, had recently experienced difficulties with an adaptation. He had made a play out of the Bret Harte story, "Salomy Jane," which was one of the hits of the 1907 season. Unfortunately he had not cleared the rights to the story with the Harte estate and he was being sued by the writer's heirs.

There were two versions of just how the O. Henry story, titled *Alias Jimmy Valentine* for Tyler's presentation, came to be written and produced with lightning speed—a matter of several weeks from contract signing to dress rehearsal. One was that Armstrong, who had written "Salomy Jane" in ten days after locking himself into a room at the Algonquin, cloistered himself in the warden's office at the Tombs to be permeated in the atmosphere of a prison, and emerged in about a week with the finished script. This was Armstrong's version.

Another was that he had collaborated with Wilson Mizner, who subsequently had one of the more protean careers of his time (Klondike gold-rusher, conman, cardsharp, briefly the husband of the heiress to a traction fortune, Florida real estate boomer, playwright, cocaine addict, Hollywood screen writer, and one of the founders of the Brown Derby restaurant in Hollywood) but whose posthumous fame rests chiefly on an endless stream of wisecracks. Mizner, while managing one of the sleaziest hotels in the Times Square district, had written a play called *The Only Law,* which had opened the 1909 season, had been blasted as a vulgar display of "sluts, scoundrels and boobies," and had closed a few days later.

According to the pro-Mizner version of how *Alias Jimmy Valentine* was written, he and Armstrong were commiserating with each other over their misfortunes in a Broadway saloon one day when they decided to collaborate on the O. Henry adaptation. Mizner was still irked at his rough handling by the drama critics; Armstrong was engaged in litigation with the Bret Harte heirs, a situation which prompted one of Mizner's more enduring witticisms. "If you steal from one author, it's plagiarism," he summed it up for Armstrong; "if you steal from many, it's research." Whether or not Mizner contributed to *Alias Jimmy Valentine*—

and much of the play's crackling dialogue, its authentic underworld atmosphere and attitudes sounded as though they had been fabricated by an expert of Mizner's standing—he and Armstrong subsequently collaborated on two other successful plays, *The Deep Purple* and *The Greyhound,* in the same mode.[7]

Armstrong and Mizner, or Armstrong alone, did a skillful job of converting the O. Henry story into a drama of redemption. They changed O. Henry's story somewhat by having the reformed safe-cracker use his burglar's tools to open a bank vault in which his fiancee's niece is trapped. The essential sentimentality of the story was concealed in its dramatic form by the soundness of the characterizations and the crackling dialogue.

Alias Jimmy Valentine opened to approving reviews and standing-room-only audiences. Among its leading players were H. B. Warner as Jimmy Valentine (later Christ in C. B. DeMille's *King of Kings* silent film) and Laurette Taylor, beginning her distinguished career, as the ingenue. *Alias Jimmy Valentine* thus began a long and lucrative run which, as Alexander Woollcott commented, was to "tweak and tantalize playgoers all over America, England, France, Spain and South Africa; and which was to breed a very epidemic of plays in which no self-respecting protagonist would think of approaching the first act without a neat murder or at least a bank robbery to his credit."[8]

Possibly as a goad to O. Henry's playwrighting ambitions, Producer Tyler every week mailed a copy of the box-office returns and another of the royalty payments due Armstrong (averaging about $800 a week) to O. Henry in Asheville. His point, thus sharpened, was that O. Henry had made $250 out of a venture from which Armstrong as adapter earned an estimated $100,000 —and the story, the plot, the characters were all O. Henry's, all but the necessary carpentry work of dramatization.

There was no doubt that O. Henry's appetite was whetted by the financial statements coming from New York every week. Indirectly, perhaps, they were responsible for his death. It would have been better for his health if he had stayed quietly in Asheville living a regular non-alcoholic life; this was the worst possible time for him to be lured back to New York, its temptations and frustrations.

Yet O. Henry didn't envy Armstrong, nor was he embittered by the personally profitless success of *Alias Jimmy Valentine*. The extraordinary generosity of his nature was illuminated by his legal adviser, Judge Jones, who went up to New York later to visit O. Henry and attend a performance of *Alias Jimmy Valentine* with him. O. Henry, he said, "applauded every act and complimented Armstrong on the dramatization. I learned that the royalties totaled $800 a week, none of which went to Porter. 'Aren't you sorry,' I asked, 'that you didn't keep a string on some of that easy money?' 'Not at all, Judge,' he replied. 'When a truly great dramatist puts a kick into one of my short stories and gets his money back I'm tickled along my entire vertebrae. The stuff I sold him is nothing compared with what he gave the public. Glad it's a hit.' "[9]

The success of *Alias Jimmy Valentine* did, however, make him determined to duplicate it with his own adaptation of one of his stories, "The World and the Door," which was included in his posthumously published volume *Whirligigs*. It was the romance of a New York broker, who fled to a South American port believing he killed a man in a saloon brawl, and a woman from St. Louis who was also a fugitive and technically guilty, perhaps, of killing her husband. It had the usual O. Henry whiplash ending, and might have had the makings of a romantic drama; certainly it had the possibility of a smashing second-act curtain when one of the presumed murder victims turned up in La Paz and jovially confronted his confused "slayer."

Suddenly O. Henry was eager to return to New York and convert "The World and the Door" into a Broadway success, though there was no reason he couldn't have done the writing in Asheville. To George Tyler, who apparently represented all his hopes at the time, he wrote that "I have been putting in all my time getting in good shape for future campaigns, and doing practically no work at all. Have entirely recovered my health and feel fine and fit. I have done barely enough writing to keep the possum from the door since I've been down here, but I think I've gained greatly thereby.

"Got a little proposition to make to you. If you'll advance me $500, I'll come to New York, establish myself in some quiet rural spot of the metropolis known only to yourself and your emissaries and go to work and finish a play. I will not let my whereabouts or even the fact that I am in the city be known to any one but you; and I will give all my time and energy to the play.

"As collateral, I can only make over to you the dramatic rights of all my stories until the work is done. The new play, 'Alias Jimmy Valentine,' inspired me to believe I can do something for both of us. . . . Of course, if you don't care to do it, it won't affect our future relations. But I want to get into the game, and I'll stick to you exclusively till we try it out."[10]

A few weeks later, early in January 1910, he again wrote Tyler, even more urgently. Tyler was regarded on Broadway as one of the more gentlemanly producers and he was probably netting a couple of thousand a week on *Alias Jimmy Valentine*, but something was making him hesitate about bringing O. Henry to New York. Possibly some of the latter's friends had urged him not to, had pleaded that O. Henry needed more of his rest cure no matter how optimistic his self-diagnosis. Or possibly Tyler wasn't at all sure that O. Henry still had the vitality necessary to turn out a play and see it through all the revisions and wranglings to production. At any rate, he seems to have balked at sending O. Henry a lump sum, which the latter now raised from $500 to $750 on some obscure principle of reversing the usual processes of negotiation—if things are going badly, don't lower your price but bluff it through and raise the ante.

"Why I want the money in a lump sum," he explained in the letter to Tyler, "is to make a quick getaway. Your proposition is better than mine, but it lacks the hastiness and expediency necessary to a big theatrical success."

He insisted that four months in the Carolina mountains had restored his health and the "cirrhosis of the liver, fatty degeneration of the heart and neurasthenia" diagnosed by various doctors were also false rumors. "But," he continued, "I am about as nervous and reflexactionary as the hind leg of a frog as shown in the magazine section of any Sunday newspaper. The country and the mountains have been worth more to me than money–I am almost as strong and tough as a suffragette."

Stopping work "on the order of the old Doctor" had left him with "about as much money lying on hand as was left lying around the box-office at the last performance of *Lo!*"

He then outlined the circumstances behind his eagerness for a "quick getaway"–largely financial as usual. "I owe something in the neighborhood of $500 down here that should and shall be paid before the obsequious porter of the So. Ry. Co. can have the opportunity of brushing the soot off the window-sill of Mr. Pullman's car onto the left knee of my new trousers. I'm not after money now–it's transportation, and a chance that I want. I can't work the proposition out in the short story line; but it's slow, Colonel, slow. I want to get into the real game, and I'll stake my reputation as the best story writer within a radius of Asheville that we can pull it off.

"Here's what I need in order to start things going. I've got to pay up everything here and leave a small bunch of collateral with my long suffering family to enable them to purchase the usual cuisine of persimmons and rabbits for a while. . . . If you will send me the necessary sinews I will start for New York on Wednesday or Thursday of next week. I will, on arrival, secure a room with privileges of bath three flights above, and phone you the next morning. Thenceforth I am yours and Mr. Ford's until results have been accomplished. I will place all my time at your disposal until the play is finished. . . .

"Proviso–Don't give it away to any magazine, or anybody else that I am there. I will be in retirement and working for you as long as may be necessary. My mail will be sent here as it has been, and forwarded there. My family will remain here during the summer. They seem to like the idea of my returning to New York, although I have been reasonably kind to them."

As always he was concerned with what he called his "front,"

his appearance, explaining, "I'm not afraid of New York police and editors; but if I arrive there in a linen suit, with helmet and tennis shoes, what would [Police Chief] Big Bill Edwards do but to shovel me in a cart and dump me into the East River?"

He added that he hated to "make any new dickers" with the magazine editors and be tied down to the delivery of new stories, and "that's why I put the matter so strenuously."

"Tell Oom Paul Armstrong," he added, "that I hope he'll crack the safe for all it's worth in 'Alias Jimmy Valentine' . . . I'm awfully sorry to have to come back to work and write a better play than Mr. Armstrong has—but I need the money—he won't mind."

And there was a postscript asking Tyler to telegraph a $750 money order—"satisfaction guaranteed—or money refunded."[11]

If he complied with the request, Tyler would have $1,250 invested in a flyer on O. Henry's unproven playwriting talent; the $750 plus the $500 previously advanced, and he had heard of O. Henry's hoydenish ways with magazine editors who advanced him money for unwritten stories.

O. Henry followed up the letter with a telegram: "LIKE TO HAVE FUNDS. DO WIRE TODAY. WILL POSITIVELY BE THERE ON TIME. HAVE CUT OUT SPENDING AND CHIANTI."

Then a second wire the same day: "WILL ARRIVE AT NOON MONDAY IF FOUR HUNDRED WIRED TODAY. EXCLUSIVE WORK GUARANTEED UNTIL SATISFACTORY."

Finally, and reluctantly, Tyler wired him $400 as requested in the last telegram, making a total of $900 advanced.

That only brought a third message via Western Union: WIRE BALANCE. AM WAITING AT THE DEPOT.

"So," as Tyler later told Alexander Woollcott, "I wired the balance, but the telephones from the modest and secluded lodgings never came. The first tidings came from a hospital. . . ."[12]

On a day late in January 1910, O. Henry stood on the platform at the Asheville station waiting with his wife and daughter for the Southern Railway train which would carry him away to the

North. Perhaps he felt much as he had the day he left Pittsburgh, also on borrowed money, to go to New York for the first time—older, wiser, sicker, but perhaps equally as hopeful. A new career was opening up. Meanwhile his wife was issuing last-minute instructions on eating and sleeping regularly, staying away from companions who would want him to drink with them. His daughter thought that they all wordlessly expressed "all the unspoken things of the past."

Probably it was a great relief when the northbound train finally came up the tracks; the mountains around Asheville seemed like prison walls keeping him in this quiet southern town, barring him from the exciting reality of life up North. Perhaps he felt as Thomas Wolfe of Asheville would feel some years later when that same train took him away from there. "Now the train was coming," Wolfe wrote in *Of Time and the River*. "Down the powerful shining tracks a half mile away, the huge black snout of the locomotive swung slowly round the magnificent bend and flare of the rails that went into the railway yards of Altamount two miles away. . . . It was his train and it had come to take him to the strange and secret heart of the great North. . . . The road to freedom, solitude and the enchanted promise of the golden cities was now before him. . . . out of the dark heart and mournful mystery of the South forever. . . ."

In a few minutes the train was carrying O. Henry through the labyrinth of passes and over the mountains he would never see again.

Chapter 11. "I Don't Want to Go Home in the Dark"

On that long train ride north, something akin to a sea change seems to have occurred in O. Henry. He had left Asheville on money advanced by George Tyler, pledging the producer, and no doubt himself, that he would seclude himself in New York and concentrate all his energies on writing the stage play of "The World and the Door." He was proud of the fact that he always, eventually, fulfilled his commitments. This last one, and the novel promised Doubleday, would be the exceptions.

Perhaps it was a failure of will, a realization that the effort of writing a play was beyond his present capacities. Or possibly he thought it was something that could be put off, a day or two, a week or two, until he had reacclimated himself to New York. Maybe, on the other hand, he simply fell off the wagon and never managed to clamber back on.

The only other explanation—which would have been entirely out of character—was that he had wangled the $750 advance out of Tyler without intending to earn it; that he had made up his mind, as some alcoholics do, to give up the struggle and go down the drain in a hurry.

One of the few old friends known to have seen him shortly after his return to New York was Harry Steger of Doubleday, who had been puzzled by his non-appearance at the workroom across the hall from Steger's apartment at the Caledonia.

One day Steger got a telephone call from the author, the subject of which predictably was O. Henry's shortage of money. "Hello, hello. That you, Colonel? Say I've got to have $58.14 at 11:20 tomorrow morning."

"Well, I'll see if I can fix you," the Doubleday executive said. "But where in thunder are you?"

"I've taken quarters at the Chelsea. Come and see me."

Next morning Steger found his errant author camping out in one of the Chelsea's huge six-room apartments, furnished only with a work table, a chair and a bed. O. Henry wore a blue dressing gown, and greeted Steger: "Excuse my negligee. My clothes are out being pressed."

"But what are you doing here?" Steger asked.

"Why, I owed them so much at the Caledonia that it got on my mind and I couldn't work there. So I've taken these rooms."

"And you've given up your rooms at the Caledonia?"

"Oh, no," O. Henry replied. "I've got those too. I just wanted temporarily to get out of the atmosphere of indebtedness. As soon as I get a little ahead I'll square up and move back."[1]

Instead of secluding himself as he had promised Tyler, he had checked into the Chelsea. Instead of working on the dramatization of his short story, he never wrote a line of it, so far as can be determined. "Once he found himself at the gates of Bagdad," as Tyler pungently expressed it to Alexander Woollcott, "he stood wide-eyed for a moment and then drifted happily off to the bazaars, stumbled on some old cronies and gave himself over to celebrating his return from exile. I never saw him again, and the great American play, 'The World and the Door,' was never written."[2]

Who those "old cronies" were cannot be discovered from the scanty recoverable facts of his last four months. Bill Williams didn't meet him until a few weeks before his death, nor do any of the other O. Henry chroniclers mention seeing him at his "celebrating." Evidently his drinking was of the deadly solitary type with little merriment and certainly no celebration. He had expected that New York would further revitalize him. When the big city failed him, he turned to whiskey—and that old vitalizer also let him down.

After his death a friend quoted O. Henry as remarking, shortly after his return from North Carolina, that New York did not seem to "agree" with him as it formerly did. That puzzled him because New York was "all the mountains, the streams, the hills and purple valleys of mother earth. All the daffodils of spring meadows are blooming here. There's more poetry in a block of New York than in twenty daisied lanes."[3]

Apparently Sara, back in Asheville, sensed that he might backslide, that being plunged into the old environment might be too much for him. As sort of a life line, she sent him a letter shortly after he left Asheville in which she touchingly promised to be as unpossessive as possible, to provide an atmosphere in which he could work without distractions whenever he felt like returning to North Carolina.

"Never again," she promised, "will I ask you to tear your affection for me out of your body and hand it over to me to look at the roots to see if your love for me is alive. I know it is, because mine is.

"Sometimes when you have disapproved of wives we know, you have looked at me with that funny, wise, cynical little smile of yours and have said, 'You're better than most.' I am going to wait ten whole years, and I mean to be wonderfully good—then some night when we get home from some place where you haven't approved of the wives' methods of managing their husbands, you're going to say, 'You are better than any.' See if you don't."

The implied appeal in that letter, she said, was unanswered.[4]

About six weeks after his return to New York, he was stricken with the flu and seemed to be contemplating the possibility of death. His old friend Anne Partlan visited him in his rooms at the Chelsea, and he told her, almost groaningly, "I don't want to die, I'm swamped with obligations." He had little faith in the hereafter or the perfectability of the human spirit. "Suppose you and I got another chance," he said, "with the experience and knowledge we have now. Wouldn't we boggle up our lives just as badly?"[5]

Seth Moyle, the literary agent who occasionally acted on his behalf, also recalled that O. Henry's paganism endured until the end and that on the subject of an afterlife O. Henry smilingly recited:

"I had a little dog
And his name was Rover,
And when he died
He died all over."

About that time he wrote a friend and former Texas colleague in Chicago, James P. Crane, that "I'm back in New York after a six months' stay in the mountains near Asheville, North Carolina. I was all played out—nerves, etc. I thought I was much better and came back to New York about a month ago and have been in bed most of the time—didn't pick up down there as well as I should have done. There was too much scenery and fresh air. What I need is a steam-heated flat and no ventilation or exercise."[6]

But the steam-heated atmosphere of the Chelsea and the "scenery" afforded by the Manhattan skyline didn't revive him either. Nor did the publication of *Strictly Business*, the last collection of short stories to be published in his lifetime. That volume contained more of his New York stories, most of them originally published by the *Sunday World*.

The reviews were lukewarm, though *Strictly Business* included some of his best stories, "The Gold That Glittered," "The Fifth Wheel," "A Municipal Report," "Past One at Rooney's," "The Poet and the Peasant" among them. The setting of "The Gold That Glittered" was one of his favorite haunts on his night rambles around the Union Square section, the Hotel America on Fifteenth Street, which, as mentioned above, he called El Refugio in the story. It was the place where Caribbean and South and Central American exiles gathered to plot their return to power, and "The Gold That Glittered" was a lively account of the Americanization of one of those fugitive revolutionaries, General Perrico Ximenes Villablanca Falcon, who "had the mustache of a shooting-gallery proprietor, wore the full dress of a

Texas congressman, and had the important aspect of an uninstructed delegate." General Falcon has come to the United States on a gun-running mission but instead falls in love with Mme. O'Brien, the "unimpeachably blonde" proprietor of El Refugio, upon which he concludes that "War and revolution are not nice. It is not best that one shall always follow Minerva. No. It is of quite desirable to keep hotels and be with that Juno—that ox-eyed Juno. Ah! what hair of gold it is that she have!" The story ends with the general's panegyric to Mme. O'Brien's corned-beef hash.

After recovering from the flu, he still found the strength, occasionally, to wander the Manhattan streets at night, almost as though searching for a lost self.

One night George Jean Nathan, co-editor with H. L. Mencken on *Smart Set* and later a renowned drama critic, accompanied O. Henry and another man on a stroll around the streets. Near Herald Square they were approached by a fairly well dressed young man with a genteel manner who asked for a quarter. Their companion gave him the money and commented, "He seemed like an honest, worthy chap."

"Yes," said O. Henry quietly, "he seemed like an honest, worthy chap to me too—last night."

Against the ebbing of his creative energy, he struggled desperately in his room at the Chelsea to produce enough work to pay his bills. Richard Duffy of *Ainslee's,* who with Gilman Hall had imported him from Pittsburgh only eight years before, advanced him money for a story during this period. A few years earlier O. Henry would have knocked off the story at one sitting.

Now Duffy received a series of notes for two weeks as O. Henry struggled to produce the story a page or two at a time and send them down to the magazine's offices as evidence that he was doing his best. A note with the first few pages over-optimistically informed Duffy that he would "receive the rest tomorrow if possible." Another few pages several days later were accompanied by the note, "I think it is better for both sides not to have it spoiled by hurry." Days later another few pages were attached to a note reading, "Here is some more of the story. I am giving all my attention to the finishing of it. I am rather sanguine of handing you all the rest of it tomorrow. All I can surely promise is that I will put all my time at it until it is completed." A fourth note was grim testimony to the effort it took to finish the story: "Here's all of the story except about 200 words. It will have to be finished tonight. I am so sick that I can't sit up. I'll go home and knock out the rest tonight if I can hold a pencil. I am hugging the radiator with an overcoat on. . . ."[7]

He moved back to the Caledonia and from then on met few persons except employees of the hotel and those he saw on a daily walk over to Madison Square and back. The last time Bill Williams ever saw him was about the middle of May, when "O. Henry called me up and asked if I could get him a certain piece of information about the reprint of some of his stories by one of the papers—where it got them, how and what was paid. I promised to find out if I could and let him know that evening. I got the data he wanted and dropped off at Twenty-sixth Street on my way home to give it to him." Instead, he ran into O. Henry in front of Trinity Chapel. O. Henry wanted Williams to come up to his room at the Caledonia but the *World* man had another engagement to keep.

"I won't keep you then," O. Henry said, "but I'm awfully glad I ran into you before you got away. I didn't expect you quite so early. . . . You've done a lot of nice things for me and I want you to know that I have appreciated all of them. . . ."

Apparently he was planning on having Sara join him in New York, because he added, "One thing you haven't done yet and that's to come to my house for dinner. I'm going to hold you to that, Bill. Mrs. Porter isn't at home just now, but as soon as she returns I want you to come over and meet her, have dinner and spend the evening. Now that's a date and I want you to set it down in your little book. I'll let you know when."[8]

Then, Williams would have poignant reason to recall very soon, "we did something I can't recall our ever having done before—I remember how it hung in my mind after I left him—he extended his hand toward me, I took it in mine and we shook hands."

There were other valedictory touches, which only later took on significance to his friends. One afternoon, long before the "regulars" appeared, he dropped in at Healy's Cafe on Irving Place, looked around wistfully, nodded to bartender Con Delaney and then wraithlike slipped away. The last time any of his friends could remember seeing him in public was at a small dinner, where one of them would recall his pathetic attempts "to talk and to summon those glints of cynical wisdom which were the salt at every table where he sat." He was pale, gaunt and haggard and his face had strikingly changed in another way. To Will Irwin, one of the diners, it appeared that he had lost control of his upper lip: "it drew up as he talked, giving a sinister change to the whole aspect of his face."[9]

How little of life remained to him was also indicated by his last grapple with the exigencies of his profession. *Hampton's Magazine* had given him an advance on a story to be titled "The Snow Man." About a third of the way through, he found he simply lacked the strength to sit up and hold a pencil. For the last story which carried his by-line, the last story in the posthumously published *Waifs and Strays* and in the *Complete Works,* he required the assistance of an editor at *Hampton's.* Harrison Merton Lyons went over to his room at the Caledonia, took notes on how O. Henry intended to finish the story, and completed the job for him.[10] The writer was so thin, Lyons later recalled, that "his neck stood on his collar like a stick in a pond, his face mercilessly lined. . . . He gave me a curious feminine impression—not effeminate—as he sat in his chair, something grandmotherly . . ."

Early in the evening of June 3, 1910, he was seized by an agonizing pain. Before he collapsed he managed to call one of his friends—Gilman Hall, by one account, Anne Partlan by another. He was found on the floor of his room at the Caledonia, semiconscious, with the telephone lying on the floor beside him.

Dr. Charles Russell Hancock was summoned immediately, saw at once that O. Henry would have to be hospitalized, and wanted to summon an ambulance from the Polyclinic Hospital on East Thirty-fourth Street. O. Henry, reviving a little, insisted that he would leave under his own power and that a taxi be called. Dr. Hancock helped him on with his clothes and began brushing his hair, when O. Henry took the brush away from him.

"You're a poor barber, Doc," he muttered. "Let me show you."

Though obviously in considerable pain, he insisted on stopping in the lobby on their way out to shake hands with the manager of the Caledonia and to say a few words to the elevator operators and bellhops who had protected him so devotedly against intruders when he was trying to work.

Dr. Hancock recalled, in an interview given some years later to a young Atlanta newspaperwoman named Peggy Mitchell, subsequently better known as Margaret Mitchell and author of *Gone with the Wind,* how O. Henry painfully managed to keep up what he had always called his "front"—an urbanity, an air of indifference to his own troubles, a gentlemanly sense of obligation ingrained to the marrow of his character. Despite spasms of pain, he chatted with Dr. Hancock as though they were on their way to dinner at Rector's instead of hurrying by taxi to a hospital.

At the hospital's emergency entrance he again insisted on walking without assistance. When the reception clerk asked for his name, he replied:

"Call me Dennis. My name will be Dennis in the morning."[11]

His friends believed that he entered the hospital under an assumed name because he didn't want any publicity, but actually it was consistent with his view of himself as a man living underground.

Finally he decided that his name should go on the hospital records as "Will S. Parker." The puzzled Dr. Hancock, who had never seen his patient before, later stated that he did not at the time know who the man was, only that he was dying and yet worried over what name he should assume. Choosing the name he did, a friend told Alphonso Smith, was "prompted by the desire to die with the name and initials given him at birth and endeared by every memory of childhood and home."[12]

He emptied his pockets of a few coins and placed them on the reception desk, saying, "Here I am going to die and only worth twenty-three cents."

For the next twenty-four hours he grew weaker. Both diabetes and cirrhosis of the liver were in their advanced stages, Dr. Hancock said. O. Henry also had the "most dilated heart I have ever seen."[13] His pain lessened and he was conscious, except for brief periods of sleep. The only visitors allowed him were Anne Partlan and John O'Hara Cosgrave of *Everybody's.* Sara had been summoned and was on her way North by train.

At midnight Saturday, June 4, a nurse turned down the lights in his room, and he was heard to murmur:

"Turn up the lights. I don't want to go home in the dark."

Dr. Hancock left his bedside early Sunday morning and returned after several hours sleep. Dawn and death were approaching. "He was perfectly conscious until within two minutes of his death," Dr. Hancock later reported, "and knew that the end was approaching. I never saw a man pluckier in facing it or in bearing pain. Nothing appeared to worry him at the last."

At 7:06 A.M., Sunday, June 5, 1910, he died, not in the dark, but with the dawn light streaming through the window. He was halfway through his forty-eighth year.

Sara arrived later that day, by which time three of his editors—Gilman Hall, William Griffeth and Harry Steger—had made the funeral arrangements. The funeral was to be held June 7 at 11 A.M. at the Church of the Transfiguration (Episcopal), better known as The Little Church Around the Corner for its literary and theatrical weddings and funerals, on West Twenty-ninth Street. The pallbearers would be Richard Harding Davis, John O'Hara Cosgrave, Dr. John H. Finley, Don Seitz of the *World,* Will Irwin of the *Sun,* and Walter Hines Page, the United States ambassador to London during World War I . . . a more distinguished company than that in which O. Henry usually found himself.

The funeral itself, with its one startling misadventure, might have been arranged by the dead man himself.

Two of the pallbearers, Davis and Irwin, arrived early at the church. They were waiting on the grounds outside the church when three automobiles, full of laughing and carefree people, parked at the curb outside the church. It was a wedding party. Among its members was the art editor of a magazine, with whom Irwin was acquainted.

Irwin asked the art editor what time the wedding was scheduled.

"Eleven o'clock," the art editor replied.

"But," Irwin protested, "that's the exact time set for O. Henry's funeral. There must be some mistake."

"A funeral takes precedence over a wedding," said the art editor. "Leave it to me. But don't say a word. I don't want these friends of mine to be married with any superstitious feeling of bad luck. . . ."[14]

The art editor whisked his friends away, but the funeral was late in starting and the wedding party had returned to the church grounds while the services for O. Henry were still in progress. They chattered away, their voices audible through the open windows of the church and providing a lively counterpoint to the solemnities inside. The unpretentious O. Henry might have objected to the naming of several of the eminent pallbearers, with whom he was barely acquainted, merely for the sake of lending dignity to the occasion, but he would surely have approved of that wedding party chattering away while the Rev. George Clark Houghton read "Crossing the Bar."

He was buried in a cemetery at Asheville overlooking the French Broad River with the hazy blue mountains in the distance. Later his daughter was buried at his feet. The headstone marking his grave reads simply, "William Sydney Porter, 1862–1910." No mention of O. Henry. That other self—more real to him, perhaps, than the Will Porter who left those Carolina mountains as a youth—is more than adequately celebrated on the title pages of the millions of copies of his books published throughout the world.

Chapter 12. The Afterglow

On the Big Board of Literature O. Henry's stock has never been lower. It is not even listed, in fact, by the more fashionable speculators. If he were alive and practicing today, and if his style were unchanged, it is difficult to imagine where his stories would be published. *Grit,* perhaps, or some other rural publication with a commercial and sentimental attachment to a vanished America.

There is nothing odd, of course, about the violent fluctuations of a man's literary reputation. The Brahmins of literary criticism are constantly reassessing, revising, reviving some writers and consigning others to oblivion. The English professors and creative-writing teachers also dig up the usable past. But none of the resurrecters has been brave or foolish enough to attempt a restoration of O. Henry.

Both his strengths and weaknesses as a writer are held in contempt—his cleverness and his sentimentality, his mastery of technique, his facility at constructing plots, his trick endings, his hyperbolic humor. All his devices are exactly what young writers aspiring to be published in the *Partisan Review* or the *New Yorker* are told to shun. At best he is regarded as an artifact of the semiliterate early-century years when the two-penny newspapers and the dime magazines were the conveyors of popular culture. At worst, perhaps, he is regarded as a hack, an opinion which O. Henry would have shared. Overpraise from the critics of his own day, such as comparisons with Poe or Maupassant, usually annoyed him; he dealt with editors, whom he depended upon to evaluate the tastes of the reading public; all others were to him merely loafers in the marketplace.

At the time of his death, in fact, O. Henry in this country, after a career of only eight productive years, was regarded as a burned-out star in comparison with Jack London, Willa Cather, Edith Wharton, Henry James and others of more prominent reputation. In popular esteem, however, he rose higher than ever in the dozen years after his death and his work was held up for adoration by such appraisers of contemporary culture as Christopher Morley, Alexander Woollcott and Carl Van Doren, the latter writing that "no writer in the language seems clever immediately after one has been reading O. Henry." Collected volumes of O. Henry were a staple in middle-class American homes; any library of as many as twenty books was almost certain to include his work. No other short-story writer except Kipling sold better in hardcover than O. Henry in the decade following his death. More than five million copies of his books were sold in the United States. During that period he also became ever more popular abroad, particularly in England, where he was heralded by Hugh Walpole as "the father of this new American literature." And he was translated into French, German, Russian, Spanish, Swedish, Japanese and Norwegian. He appealed particularly to the Russians, both before and after the Revolution, and was regarded as the founder of a new literary school, as a writer to be ranked with Chekhov and Turgenev.

To American readers before and just after World War I his collected works—O. Henry must be taken *in toto* or not at all—constituted the body of a revealed myth, a concept of themselves they accepted and liked. His optimism about the eventual success of the American experiment, always implicit even when he described the inequities and injustices of the social system, exactly suited the national mood.

It may seem incredible to those who associate O. Henry only with literary entertainment of the more meretricious sort, but on the popular level he was a social commentator of considerable impact. In *Postscript to Yesterday,* the late Lloyd Morris discussed most perceptively O. Henry's penetration of the American scene. "He turned away from the prosperous levels of society, so popular at the time as a subject for fiction. He ignored the Four Hundred to deal with the four million. This choice was more the result of his previous misfortunes than of any interest in social reform, but its net effect was to produce an optimistic social myth. His stories mainly turned on the fortunes of humble folk, shop girls and clerks and mechanics; a group that, on the whole, had been anonymous and inarticulate in American life, and absent from American fiction. They formed the group that a later generation was to describe as 'the little people,' and that politicians would aggregate as the 'forgotten man' and 'common man.' In the rapid urbanization and industrialization of American life, their numbers were constantly increasing. They were the vast, hard-pressed, hard-working lower middle class of the great cities, to whom the present was usually precarious and the future equivocal.

"It was O. Henry's special gift to portray them as they saw themselves. They did not consider themselves proletarians, victims of an exploiting social order, tragic subjects for rescue or salvage. Although this interpretation of their condition might be made by political radicals like Emma Goldman and social reformers like Jane Addams, by the muckraking journalists and the young school of writers, it was not acceptable to them. Did not the old tradition of American life hold out the assurance that they might rise in the social circle? Did not the American Federation of Labor teach that every skilled worker might, in time, become a member of the bourgeoisie? However hard pressed, they were still hopeful. 'It ain't the road we take; it's what's inside us that makes us turn out the way we do.'"

O. Henry was very much a part of that lower middle class himself and an earnest subscriber to its moral view. Until the last years of his life he had never earned more than twenty-five dollars a week, and it has usually been money that fixes an American's social position. It was the bank clerk speaking when Al Jennings urged him to call the lady blackmailer's bluff, and O. Henry replied, "I have much to lose. I don't look at things as you do." And it was the bank clerk, not the world-famous writer he had become, who devoted so much thought and energy to concealing the shame of having been convicted as an embezzler.

Russian Communism's approval of him as a proletarian writer is, of course, a misapprehension. (Russian publishing figures are not readily obtainable, but the State printing presses turned out ninety-four printings of his works between 1920 and 1945, for a total of 1,403,500 copies. In 1953, for instance, the Soviet Union published 900,000 copies of American writers' books, and of these, 225,000 were O. Henry's, exactly one fourth of the total output. Deming Brown, the American expert on such matters, has written that "One may speculate on the motivation of the Communist Party" in keeping O. Henry alive in Russia but "it is clear that, despite years of constant indoctrination, Russian readers still like to seek release in a good yarn.") He did attack the abuses of capitalism, but that was hardly a radical social or political stance to assume. The journalistic exposé of conditions in the factories and sweatshops, glaringly highlighted by the flames which destroyed the Triangle Shirtwaist Factory in lower Manhattan, had aroused not only O. Henry but such disparate crusaders as Anne Morgan, Alfred E. Smith, Henry L. Stimson, R. Bayard Cutting and Henry Morgenthau, Sr. "But his indictment," as Lloyd Morris has written, "though it indicated general social sympathies which recommended him to the reformers, implied no such social skepticism as other young writers were beginning to express. The workers of his stories had confidence in their future, and he appeared to share it. He gave the old dogmas a new sanction in terms of the commonplace. His myth was the one which most Americans lived by, and wanted to believe. In an age of wealth for the few and poverty for the many, it asserted that all things were still possible to the common man, and that most of them would turn out to be good."

There was, in fact, something for everyone in O. Henry's stories about the urban masses. "Social reformers," Morris continues, "counted him sympathetic to their aims. Apologists for an expanding capitalism found their complacency reinforced by his optimism; and, because he seemed to be a conservative, they were quite willing to praise him for being a democrat. The class about whom he wrote liked him for shedding on their existence a light of romance."

The range of his admiring readership was indicated by an incident that occurred in the fall of 1906 outside a bookshop in Cambridge just off the Harvard Yard. In the window was a display of O. Henry's recent works. A Harvard freshman and an elderly bearded gentleman, though strangers, began excitedly discussing the author and his stories. It developed that both considered O. Henry their favorite writer. The older man was William James. The freshman was John Reed, who was to become a radical prophet, author of *Ten Days That Shook the World,* and one of the few Americans buried under the Kremlin wall.

Shortly after his death, Hildegarde Hawthorne, writing in the New York *Times* (June 18, 1910) rather neatly defined O. Henry as "the Bret Harte of the City," adding that "his style was perfect; it was the man himself; nervous, picturesque, quick, supple, with easy, inevitable metaphors." There was something of Bret Harte in the humanism, the gallant humor, the technique of the surprise twists, the mechanism of his plotting. As Bret Harte was the literary discoverer of the West for the ordinary reader, O. Henry was the explorer of the cityscape. He pictured New York as the outlanders wanted to see it, the thundering metropolis of "four million mysterious strangers," the magical place they would see from the upper deck of a rubberneck bus or more likely through someone else's imagination. To Van Wyck Brooks (*The Confident Years*) he "shared Dickens's vision of a happy domesticity, sharing as well his feeling for the city streets, for the crowds and the lights of the metropolis, the night-blooming cereus unfolding its dead-white heavy-odoured petals." Brooks considered him "too hard or too soft in the wrong way," but conceded that "O. Henry was occasionally an artist, nevertheless, who escaped from the mechanical formulas of the cheap magazines, the last to vindicate Howells's belief that the 'more smiling aspects of life' were the most characteristic of America, as no doubt they had been."

A definite slippage in O. Henry's standing was to be noted in the early twenties, with writers such as Sherwood Anderson and James Branch Cabell, with their greater subtlety, already on the scene, along with the young Scott Fitzgerald, and Ernest Hemingway just around the corner. H. L. Mencken wielded a bludgeon on both O. Henry and Richard Harding Davis as the "cheesemongers" of the Edwardian years. In his *Prejudices: Second Series* (1920) Mencken charged O. Henry with a "smoke-room and variety show smartness" and declared that "In the whole canon of O. Henry's work you will not find a single recognizable human character; his people are unanimously marionettes; he makes Mexican brigands, Texas cowmen and New York cracksmen talk the same highly ornate Broadwayese."

A few years later the task of dismantling O. Henry as a popular idol, and perhaps more particularly as a writer to be taken seriously (as he was) in high school and college English studies, was taken up by F. L. Pattee, the literary historian. In *The Development of the American Short Story* (1923), Professor Pattee declared, "The elements of his art were not many. He knew precisely how much of the sugar of sentimentality the great average reading public must have, and how much of the pepper of sensation, and the salad dressing of romance. . . . But brilliant as was the possibilities of his powers, and distinctive as was his technique, his final place can never be high even among the writers of short stories. He did not take literature seriously; he was a victim of Momus and the swiftly ephemeral press. His undoubted powers were completely debauched by it. He became exclusively an entertainer, with no thought but of the moment, and no art save that which brought instant effect upon his reader. To accomplish that he would sacrifice everything, even the truth."

In later times O. Henry was not even given the reverse accolade of being exhaustively criticized, but was dismissed with a paragraph in the magisterial *A Literary History of the United States* and a slightly longer analysis of his methods, using the story "The Furnished Room" as their model, in Cleanth Brooks' and

Robert Penn Warren's *Understanding Fiction.* To much of this criticism, Prof. Eugene Current-Garcia, in his study *O. Henry* (1965), has succinctly replied that "To condemn O. Henry's stories *in toto* for not being realistic and serious, for depending too heavily on coincidence, and for playing to the gallery is an evasion of the critic's responsibility—unless it can be shown that these characteristics invariably result in badly written stories. This, O. Henry's severest critics have seldom been willing to do. His intention rather than his achievement has been the object of their censure. . . ."

All this scholarly and literary and academic discussion of O. Henry's work is, of course, beside the point and beyond the notice of the ordinary reader, for whom O. Henry labored. Judging by the publishing history of his collected stories, including the 1,692-page, one-volume leviathan (*The Complete Works of O. Henry*) published a few years ago, he continues to be read for pleasure by considerable numbers of people.

In this manner he is still a "live" author, as Stephen Crane and Jack London are, regardless of the changes in literary fashion.

One way of measuring his literary importance is to examine the gap that would be left in popular literature if he had been content to compound prescriptions for the rest of his life in a Greensboro drugstore. Certainly he encouraged Americans to take a gentler view of the unorganized, non-violent criminal in such stories as those contained in *The Gentle Grafter.* In many of his western tales he modified the dime-novel view that the West was settled exclusively by good guys with guns and bad guys with more guns. In *Cabbages and Kings* he provided a brilliantly lit picture of Central America in its banana-republic heyday, and of the "culture shock" provided by an American colony consisting of two murderers, an army paymaster afflicted by a shortage in his accounts, two bank presidents with similar problems and a mysterious widow. But it was in the 140 stories with a New York background that he passed along a storyteller's heritage of continuing value to his readers. With them one can reconstruct a fairly accurate panorama of the nation's first city during those years when it was being packed by hundreds of thousands of immigrants, both from the American hinterland and from Europe.

He was New York's biographer. In his stories one can grasp exactly how people lived, struggled, survived and eventually bettered themselves in the pre-welfare state. If the city had a soul, O. Henry was the man who understood it.

Himself an outlander, he was able to merge with the ordinary people. Even better, he was able to observe the city with a fresh and sustained curiosity, illuminated by an unflagging imagination. Who but O. Henry could have conceived a conversation (as he did in "The Lady Higher Up") between the revolving statue of the naked Diana atop Madison Square Garden and the Statue of Liberty a few miles down the bay? Or conveyed so much of the city's essence in a few sentences that preceded that lofty conversation: "Three hundred and sixty-five feet above the heated asphalt the tip-toeing symbolic deity on Manhattan pointed her vacillating arrow straight, for the time, in the direction of her exalted sister on Liberty Island. The lights of the great Garden were out; the benches in the Square were filled with sleepers. . . . The statue of Diana on the tower of the Garden—its constancy shown by its weathercock ways, its innocence by the coating of gold that it had acquired, its devotion to style by its single, flying scarf, its candor and artlessness by its habit of ever drawing the long bow, its metropolitanism by its posture of swift flight to catch a Harlem train—remained poised with its arrow pointed across the upper bay. Had the arrow sped truly and horizontally it would have passed fifty feet above the head of the heroic matron whose duty it is to offer a cast-ironical welcome to the oppressed of other lands."

One cannot help but wonder how much better O. Henry would have done if he had not turned out his stories in hot haste, under the constant prod of creditors and obligations; if he had been able to rewrite and reconsider instead of sending off the first draft to impatient editors. But that has been the fate of many writers. O. Henry, such is his enduring charm, is as lovable for his artistic failings as he was admirable for his successes. The afterglow of that hectic eight-year career will continue to linger in the global village whose beginnings he glimpsed in brownstone New York, in a more innocent and hopeful age.

Notes of Sources

Chapter 1. Salad Days

1. Smith, *The O. Henry Biography,* afterward referred to as *Smith,* pp. 18–22.
2. Greensboro *Patriot,* May 30, 1832.
3. *Smith,* pp. 66–67.
4. *Waifs and Strays,* a collection of brief memoirs of O. Henry, no editor given, pp. 130–31.
5. Quoted in *Smith,* p. 76.
6. Quoted in E. Hudson Long's *O. Henry, The Man and His Work,* pp. 22–23.
7. Greensboro *Daily News,* April 16, 1963.
8. Edmund King, *The Great South,* pp. 178–79.
9. San Antonio *Daily Express,* March 20, 1911.
10. Quoted in *Smith,* pp. 98–99.
11. Smith Papers, Greensboro Public Library.
12. Quoted by Arthur Page, "Little Pictures of O. Henry," *The Bookman,* October 1913.
13. Smith Papers.
14. Quoted by Page, op. cit.
15. *The Complete Works of O. Henry,* p. 1078.
16. "Bexar Scrip No. 2692," first published in *The Rolling Stone,* May 5, 1894; *Complete Works,* p. 1053.

Chapter 2. The Girl in Dimity

1. Davis and Maurice, *The Caliph of Bagdad,* hereafter *Davis,* pp. 348–49.
2. Smith Papers.
3. *The Rolling Stone,* April 27, 1895.
4. Ibid., May 12, 1894.
5. Ibid., April 27, 1895.
6. Ibid., June 2, 1894.
7. Page, op. cit.
8. Langford, *Alias O. Henry,* hereafter *Langford,* p. 71.
9. *Smith,* p. 126.
10. Department of Justice files for 1895, National Archives.
11. Quoted in Page, op. cit.
12. Ibid.
13. Houston *Post,* November 5, 1895.
14. Ibid., June 6, 1910.
15. Ibid., October 26, 1930.

16. Wilson, *Hard to Forget*, p. 194.
17. *Smith*, pp. 144–45.
18. Jennings, *Through the Shadows with O. Henry*, passim.
19. Ibid., p. 90.
20. Quoted in *Smith*, pp. 141–42.
21. Jennings, op. cit., p. 94.
22. *Complete Works*, p. 563.

Chapter 3. Federal Prisoner No. 30664

1. *Langford*, pp. 124–25.
2. Quoted in *Smith*, pp. 147–48.
3. Ibid., pp. 154–58.
4. Jennings, *Beating Back*, pp. 175–76.
5. Smith Papers.
6. Quoted in *Smith*, pp. 148–49.
7. Ibid., p. 148.
8. Ibid., p. 163.
9. Jennings, op. cit., pp. 244–47.
10. Smith Papers.
11. *Smith*, p. 153.
12. Jennings, *Through the Shadows with O. Henry*, pp. 133–34.
13. Jennings, *Beating Back*, pp. 249–50.
14. Jennings, *Through the Shadows with O. Henry*, pp. 253–54.
15. *Complete Works*, pp. 1090–93.
16. George MacAdam, "O. Henry's Only Autobiographia," *O. Henry Papers*, hereafter *MacAdam*, p. 17.
17. Pittsburgh *Post* interview with Jamison, March 28, 1930.

Chapter 4. One of the Four Million

1. *Davis*, p. 174.
2. "The Trimmed Lamp," *Complete Works*, p. 1366.
3. Churchill, *Park Row*, passim.
4. Quoted in Page, op. cit.
5. Article by William Griffeth, Dearborn *Independent*, November 14, 1925. Griffeth was a friend and editor of O. Henry.
6. Quoted in Page, op. cit.
7. *Smith*, pp. 178–79.
8. Ibid., p. 176.
9. Ibid., p. 177.
10. *Davis*, p. 206.
11. Ibid., p. 274.
12. Ibid., p. 266.
13. *MacAdam*, p. 14.
14. Quoted in Page, op. cit.
15. Quoted in Wagnalls, *Letters from Lithopolis*.
16. *Davis*, pp. 201–4.
17. Williams, *The Quiet Lodger of Irving Place*, hereafter *Williams*, pp. 25–38.
18. *MacAdam*, p. 6.
19. Article by Cullen, New York *Sun*, January 10, 1915.

Chapter 5. The Quiet Man of 55 Irving Place
1. *Davis,* pp. 210–14.
2. *Williams,* pp. 41–53.
3. Ibid., pp. 63–64.
4. Ibid., pp. 71–74.
5. Partlan, op. cit.
6. Anne Partlan in *The Writer,* August 1914.
7. *Smith,* p. 184.
8. *Smith,* pp. 185–87.
9. Arthur Maurice, *The Bookman,* January 1916.
10. *Smith,* p. 233.

Chapter 6. Fresh Out of Money
1. *MacAdam,* p. 22.
2. Black, *American Husbands and Other Alternatives,* p. 143.
3. Quoted in *Davis,* pp. 258–60.
4. *Complete Works,* pp. 1084–85.
5. *Critic,* February 1904.
6. Quoted by Paul Adams, "O. Henry and Texas," *Bellman,* September 22, 1917.
7. *Davis,* pp. 362–63.
8. *Williams,* pp. 206–7.
9. Ibid., pp. 135–38.
10. O'Connor, *Hell's Kitchen,* p. 90.
11. *Williams,* p. 217.
12. Quoted, ibid., pp. 211–12.
13. *Davis,* pp. 299–301.
14. Quoted in *Davis,* p. 307.
15. Black, op. cit., p. 188.
16. *Davis,* pp. 307–9.

Chapter 7. Fame If Not Fortune
1. Quoted in *Langford,* p. 194.
2. Quoted in *Davis,* pp. 305–6.
3. *MacAdam,* pp. 13–14.
4. *Williams,* pp. 169–70.
5. Quoted, ibid., p. 198.
6. Ibid., pp. 165–69.
7. *Davis,* pp. 331–32; *Williams,* pp. 189–91.
8. Quoted in *Davis,* p. 130.
9. Quoted in *Williams,* pp. 179–80.
10. *Atlantic Monthly,* January 1907.
11. Jennings, *Through the Shadows with O. Henry,* p. 282.
12. Ibid., p. 296.
13. Ibid., p. 107.
14. Ibid., p. 313.

Chapter 8. "Train's Late for Happiness"
1. *Davis,* p. 275.
2. O'Connor, *The Scandalous Mr. Bennett,* pp. 272–74.
3. The whole story was told by Ethel Patterson in "O. Henry and Me," *Everybody's Magazine,* February 1914.

4. Quoted in *Smith*, p. 190.
5. Smith Papers.
6. *Williams*, p. 245.
7. O. Henry to Gilman Hall, *Complete Works*, pp. 1085–86.
8. Quoted in *Davis*, pp. 251–54.
9. Margaret Porter, "My O. Henry," *The Mentor*, February 1923.
10. Interview with Sara Porter, Raleigh *News & Observer*, November 25, 1934.
11. Sara Porter, "The Gift," *Delineator*, May 1912.
12. Ibid.
13. Quoted in Jennings, op. cit., pp. 309–13.
14. *Williams*, pp. 247–48.

Chapter 9. A Reach for the Laurel

1. Henry James Forman, "O. Henry's Short Stories," *North American Review*, May 1908.
2. *Davis*, pp. 319–21.
3. Quoted in *Williams*, p. 175.
4. Interview with Sara Porter, loc. cit.
5. *MacAdam*, p. 15.
6. New York *Times*, April 4, 1909.
7. Ibid.
8. *World's Work*, June 1909.
9. *Complete Works*, pp. 1089–90.
10. Sara Porter, "The Gift," loc. cit.
11. Margaret Porter, op. cit.
12. Quoted in *Davis*, pp. 368–69.
13. Quoted in Arnett, *O. Henry from Polecat Creek*, pp. 17–18.
14. Margaret Porter, op. cit.
15. Ibid.

Chapter 10. A Dalliance with Broadway

1. Woollcott, *Shouts and Murmurs*, p. 211.
2. *Waifs and Strays*, p. 228.
3. Ibid., p. 205.
4. Woollcott, op. cit., passim.
5. Quoted in *Davis*, p. 369.
6. Ibid., pp. 387–88.
7. Churchill, *The Great White Way*, pp. 152–53.
8. Alexander Woollcott, "O. Henry, Playwright," *The Bookman*, October 1922.
9. Quoted in *Davis*, p. 369.
10. Woollcott, op. cit.
11. Ibid.
12. Ibid.

Chapter 11. "I Don't Want to Go Home in the Dark"

1. Quoted in *MacAdam*, p. 15.
2. Woollcott, op. cit.
3. Interview with Flo Field, New York *Tribune*, July 24, 1910.
4. Sara Porter, "The Gift."

5. Quoted by Will Irwin, "O. Henry, Man and Writer," *Cosmopolitan,* September 1910.
6. O. Henry to James P. Crane, quoted in *Smith,* p. 248.
7. Quoted by Page, "Little Pictures of O. Henry."
8. Quoted by *Williams,* pp. 249–50.
9. Irwin, op. cit.
10. Editorial precede to "The Snow Man," *Complete Works,* p. 1680.
11. Dr. Hancock gave this account in an interview with Margaret Mitchell of the Atlanta *Journal,* January 3, 1926.
12. *Smith,* p. 250.
13. Ibid.
14. *Davis,* pp. 397–98.

Bibliography

Arnett, Ethel Stephens. *O. Henry from Polecat Creek*. Greensboro, N.C., 1962.

Black, Alexander. *American Husbands and Other Alternatives*. Indianapolis, 1923.

Brooks, Van Wyck. *The Confident Years*. New York, 1923.

Brown, Deming. *Soviet Attitudes Toward American Writing*. Princeton, 1962.

Churchill, Allen. *Park Row*. New York, 1958.

——. *The Great White Way*. New York, 1962.

Coleman, Sara Lindsay. *Wind of Destiny*. New York, 1916.

Current-Garcia, Eugene. *O. Henry*. New York, 1965.

Davis, Robert H. and Arthur B. Maurice. *The Caliph of Bagdad*. New York, 1931.

Harrell, Mary S. *O. Henry Encore*. New York, 1939.

Jennings, Al. *Beating Back*. New York, 1927.

——. *Through the Shadows with O. Henry*. New York, 1921.

King, Edmund. *The Great South*. New York, 1874.

Langford, Gerald. *Alias O. Henry*. New York, 1957.

Lewis, Alfred Henry. *The Apaches of New York*. New York, 1912.

Long, E. Hudson. *O. Henry, The Man and His Work*. Philadelphia, 1949.

Maltby, Frances G. *The Dimity Sweetheart*. Richmond, Va., 1930.

Marcosson, Isaac. *Adventures in Interviewing*. London, 1920.

Mencken, H. L. *Prejudices: Second Series*. New York, 1920.

Morris, Lloyd. *Postscript to Yesterday*. New York, 1947.

Moyle, Seth. *My Friend O. Henry*. New York, 1914.

O. Henry Papers (no editor listed). New York, 1924.

O'Connor, Richard. *Hell's Kitchen*. Philadelphia, 1958.

——. *The Scandalous Mr. Bennett*. New York, 1962.

Parry, Albert. *Garrets and Pretenders*. New York, 1933.

Pattee, F. L. *The Development of the American Short Story*. New York, 1923.

Porter, William Sydney. *The Complete Works of O. Henry*. New York, 1953.

Sinclair, Upton. *Bill Porter: A Drama of O. Henry in Prison*. Pasadena, Calif., 1925.

Smith, C. Alphonso. *The O. Henry Biography.* New York, 1916.
Swanberg, W. A. *Pulitzer.* New York, 1967.
Wagnalls, Mabel. *Letters from Lithopolis.* New York, 1922.
Waifs and Strays (no editor listed). New York, 1917.
Williams, William Wash. *The Quiet Lodger of Irving Place.* New York, 1936.
Wilson, Lollie Cave. *Hard to Forget.* Los Angeles, 1939.
Woollcott, Alexander. *Shouts and Murmurs.* London, 1923.

Index